Moroccan Households in the World Economy

MOROCCAN HOUSEHOLDS
IN THE WORLD ECONOMY

Labor and Inequality in a Berber Village

DAVID CRAWFORD

LOUISIANA STATE UNIVERSITY PRESS

BATON ROUGE

Published by Louisiana State University Press
Copyright © 2008 by Louisiana State University Press
All rights reserved
Manufactured in the United States of America

LSU Press Paperback Original
First printing

DESIGNER: Michelle A. Neustrom
TYPEFACES: Tribute, Old Claude LP
PRINTER AND BINDER: Thomson-Shore, Inc.

Except where otherwise noted, photographs are by the author.
Maps and charts are by Mary Lee Eggart.

LIBRARY OF CONGRESS CATALOGING-IN-PUBLICATION DATA

Crawford, David, 1965–
Moroccan households in the world economy : labor and inequality in a Berber
Village / David Crawford.
    p. cm.
Includes bibliographical references and index.
ISBN 978-0-8071-3372-9 (pbk. : alk. paper) 1. Income distribution—Morocco. 2.
Households—Economic aspects—Morocco. 3. Berbers—Morocco. 4. Globalization—
Morocco. I. Title.
    HC810.Z9I516 2008
    339.2'20964—dc22

                                                              2008017782

FIELDNOTES, AUGUST 10, 1998

◈ ◈ ◈

This land is an organic machine, run by the sweat of women and men, fed by their shit, and the shit of their herds. The water is from God, who stores it high in the Ouanoukrim and parcels it out through the summer. But the *targas* that carry the water are of men, and the fields too . . . a slow history of being hauled into place stone by stone. It is here in the wet river bottom that the men plant the barley and corn, where [the women] cut the *tooga* that feeds the cows, that feeds the children, that readies the bodies of a new generation of work-ers. Before [children] are three they know their work. They waddle around the village carrying water, carrying wood, carrying food to the men working, carrying children even younger than themselves. They will grow to run the machine, to replace the parts of the *targas* [that] floods carry away, to build new fields to feed new babies, to re-plant the crops eaten by frost, to nurse back the herds decimated by early winter storms. They will not be saints . . . they will not be lords. They may go work in the city and send home money for a new tea set, for cement to fill the cracks in the stone houses, for pipes to carry water places too steep to walk. But mostly they will grow to be the fire in the machine, the "living, breathing fire" that works against time and nature and death.

Contents

Illustrations and Tables

TABLES

Preface

Notes on the Practicalities of Growing a Book

This ethnography examines the transformation of a village in the High Atlas Mountains of Morocco, one hundred kilometers south of Marrakech. The village is called Tagharghist, though in the text I refer to it as "Tadrar." The reason I do so is that English speakers tend to pronounce "Tagharghist" ("the place of the steep gorge") as "terrorist." My apologies to the villagers of Tagharghist/Tadrar for the presumption of changing the name of their home.

Few other pseudonyms are employed in the text. Most people in Tadrar know who I talked to, and the local government agents know virtually everything I did and everyone who gave me information. Everybody was aware that I was "writing a book," and I was publicly, constantly writing things in my notebook. Nothing I say here is much of a secret in the mountains, and there is little to be gained by disguising names. Pseudonyms might protect me from being responsible for getting the story straight, but it would take no serious effort to figure out who I am talking about. Some villagers, in fact, adamantly insisted that their words be credited to them, and so they are. The one exception concerns the transcript of my fieldnotes in chapter 6. Here I disguise the names of government and development agents about whom I have unkind things to say. None of these people work any longer in the region, so I do not think I am compromising their careers.

The people of the High Atlas, like most of the mountain people of Morocco, are referred to as "Berbers." *Berber*, from the Latin for "barbarian," is the English word for the majority population of North Africa in historic times and is also the word for the language they speak. Most scholars refer to Berbers as the "indigenous people of North Africa," and the culture does seem to have very deep roots in the region (Brett and Fentress 1996). Today you find Berber speakers across North Africa, from Egypt to Libya, Tunisia,

Algeria, and Morocco, and down to Mauritania, Mali, and Niger. The largest population of Berber speakers is in Morocco, and is said to equal somewhere from 20 percent to 40 percent of the population (Crawford 2005). They do not only exist in rural areas, but in all of Morocco's cities and all social classes. There is also a large Berber diaspora in Europe, especially in France, the Netherlands, and Belgium. Since the arrival of Islam in the eighth century, ever more North Africans have come to consider themselves "Arab" and speak Arabic—whatever their family history. The vast majority of Berbers are Muslim.

The issue of the place of Berber language and culture in North Africa is widely debated (Boudraa and Kraus 2007; Boukous 1995; Chaker 1989; Crawford and Hoffman 2000; Crawford 2002; MacDougall 2006). Some activists object to the term *Berber* because it is exogenous to the people being described, and because of its link to barbarism. Contemporary activists and some scholars use *Imazighen* (singular, *Amazigh*) to refer to the general, contemporary Berber-speaking population, though, confusingly, *Imazighen* is also the name for the Berber-speaking people of the Middle Atlas Mountains in Morocco. Contemporary scholars often use *Amazigh* to refer to the family of Berber languages and the associated culture. However, the *Amazigh* people of the High Atlas, where Tadrar is located, refer to themselves as *Ishelhin* (pronounced Ish-al-heen) and their language as *Tashelhit* (Tash-al-heet). I use various combinations of these terms in the book, depending on whether I am taking the local perspective (*Ishelhin*), suggesting a wider and more politicized way of thinking (*Amazigh*), or am trying to be as clear as possible to English-speaking readers (when I use the most common term, *Berber*). I do not believe that *Berber* has any negative connotations in English (Sadiqi 1997).

Throughout this book I have tried to use the most comprehensible transliterations of Berber words that I could manage. Morocco was a protectorate of France during the early part of the twentieth century, and many Moroccan words—both Arabic and Berber—have developed standard spellings in Latin characters. If there is a common French spelling, I try to use it (thus "Marrakech" instead of "Marrakesh"), but in many places I have had to rely on my own imperfect ear for the best rendering of *Tashelhit* as it is locally spoken.

The bulk of the research for this book was undertaken in 1998 and 1999 while I was preparing my Ph.D. dissertation, though I visited Tadrar once before that in 1995, and have returned since 1999 almost yearly. During the main phase of research I moved back and forth between Taroudant (where I rented a room from a fellow researcher) and Tadrar (where I rented a room from a villager who had migrated to Taroudant). I rarely stayed in the village for more than a week at a time, instead leaving for short periods to write or check e-mail, and to make visits to other parts of the country. I sometimes hitchhiked, and met some very interesting characters that way, and sometimes I traveled by foot, bus, and local taxi. The exposure to other travelers in the region was crucial to my understanding of the particularities of Tadrar.

Methodologically, most of the observations herein rely on "participant observation," by which I mean eating, sleeping, talking, and working with villagers in Tadrar as they went about their lives. I conducted a small number of taped, in-depth interviews about life in the mountains. These tapes were transcribed into *Tashelhit* written in Arabic characters, then translated into English by Latifa Asseffar as I typed them in Latin characters. Without Latifa this book would not have been possible; she and her husband, Said, have been wonderful friends and colleagues. Of course, I remain responsible for what errors remain in the texts of the interviews.

To augment the interviews, I conducted a series of household censuses in 1999, 2002, 2004, and early 2007, counting the household members of different ages as well as the number of migrants, and gathering other information, such as ownership of cattle and solar power panels. I mapped each of the fields in Tadrar in 1999, and assessed their ownership, whether or not they were irrigated, and whether the field was used for crops or fodder. I counted each almond, walnut, pomegranate, and carob tree owned by the villagers, and determined who owned which of them, a project that was complicated by various types of communal ownership in some areas. I mapped the canals, and determined water rights and irrigation rotations on all of them, and computed the comparative amount of time households owned on each canal. I also assembled a genealogy of all members of the village.

One of the greatest challenges faced by any anthropologist is finding ways to compensate our research partners. Different people in Tadrar helped me in different ways and to different degrees. Some fed me, some helped me draw maps or explained things, others loaned me blankets, helped me clean, or nursed me when I was sick. Some warned me of various dangers and some encouraged me in my work. Many of them spoke with me, explained things, or corrected explanations others had given me. How can I pay people back for this? A collaborative project like this makes it difficult to know who is owed what, and yet these mostly illiterate villagers have, in effect, given me a career.

For shelter I rented a room from Hamad Lukstaf, who had migrated to the city. I paid him the equivalent of $30 a month in a purely formal relationship. Meals were more complicated, however. When I first arrived I benefited from a kind of competitive generosity. Multiple families attempted to feed me or deliver food. I sometimes ended up wasting things I could not eat, or eating three dinners, then no breakfast or lunch, and I knew many of my neighbors were desperately poor and had no food to waste. My solution was to choose three families—one relatively wealthy, one in the middle range of village families, and one poor—and deliver food to them. Every market day I would travel twenty kilometers to buy meat, coffee, spices, and other items, which I would bring back and deliver in bundles to the three main households where I ate—the houses of Abdurrahman Ait Ben Ouchen, Mohammed Lukstaf, and Mohammed Belaid. I would either send the bags with children to deliver, or allow myself to be invited in for tea and then casually leave them behind. This ensured that I was not subtracting calories, and especially protein, from families that had little to spare, and allowed them to be generous hosts for the duration of my research. I was invited to dine by at least one of these households at every meal, but they were all compensated equally whether or not I ate with them. Sometimes I would eat many meals in a row at one house, sometimes I ate with other neighbors, but in general I think I managed to eliminate any sense of "buying" meals without inconveniencing people or unduly taking advantage of them.

I did pay some individuals in cash for specific tasks performed. One woman did laundry for me, a few girls cleaned my room once or twice, and I compensated Abdurrahman by the hour to help me map fields and collect genealogies. My normal rate was approximately minimum wage in the United States. I also chipped in for medicine, bandages, or funeral expenses when people needed help, I donated clothes, and when there was a villagewide collection for a wedding or communal meal I paid as a separate household. For people who wanted them, I took photographs, then returned with copies. This was especially popular with mothers, and so a disproportionate number of my photos feature babies and children.

To compensate people who did not work with me directly, neighbors who helped me in diffuse or intermittent ways, I opted to donate money and technology to the village as a whole. I paid for a solar power panel, lights, and batteries for the mosque so that students could study in the evenings. I obtained a grant for a solar hot water heater in the mosque to lessen the amount of wood the women needed to gather to heat water, and over the years I have made infusions of cash to the village assembly, either my own or sometimes money given to me by students or friends specifically to better the welfare of the village. I continue to support Tadrar when I can, usually with funds that the villagers decide how to spend on their own. I do occasionally make suggestions of things I think might benefit the most people, but I do not control what happens to monies I contribute. In the somewhat unlikely event that this book makes a profit, I will split it with the families of Tadrar.

During the 1998–1999 research I was unmarried, a fact that impacted the ways in which I could interact with villagers. It was very difficult to talk to women or unmarried girls, for instance, or at least it was difficult to talk to them about anything other than getting married. In 2002, I finally did get married, and later that year my wife gave birth to our son, Calum. In December of 2003 my wife further interrupted her own Ph.D. research to bring our daughter, Lula, into our family. We all flew to Marrakech a couple of weeks after Lula was born in December of 2003, and some of my village colleagues came down to visit us there; we visited them, too, at *souk* in the mountains, and my family and I returned to Tadrar expecting to stay for the summer of 2004.

Coming to Tadrar with a family was a huge relief for my friends there. *Finally* I had managed to end my incomprehensible bachelorhood and—with God's blessings have children. My village friends were thrilled, and I hoped that this would put me on new footing to discuss new issues, and indeed it did. However, I also came to see the difficulties of village life in a much more arresting and visceral way. While doing research alone in Morocco I had been hospitalized twice, but I was young at the time (or at least younger) and thus relatively oblivious to my own mortality. Summer of 2004 was different. My son nearly fell off a roof to what would surely have been his death, my neighbor Fatime died by snakebite, and my wife was evacuated by four-wheel-drive "ambulance" with dysentery and dehydration. I was not emotionally prepared for this, and I regret that since then I have done no research in Tadrar with my family. I have continued to stay informed by making short trips without them, and by hosting villagers when they visit me in Marrakech, Taroudant, or Essaouira.

This book was drafted in Auckland, New Zealand, during 2005 while I was on sabbatical from Fairfield University, and finalized in the summer of 2007 in Connecticut. Research and travel money has come from Fairfield University, the American Institute of Maghrib Studies, the Near and Middle

East Studies section of the Social Science Research Council, the Fulbright Scholar Program, and the University of California at Santa Barbara.

The text was helpfully critiqued by Mark Schuller, Hillary Haldane, Sandy Robertson, Fatima Gebrati, Paul Silverstein, Gary Martin, and Ramon Guardans. Ramon and Hillary have also followed me up and down the hill, for which I am deeply thankful. Helen Regis provided page by page microediting as well as terrific broader suggestions for making several of the chapters more comprehensible. I owe her and the anonymous reviewers for Louisiana State University Press a great deal. Susan Slyomovics has been an inspiration throughout this work, Paul Silverstein offered timely words of encouragement, and Dale Eickelman and Henry Munson have kindly responded to last-minute e-mails on questions large and small. My colleagues in sociology and anthropology at Fairfield University have built a workplace that is almost too much fun, and I want to thank them for this. Joe Powell has been a patient and pacific editor at LSU Press, and has my deep gratitude. Derik Shelor masterfully copyedited the manuscript and made a number of insightful suggestions and improvements. Anne Frank drafted the index. Andy Shimizu has now been serving as my permanent address and paying my bills for a decade. I can only roam because he does not, and all he ever gets in return are short sentences in obscure acknowledgments.

My honors students at UCSB and Fairfield University read early drafts of this book and submitted poignant commentary, as did my teaching assistants at UCSB. Their hard work has, I hope, made this text more readable for future students. The Arbuz, Idzdo, Id Baj, Belaid, and Ben Ouchen families have been warm and accommodating of my repeated visits to their homes and fields in Tadrar, and have patiently endured my endless, poorly articulated questions. With some of them I have now become *zound famila,* like family, for better and for worse. As will be apparent in the text, I owe a very special debt to Abdurrahman Ali Ait Ben Ouchen. This book is as much his as mine, and I hope I have done justice to his insights on the world we try to explain. My wife, Hillary, has lived with this project as long as she has lived with me. For the time, editing acumen, insight, love, and sacrifice of being married to a growing book, I am eternally grateful. Calum and Lula have grown up with this project, too, and fought valiantly to distract me. I thank them for their lessons in perspective.

I dedicate this book to Sandy, who taught me, and to the people of Tadrar, who tried.

MOROCCAN HOUSEHOLDS IN THE WORLD ECONOMY

Morocco

INTRODUCTION
Timeful Lives

Every human problem must be considered from the standpoint of time.
—FRANZ FANON

This book is about the changing lives of Berber-speaking farmers in the mountains of Morocco—the way people living in one village organize themselves to meet the challenges of changing times. This kind of inquiry in a place like highland Morocco necessarily invokes the crude dualism "tradition and modernity," along with a raft of other much-freighted terminology: globalization and Islam, capitalism and the subsistence economy, wage labor and tribal affinities, development, poverty, patriarchy, inequality, culture. Such terms are vital to contemporary thinking about our time—and what it is not; they are unavoidable if we are to make sense of how rural Moroccan *Imazighen* experience our shared, globalizing epoch.

But if terms like *traditional* facilitate some sorts of thinking, they also constrain and canalize it. Contemporary writing on out-of-the-way places, and, in particular, anthropological writing, has a tendency toward what Fabian calls a "denial of coevalness" (1983) or, as Eric Wolf would put it, conceptualizing other cultures as lacking "history" (1982). There is thus some confusion built into examining a culture many would consider "traditional," because its opposition to "modern" implies that the lives of subsistence farmers are static, while "we" (modern folks who read books) are new, evolving, contemporary, and dynamic. Since farmers in the village of Tadrar and stockbrokers in Manhattan are both living at the same historical moment, the *now* that we all share, terms like *traditional* impute a false rural atavism, a dull timelessness.

1

This dualistic way of categorizing the first and third worlds is similarly problematic on a smaller scale too, within Morocco itself. Moroccan scholar Ahmed Lagnaoui writes that his country has two separable cultures, "traditional and modern," with the traditional, rural, patriarchal culture characterized as "stagnant" and "lacking a spirit of initiative" (1999). *National Geographic* magazine refers to Morocco as "a timeless Mosaic" (Zwingle 1996), though the "timeless" part of the mosaic is not Casablanca—the main commercial center—but the older parts of venerable cities like Fes, and most especially rural areas. In other words, the contours of rural life in Morocco are read by urbanites within and outside of the country to mean the countryside is "behind" the *timeful* world of people who read English and French, the literate consumers who are "ahead" in a progression toward a future defined as what the West is now. In these terms, "traditional" amounts to a fantasy rearview mirror, a staid past juxtaposed to the dynamic present and the postmodern future. This is one way the self-consciously modern world understands itself: by constructing rural life as what the modern world is not, and especially what it is *not anymore*.

Thus, examining social transformation in a High Atlas village requires us to think seriously about time, to examine how we in wealthier social positions think about stability and change, how we understand our collective lives in time, and how we comprehend the globally interconnected era we live in. If we want to move beyond seeing rural Others as a lagging and dusty shadow of ourselves, it makes sense to engage the way rural people actually think and behave, the differences with urban life, but also the similarities and the dynamics of interconnectedness. Put another way, if we want to understand the dynamics of "globalization," we need to assess places that we believe are freshly globalized, in the example here a place newly, differently, and more intensively engaged with the wage labor economy, international NGOs, and the Moroccan state. Of course, as Max Gluckman has written, "all real societies in real time are always changing and have always been changing," and our job is to discern "what is changing, what the changes are, and how far the changes go, in affecting structural forms" (1968, 223). A village ethnography is one good way to fathom what is changing in our world, what the changes are, and how far they really go in transforming deeper patterns of culture and behavior. The village of Tadrar is one place to begin such a project.

My way of looking at the processes through which the people of Tadrar integrate themselves with the larger world economy will be somewhat eclectic and determinedly micro-social, linking household economies to local kinship dynamics and the larger political economy, and putting interpretive anthropology to work on the exigencies of material poverty, development, and wage labor. I will disagree with writers on globalization who contend that "the world is flat" (Friedman 2005), that the dominant economic processes of the West transfer largely uninflected to other contexts, that the world is coalescing under a single, transparent, competitive logic through the decentralization of skills and the compression of time and space.[1] But if I disagree with this Liberal vision, I also take issue with scholars and activists like Vandana Shiva who criticize the glorification of "the global" over the local, but still credit corporate capital with a totalizing power I do not believe it has.[2] This is not a simple story of good or bad capitalism, but of how villagers decide to become involved in the larger world economy, and what it does for them and to them.

This account of very poor Berber farmers is meant to add a richer, more intimate picture to grand analyses of the world economy; the welter of everyday life will serve here to leaven more general studies that summarize rural household organization as "income pooling units" alternately "resisting" the global economy and being shaped by it (Smith and Wallerstein 1992). I will show how some poor Berbers endure the exigencies of their economic position and the depredations of the political states in which they live, how they make what they can of their world, by demonstrating how poor farmers *engage* their political-economic reality—culturally, to be sure, but actively and intelligently.

I made my first brief visit to the village of Tadrar in 1995. I went back to do research and stayed off and on in 1998 and 1999, and then returned several more times through 2007. My main interest during this period has involved the way villagers organize the labor necessary for the difficult, life-sustaining task of farming barley. Farming in Tadrar is hard. It requires drawing water from a plunging river of snowmelt, channeling it hundreds of meters across precipitous mountainside, and portioning it out to over eleven hundred tiny plots. Especially in drought years, there is little to waste, and ensuring each

---

1. In fact, in my view, life in the mountains moves *faster* in some ways. See Crawford (2007a).

2. See http://www.tamilnation.org/oneworld/shiva.htm. I agree with Shiva that "flat vision is a disease," but I do not find in the Moroccan context that regular farmers are in any way averse to the advantages they might gain from engaging the world beyond the mountains.

field gets what it needs when it needs it requires a symphonic synchronization of rock, mud, and water by teams of carefully coordinated men. Once grown, the barley has to be cut, dried, and transported back to the village on women's backs, threshed by teams of mules, winnowed, stored, then ground into flour, kneaded into bread, and baked in wood-fired ovens— ovens that require women to cut, gather, and haul wood down from distant forests along dangerously steep, sometimes nearly invisible trails. Only then, circled on the floor around the common family bowl, can the warm bread be torn into pieces, apportioned by need, and eaten. In Tadrar, bread—and by extension life—does not come from a store.

Or at least it has not. A dirt road was built to Tadrar in 1996. Now more people move more frequently because truck service means the seventeen rocky kilometers down to the paved road are not the barrier they used to be. In 1998 villagers received a government school, and while the Arabic taught at the school has yet to take hold among these Berber speakers, children are now being consistently exposed to the national language for the first time. In 1998 the U.S. Peace Corps contributed the materials to install a potable water system, and a World Bank–funded development project brought cement for one of the canals by 2003. By 2004 there was a diesel-powered grain mill, also courtesy of the Peace Corps, a mill that replaced the ancient, defunct watermill beside the river. By my most recent visit in early 2007, some families had solar power panels, televisions, indoor plumbing, and even video disk players and satellite dishes. Television reception is very limited for most people, but recorded disks of Berber-language comedies, music videos, and tapes of the singing and dancing at weddings have become a popular new kind of entertainment.

We might surmise, then, that this "traditional" village is becoming "modern," more like or at least on the road to being like the rest of Morocco, like the cool, clean, electrified mosques of the old city in Fes, the bars and cafés of the seaside *corniche* in Casablanca, or the kite-surfing, Mercedes-driving Moroccan families vacationing in Essaouira. Urban Moroccans themselves often make a distinction between the modern and traditional parts of their country, and assume (like many other people around the world) that their rural brethren represent a kind of contemporary past: living folklore clinging stubbornly to the mountain valleys, partly enviable (for piety and presumed social cohesion) but also pitiable (for being backward, stubborn, impoverished, ignorant). In this view, the villagers of Tadrar are on the "frontiers of the modern" (Lagnaoui 1999), the interface between a kin-built social world of subsistence agriculture and a febrile global economy organized through individualism, anonymity, mass media, and wage labor.

I will argue that Tadrar illustrates not a holdover from a different era, but the way a continuously reconstituted traditional order meshes with the (also continuously reconstituted) world of state power and capitalist wage labor. In this confrontation the rural social order is sometimes fragmented, absorbed, or undermined, but it is also sometimes structurally durable, only superficially transformed by larger social dynamics. It is not the case that migration and money lead simply to "a changing culture" (Petrzelka and Bell 2000, 348).[3] Instead, as I will show, different villagers put development efforts and the wage labor economy to work for different purposes, and these different purposes influence how the interaction takes place, how the participants make out, and ultimately how the village is transformed. Merely observing the arrival of satellite dishes and cellular phones tells us little about how such technologies are incorporated into a local social, political, and cultural order, or how that order is changing.

In this book I will consider "modern time" not as a historical period, but as a modality—a complex of trajectories and periodicities within the broader arch normally subsumed under "history." My point is that all lives are *timeful* lives, and the issue is what sorts of time we are talking about. I will borrow from Jonathan Friedman, Katherine Verdery, and others the idea that economic modes have distinct temporal complexes, specific rhythms and periodicities by which they operate, and I want to show how different temporal orders are integrated. In the way I am using the terms, *traditional* and *modern* specify different ways of organizing time, not different times in which people are organizing. I hope this becomes clearer throughout the book.

Returning to Tadrar, and relying on the changes I observed in this village between 1995 and 2007, I will examine some of the assumptions that underpin a variety of scholarly explanations for how the global order is thought to expand, how the economic system called capitalism is seen to penetrate, poison, and overwhelm the traditional social world. To do this I will eschew the typical metropolitan view and instead begin with the dynamics of Tadrar itself—the way villagers sustain themselves through households they cleverly stitch into larger forms of community. My supposition is that unless

3. See Parry and Bloch (1989) for a set of articles detailing the different ways that money is made sensible in local cultural and social terms.

we understand how people collectively stay alive and reproduce themselves, we will have great difficulty understanding how they find meaning in their lives. In the words of Clifford Geertz, "The danger that cultural analysis, in search of all-too-deep-lying turtles, will lose touch with the hard surfaces of life—with the political, economic, stratificatory realities within which men [sic] are everywhere contained—and with the biological and physical necessities on which those surfaces rest, is an ever-present one. The only defense against it, and against, thus, turning cultural analysis into a kind of sociological aestheticism, is to train such analysis on such realities and such necessities in the first place" (1973, 30). This is my intention. Cultural analysis cannot be *only* cultural since ways of thinking and feeling exist in a tough material world that demands engagement. The daunting precariousness of rural life in Morocco is well documented, longstanding, and pervasive (Rosenberger 2001). The energetic creativity employed by rural farmers to deal with this precariousness, with the "hard surfaces" of their lives, forms the core of this book.

Fickle weather and ruthless national politics are only some of the conditions farmers engage, however. The arrival of the global economic order is arguably a tectonic shift, substantively new ground that families can, or in some cases must, work to sustain themselves. While this region has been articulated into a larger "world system" for a very long time (Mojuetan 1995; Wallerstein 2004), there are indications that the present moment is qualitatively distinct. The intrusion of development agencies, and the decision by ever more local patriarchs to send their children to the cities for wage labor rather than loan them to relatives who need help, signals a newly significant articulation between the rural and urban sectors of Morocco. Long-term village reciprocity is being abandoned for short-term gain.

Rather than view globalization from the perspective of urban migrants, people who have opted out of, or been driven from, their mountain mode of production, I want to get the view from the highlands, the perspective of people at the interface between local, longstanding forms of social organization and the "new world order" about which so much is written. I hope to illuminate a wide field of contemporary social transformations through a very narrow, specific focus, though I should admit that I am nervous about what general insights we might take from such a restricted case. I am, after all, writing about an encounter and not a microcosm. My hope is that readers see in Tadrar some of the intriguing, and to most of us quite alien, ways that some of our distant contemporaries are coping with the agony and exhilaration of the twenty-first century.

The remainder of this book is divided into chapters meant first to elicit a visceral sense of life in Tadrar, and then to make a set of arguments about how and why it is changing. I begin impressionistically, then become more analytical and theoretical along the way, and finally advance some conclusions and return to my early impressions and sentiments.

Chapter 1, "A Place in Time," introduces the village from its regional context to specific paths, houses, and rooms. Some contemporary ethnographies pass too quickly over the actual places under discussion, or at least students complain to me that they have a hard time getting a "sense of place," a feeling for what life is like in a world that seems so different. This chapter begins the process of drawing out what it is like to pass time in the Moroccan mountains, what it is like to eat and work, live and love in a mud-walled village, and something of the specific individuals who become the sources of my understanding. I want to start with this, to evoke a sense of daily life in Tadrar and set the village in a spatial context, in order give some idea how I came to know the place. This requires me to describe the particular spaces that I moved through, the houses and rooms where I did my work, the places that allowed me to understand how villagers do their work. How I came to know Tadrar has much to do with what I claim to know, so my description of space and movement through it is also a kind of methodological statement.

Admittedly, contemporary anthropology has moved away from the "village study" approach I adopt here, and there are some good reasons for this.[4] Still, I contend that Tadrar is worth treating as an entity because it is both a complex, physical place and a locus of identity. It is not that Tadrar is sealed off from other villages (quite the contrary) or that its boundaries are in all cases firm and uncontested. But the village *qua* village does play an important role in local self-identification; it is an important legal entity in terms

4. See Marcus (1995) for an early discussion of "multi-sited" ethnography and the value of working across spatial scales. Goodman (2005) notes that "the village" has long been a way of thinking about Berbers, at least in Algeria, and this serves to obscure important larger dynamics. Some very interesting contemporary ethnographies take the constitution of the object of study as central to the study itself (see Hayden 2003), but in the case of Tadrar my interest lies elsewhere.

of rights to pastures and obligations for the upkeep of communal property ranging from trails and irrigation canals to the mosque and its attendant rituals. In other words, Tadrar is an identifiable place (a cluster of buildings, fields, canals, and pastures), a place that comes with rights and obligations, but also a place specific people identify as being their own. My aim is to make the relationship between these physical, emotional, and conceptual phenomena clear, and to set this complex, physical, and notional "village" in a broader social, political, and economic context.

The spaces of Tadrar feel quite stable, or felt stable during my initial fieldwork. The village appears in my older photographs to be from another time, frozen. However, exposure over a number of years has shown this to be quite wrong. Tadrar now seems to me remarkably fluid, with rock, dirt, water, animals, and humans flowing through it, coming into this world and leaving it, being pushed up and pulled down, reconfigured, undulating in rhythms and transformed across slow pathways beyond the limits of immediate perception. Understanding how spaces are physically reproduced (fields and canals rebuilt, houses shored up) and transformed (old trails abandoned, new houses built, infrastructure improved) is one way to begin thinking about social transformation. Change is nowhere singular or simple, unidirectional or predetermined. Transformation and reproduction of the physical spaces of Tadrar can help us to think about kinds of change generally, and thus the kinds of change that are, and are not, wrought by the larger set of forces glossed as "globalization."

Chapter 2, "Intimate Matrices," moves from the fundamental spaces of Tadrar to the basic social unit, the household. There has been intense academic interest in the household in other parts of the world, but not in Morocco. Classic scholarly writing about the social world of the Moroccan mountains has focused on tribes and moieties, religious organizations, powerful warlords, and village assemblies. These are all interesting modalities of social organization, and in various ways in different times and places they are all important. Still, I believe they are better understood if we begin with the dynamics of household production and reproduction. Recent scholarship has moved away from tribal fixations and has tended to focus on "the state" and issues of power (Bourqia and Gilson Miller 1999; Slyomovics 2005a). Here too, however, I think a household perspective deepens our understanding not only of quotidian life, but of larger processes up to and beyond the machinations of the state.

In Tadrar the elemental form of labor organization is the household, or *takat*. This is where a villager's activities over a day are coordinated, as well as many of the most important decisions of her or his lifetime. The particular villagers with whom you eat, work, and sleep are your household members; households care for the young and old, they produce the workers who sustain the household, the village, and indeed the world economy; households are the preeminent locus of production, consumption, and reproduction. Households are built of people—the people with whom you share love, labor, warmth, shelter, and food over many years, people with whom you share *life*. Like the humans who constitute them, households have a life cycle; every villager's mortal existence is embedded in the life cycle of one or a sequence of households.

A *takat* is not the same as "family," though family ties (and the profound emotional resonance of the concept of family) are important to the economic constitution of households. Some scholars discuss households in terms of "family," the "conjugal family," or the "nuclear family," and this can be misleading (Berque 1955, 40; Michel 1997, 244; Pascon 1979, 109). Households are *economic* organizations, and family members, even emotionally close family members, may or may not belong to the same *takat*. Everyone belongs to some *takat*, however, and everyone knows who belongs to which.

Households are not generic. Labor is divided principally by sex and age, such that boys and girls travel distinct routes over the course of their lives. Households are not constituted the same, and while they move through identifiable "stages," no two household histories are exactly alike—an important point about households generally (Conley 2004; Mundy 1995; Robertson 1991). I will try to give some sense of these trajectories and histories, the way actual people manage the exigencies of biology and political economy with what strategies can be made culturally sensible. I will also try to capture the subtle power dynamics of the patriarchal household, where older people rule over younger, and men over women, though not in the way that bosses rule over laborers in the city.

One main theme of the book is that the temporality of households—the way household members manage daily labor through the slow unfolding of human life—is fundamental to all larger social processes, including the question of global integration. Women's labor in particular has been relatively understudied in Morocco, and is especially important to the constitution of households. Understanding women's labor behind the scenes of the male public world is crucial to understanding the more ethnographically visible masculine forms of political and social labor discussed in subsequent chapters.

All enduring societies must reproduce themselves, and households are typically the way they do so. Placing households at the base of our analysis helps us to make sense of the differences and commonalities between the social orders of the cities and the mountains, and the expansion of the global economy in novel social and cultural environments.

Chapter 3, "Household Inequality," examines the economic differences between households, and specifically how property devolves to create very different capacities for political action. The inequalities between households are hard to assess. Berbers are famously egalitarian, and villagers do not typically display their economic status in the same way that urbanites might; there has been little conspicuous consumption in Tadrar until recently. Nonetheless, economic inequality here is well understood by villagers themselves, and is important; it is impossible to make sense of larger, villagewide political dynamics (much less state-sanctioned development projects, or migration for wage labor) without accounting for the inequalities among households. I will try to transcend the notion of a generic poor villager to give a more nuanced sense of how subtle, shifting configurations of poverty frame decisions across households and across time.

Much of this chapter deals with methodology—how to gauge economic differentiation in an interdependent economic system. In Tadrar, property is diffuse and widely distributed, with fields ranging from the size of a closet to something closer to forty meters across, with trees of all sizes, from saplings to four-story-high walnuts, and herd sizes ranging to several hundred. Owners of property can be individual persons, but owners are sometimes lineage groups, sharecropping partners, absentee migrants, distant religious lodges, or the Moroccan government's department of religious affairs. Public property like canals can be used by village men for specified times. Pastures might be available to all village members for certain seasons or only after certain dates, and other pastures are available for all residents of the whole valley, again during certain times. Sometimes rights can be transferred, as when fields are sold or trees given away, further complicating the picture, but some rights cannot be transferred, as when outsiders are prevented from using Tadrar's pastures even when invited by a particular villager. The irreducible particularity of property, the complexity of ownership, and the complicated agreements about who labors for whom (and when, where, and why) all converge to make assessing something as seemingly straightforward as "wealth" a deeply confounding exercise. I try to show why such an exercise is necessary for comprehending social change.

Chapter 4, "Arranging the Bones," moves from household property to household labor, and examines the ways household labor reserves are tapped for villagewide projects. In Tadrar there is a tradition of dividing labor responsibilities for village-level projects into five work groups. These groups are in some sense based on agnatic tribal affiliations or lineages, that is, kin relations through the male line. These are the *ighsan* (singular, *ighs*), or "bones," of the village. Public work groups are built from—but are not the same as—the bones, and these groups have traditionally been used to build dams during summer droughts, for repairs on the village mosque, or to construct trails up the steep cliff faces to higher pastures and fields. More recently, these groups have been employed for various development projects, from installing a potable water system to rebuilding rock and mud canals using cement. Such long-established patterns of communal labor are thus *increasingly* important because of development interventions by the Moroccan state and international NGOs.

There are a number of points to make about how work groups are formed and how the process of formation is altered in new political and economic conditions. The key element is that the constitution of the groups is based not only on specific kin relations, but also on a local understanding of fairness, one that is interestingly tied to the long-term rhythms of village life. As households are born, expand, wither, and die, the labor responsibilities of households are adjusted, seemingly to ensure a balance among the bones. In this way the temporalities of household labor are important to extra-household community organization, an organization that is not a simple manifestation of a cultural script, but a negotiation between contradictory cultural principles and what exigencies of demography cannot be controlled.[5]

Presently World Bank projects are invigorating the use of the *ighsan* and expanding their salience, benefits, and social costs beyond traditional domains. Here we see one way that global processes reinvigorate particular local social dynamics rather than eradicating or absorbing them; we see how local social forms shape why and how global forces impact the village.

5. I borrow this critique of "text" as a metaphor for culture from William Roseberry (1989), and while it is true that demography is culturally mediated, villagers cannot entirely control their fertility or choose the sex ratio of their children.

Chapter 5, "Seeing and Being Seen by the State," extends this treatment of how the village as a whole is changing through interactions with "the outside."[6] Here I will agree with scholars who have shown that villages have long been connected to various kinds of "outsides" (Braudel et al. 2001; Mielants 2007; Mojuetan 1995; Wallerstein 2004). If Tadrar is out of the way, it has never been isolated. To establish this point, I outline some histories of local connectedness and sketch some of the ways that people in Tadrar have used resources from, and contributed to the history of, places beyond their village and valley (Mayer 2002).

Now, however, the national government is taking far more sustained interest in its hinterlands than ever before, and state and international development agencies are keen to transform the nature of village life (making it more healthful, less poor, and affording formalized educational opportunities). But if state-sanctioned development has necessitated a more intimate relationship with the central government, this has not always been welcomed locally, nor is it easy to understand. Anthropological writing on power in Morocco has been oddly divided between rural work on lineages and tribes (where the state is absent or thought to be unimportant) and urban work (where the state is thought to be all-powerful). The cultural mores associated with each political mode are likewise polarized in the literature, with "egalitarianism" reigning among the mountain tribes (cf. Gellner 1969; Kraus 1998), and "authoritarianism" infusing all social relationships in the plains (Bourqia and Gilson Miller 1999; Hammoudi 1997). As the state comes to take a more active role in rural affairs, making sense of how the Moroccan state works—and how local people understand it to work— becomes important to explaining the contemporary dynamics of village life.

I will suggest that in Tadrar the way that "development" has progressed illustrates how two distinct modalities of power in highland Morocco (egalitarianism and authoritarianism) are parts of an integrated cultural system. The genealogical order of the mountains (what has been called tribal organization) is egalitarian among brothers and cousins, but depends on a deep authoritarianism between fathers and sons. Households are internally hierarchical, not egalitarian; it is household heads—patriarchs—who are equal to one another in the village council. When social groups are calculated by patrilineal reference to shared dead ancestors, the people remaining (and doing the calculating) are necessarily equal, that is, sublineage groups are

6. The title of this chapter is taken from James Scott's *Seeing like a State* (1998).

all descended from and would owe deference and fealty to a patriarch, but he is dead. These groups are all nominally equal to one another—like cousins among cousins rather than like fathers to sons. From the perspective of Tadrar, power is conceived much like this, with chains of men linked up one above the next in a hierarchy that leads to the king. The difference, of course, is that the state hierarchy exists in the present; it is not calculated through ancestors. State officials are thus like ancestors come alive, and obeisance to state agents is analogous to obeisance to ancestors, at least ideally. Men from the government cannot be dealt with as equals; they are, as people say, *imqor*. *Imqor* means at the same time to be big (like an adult), to be powerful (like a government agent), and to be old (like a venerable patriarch). Such concordance is not random.

I will not suggest that the Moroccan state draws its power simply from these cultural understandings. Secret prisons, torture, the use of the military power against civilians, and a persistent pattern of corruption mean that from the perspective of the poor the state has power because it has the power to punish, to take things away, to imprison, to kill (Slyomovics 2005a). It is not that the state has no legitimacy, but in development work, as in other domains, people render their actions sensible in particular cultural contexts. In the village, what is important is the way men interact to get things done, the "how of power" rather than the fact of it (Foucault 1983). In rural Morocco, interactions between men take the form of haughty domination over those "below," exaggerated servility to those "above," and fierce maintenance of parity among "equals." Cultural modalities necessarily inflect how local development gets done, and what gets done with it. Again, local understandings shape larger processes as much as the other way around.

Chapter 6, "Globalization Begins at Home," ties the local dynamics of households, lineages, and village-level labor groups and development into an argument about globalization.[7] By this I do not mean a macroeconomic and broadly political argument, the way that globalization is typically discussed. The general terms of our global age are clear enough: increasing freedom of capital, rising and ever more desperate labor migration, technological innovation, especially in communications and transport, the decline of state-controlled economic regimes, and a swelling faith in the transcendental wisdom of markets. I will not challenge this as a kind of summation from above, a catholic portrait of our time. But analysis at this resolution

7. The title phrase is lifted from Homi Bhabha (1994, xxv).

tells us little about how ordinary people, especially farmers, experience this global age, much less why and how they involve themselves with it.

We see in Tadrar that participation in the wage labor economy is the main way that poor people become part of "the global." Jobs at clothing factories in Casablanca, orange picking in the Sous Valley, or construction of tourist hotels in Marrakech mean that certain villagers are contributing their labor to the production of things that will travel far, and benefit variously fortunate middlemen. Many of these middlemen will never meet or even conceive of the lives villagers contribute to the commodity chain; nor, of course, will the ultimate consumers have any idea who has had a hand in their orange juice or the walls of their vacation bungalow.

But who does these jobs, and why? What are the effects of their decisions? Most analyses of why globalization happens have focused either on the desirability of the wage labor economy (so that people choose to participate in it for sensible material reasons) or on the implementation of the capitalist system against the wishes of everyday people (so that they have no choice but to participate in it). What these positions share is the assumption that individuals are the unit of analysis. As I argue throughout this book, however, in rural Morocco the social unit that matters is the household, not the autonomous individual. In Tadrar some people are indeed choosing to be involved in the wage labor economy, but the people doing the choosing are usually not the ones doing the laboring. Fathers *send* children to work in the city, and children's wages support the rural, patriarchal household. The wage labor economy and the rural patriarchal household are not antithetical, are not counterpoised to one another as modern to traditional, but are instead mutually sustaining. The rural household provides very cheap labor for the global economy, and the global economy relinquishes small amounts of cash that find their way up to the mountains.

But this is not uniform. Different villagers end up in the city for different, and sometimes contradictory, reasons. Sometimes men and women abandon their patriarchal households, but sometimes the city is their best chance to start their own. Some young people escape to the city while waiting for their rural fortunes to change, and at the death of a patriarch they return to claim their rural patrimony. Patriarchs themselves send girls and boys to the city to tap the urban economy to consolidate their rural power. There are thus many different reasons villagers spend time outside of the village, many reasons they are busy developing new sorts of skills and bending older social connections to new ends, and this works in tandem with new sorts of self-understanding. Villagers are now much more consciously Muslim than ever before because they interact with some non-Muslims and they experience urban debates about the meaning of Islam in contemporary life; villagers are more conscious of being Berber speakers because they interact with more Arabic speakers; and they are more aware than ever before that they are poor because nearly everyone who arrives from the outside is very apparently better off than any villager. Now one of the main ways that villagers describe themselves to outsiders is as *miskin,* poor.

That fathers send children out to support the household is related to material poverty, surely, but poverty in a rural form that city dwellers do not always recognize as such. Poverty is always a question of proportion—too much of one thing and too little of another. In urban Morocco, there is too little work and what work there is pays too little, and thus there is too much time. Armies of men sit sullenly in cafés day after day nursing cups of tea, sharing newspapers, bumming cigarettes from friends who are slightly less unlucky. The *bidonvilles* of Casablanca are swollen with an army of the desperate. Women labor in sweatshops or middle-class homes, or dwell in their own homes wondering if they will ever marry, if they can find a husband with the meager enough resources to support children. The shantytowns stew with men and women unable to form households, unable, in other words, to become full members of Moroccan society, where producing children is a cultural ideal—even in the city, where bearing young workers is not an economic incentive.

In the mountains the dilemma is in some respects similar, but here there is too much work rather than too little, too little time rather than too much, and children are a net economic asset to their households from a very young age. Young village men and women are pressed into labor from predawn until after dark. There is little time to socialize, little time to play, and while they might be able to marry, the decision is entirely up to the fathers, the patriarchs, who control all the land and thus the ability of young people to become adults, to have sex, to bear children. It is not surprising that for young village women the city almost always looks desirable. They dream of indoor plumbing, a gas stove as opposed to a wood oven, indoor rather than outdoor work, a cement roof and a room with furniture rather than a leaky mud roof in a room bare except for some old carpets to sit on. For young men the decision is tougher. The mountains guarantee some security (they will inherit land once their fathers die), but often a very long wait is required.

This is not to say that urban labor is anything like ideal. There is growing recognition of the appalling conditions under which young men and
women work in urban Morocco.[8] Activists, NGOs, and scholars have criti-
cized the way rural children are treated in the urban economy, where a lack
of education is the norm, work hours are brutally long, and children suffer disproportionately from physical and sexual abuse. However, here I am
interested in how those children end up in the cities in the first place, and
how they impact the rural, household-based social order when they remain
attached to their natal households.

The concluding chapter, "The Market Has No Memory," extends this
discussion to consider the deeper, more abstract implications of the preceding chapters.[9] It also returns to some of my initial fieldnotes, with an aim
to leaving readers with my own ambivalent feelings about the beauty and
the drudgery involved in contemporary rural life in Morocco. If chapters 1
through 6 made the case for why and how globalization operates on one
of its frontiers, my final chapter asks what larger lessons this holds. To my
mind this begins with the temporal dynamics of society, the importance
of differently empowered social actors, and cultural values that cannot be
reduced to instrumental economic rationality. In this final section I make
explicit why I think the temporality of inequality is a useful framework for
examining society, why it helps us to more clearly see the potential and peril
of our global age.

To begin such an argument, I assert that all societies are structured of
inequality. The set of processes we call globalization are thus usefully understood as a transformation of inequality, and especially the temporalities
or time frames by which inequality is expressed. The wage labor economy
relies upon a social unit (the individual) selling labor for immediate return.
It makes no promise for the future and expects none in return. The individual is expected to provide for herself, for sickness or physical disability,
and certainly for the infirmities of old age. Sometimes larger social collec-
tives we call "governments" step in to assist here, but not normally in poor
countries like Morocco. Thus the wage labor economy is made up of very
short-term relationships (hourly wages, immediate sales) between anonymous actors (workers identified by a number, customers who are categori-
cally "sir" or "madam") who are differently empowered (the owner of

---

8. A simple Google search on "child labor Morocco" makes this clear.

9. I borrow the title of this chapter from Kim Hopper's *Reckoning with Homelessness* (2002, 48).

capital or a commodity, laborer, or customer). This stunning simplicity is part of what gives capitalism its expansive power and its explosive fecundity. It is relatively easy to make a farmer a worker, and very difficult to make a worker a farmer. The difficulty lies partially in *mētis* (Scott 1998), the intimate, practical knowledge required to farm in a particular vertical environment, but also in the deeply complex organization of village labor over time periods that extend from a few hours to multiple generations. Community must be built and maintained along with the land it lives on and through. This is hard work.

Tadrar operates with its own temporalities and inequalities. Relationships are lifelong or even beyond. One *owes* parents and grandparents labor as long as they are alive. One may even owe labor to distant religious lodges or saintly lineages or urban relatives that one has never met; portions of what one produces may be claimed by others because of promises uttered by long-dead ancestors. No person can escape these long-term dynamics; they are the foundation of rural society. A young person will only become empowered once she or he becomes old, once children and grandchildren and great grandchildren have been produced to serve. Fertility is thus a main form of wealth—at least as important as productive land.[10] Children are economic necessities *and* a preeminent cultural value.

This is why I argue that globalization—or any transformation of production and reproduction—is usefully conceived in terms of the types of regnant inequalities and their associated time frames. Young migrants who leave Tadrar are exchanging one time frame of inequality (rural, long-term) for another (urban, short-term), one kind of exploitation (of parents over children) for another (owners over workers). Young women are trading the hard life of the mountains for the physically easier (though more isolated and socially restricted) life of the cities. Older men and women are attempting to capture the short-term benefits of exogenous wage labor and integrate it into the longer-term dynamics of household cycles, trying to retain and augment their relative security without leaving the mountains. Others are trying to inject capital into the village from the outside in ways other than wage labor, by drawing government or international development efforts. And still others are resisting, holding out, limiting their participation to cling tenaciously to the rhythms and values of an economy based on the durable

10. See Donald Donham for a discussion of fertility as the "master symbol of Maale [a society in Ethiopia] political economy" (1999, 94). Much of my thinking here on "productive inequalities" also comes from Donham.

loyalty of kin rather than money and commodities.[11] Some do reject participation in the economy of the flatlands, after all; I have met grown men who
claim to have never left the mountains, never seen the ocean or an airport,
or even Marrakech only one hundred kilometers away. Importantly, in an
economy based on the patriarchal household rather than the free individual,
the diversity of responses to capitalist opportunity is filtered through the
social institution of the household, and only makes sense in reference to it.

To my mind, this diversity of integration opens up conceptual possibilities for all of us. Certainly change is inevitable, but perhaps not in the way
that we think. Durable traditions are patterns that we identify as "old" being enacted by new people. "Tradition" is thus about faithful reproduction
of some element or practice that we value in conditions that have changed.[12]
Both reproduction and transformation are common, everyday, inevitable,
ubiquitous. The issue is what is changing, what is not, how change happens,
why, and how fast—a knotty issue social theorists do not seem close to un-
raveling.[13] But just because change is fundamental to human experience does
not mean that the direction or pace of change is predetermined. We are not
compelled to accept every new technology that is invented, to make every
trade that is monetarily profitable, to use any particular resource simply
because it exists, or to exterminate every inefficient, but perhaps intriguing, difference between us. We are not compelled to bow to monetary logic
as if we lived for the economy rather than making it work for our common
needs and desires.

Farmers in Tadrar understand that there are costs to what they seek
from the larger world. They are not mystified, they are not blindly accepting of every gadget and gizmo produced by American corporations in Chinese sweatshops; nor are they ignorant of the savagery of an atomized wage
labor economy based largely, for the poor, on mindless drudgery. Villagers
face desperate circumstances with distressing regularity, however, and thus
are not so quick as Western progressives to abhor what the cities have to offer. Children in Tadrar die at alarming rates, winters are freezing, clothes
are purchased second-hand and fall apart quickly, cheap plastic slippers do
little to protect anyone from rocks, much less snow. The experience of such
a world is certainly, as any anthropologist would contend, "culturally con-

11. For the literature on "resistance," see Scott (1985) and Fletcher (2007).
12. See Graeber (2001) for a sophisticated musing on "value."
13. On the anthropology of time, see Gell (1992), Gluckman (1968), and Munn (1992),
among others.

structed," but cultural constructions engage a material world. The distinction between an ideal and material world is, of course, itself a cultural construction. Scholars no less than farmers are stuck thinking with the tools available, the ideas they have inherited to think with.

In our own scholastic terms, the bodily experience of a difficult life, the ache of overworked backs, numb feet in cold river water, the pain of dentistry without anesthetic, of childbirth without hospital care, the slow-leaking, ineluctable physicality of our human lives: these cannot be dissolved in pools of pure meaning. To bring the experience of contemporary rural poverty into some focus we must bring our own notions (such as "culture," "poverty," and "meaning") into conversation with important concepts in Tadrar (like *takat, ighs,* and *miskin*). One useful way to do this, to try and find a schema that will accommodate rural Berber understandings in contemporary English, is to marry understandings of inequality to temporality. Sometimes this relies more on evocation than explanation, empathy more than intellect. We are all mortal, we live, as one Sufi teacher put it to me, on a narrow bridge of light between two black and fathomless voids—the darkness before birth and the one after death. All of us live in societies that operate in time on this narrow bridge, societies we must reproduce in time as the light pushes back the darkness and the future becomes known; all people, all societies prepare for their future, and do this by synchronizing complicated rhythms of inequality, by organizing undulations of power and weakness, strength and dependency. Approaching social change from the perspective of the temporality of inequality offers a way to grapple with reproduction *and* transformation in both the frenetic world of well-heated houses and the cold dirt huts of farmers negotiating modern time.

Why Tadrar? It was a question that villagers asked me repeatedly as I came to know them during the course of my Ph.D. fieldwork in cultural anthropology. I am not sure how sensible my explanation was to them then or is to the reader now. As a profession, anthropology is quite diverse, but one strand of it has archetypically involved traipsing off to the poorer, less visible regions of the planet to write about what "the natives" are up to. The best way I could think to relate this to the people of Tadrar (who had little idea what a "university" might be, much less anthropology) was that I was going to write a book about life in the mountains. This sounded, in a word, insane. Given the experience of the villagers that the people who write things down tend also to be people who take things away, my plan to write a book did not seem like a good idea to the villagers of Tadrar. So I came to add that (1) the job of a "university" was to write books about every single place in the world, that (2) Tadrar was my assignment, and that (3) the city people who populated universities did not seem to understand the rural world. The third reason was the only part villagers ever found very convincing; even people not so keen to help me still felt strongly that urbanites had no clue about the rural world. Thus began my collaboration with at least some of the people of Tadrar, and our attempt to explain how their part of the rural world works.

From the beginning of anthropology, this sort of collaboration has been a strange way for strange scholars to produce a strange kind of knowledge. As social science this "method" has weathered much abuse in the last few decades, from within and without the guild, but the strident debates about the politics and morality of studying "Others," about whether it is reasonable, desirable, or even morally defensible to leave our cozy natal niches and try to understand people elsewhere, are no longer very interesting—even to most of us who *are* anthropologists. There are exceptions, but most of us today would agree that what anthropologists have called "fieldwork" remains important, that you can do it in your own society or elsewhere, and you can try to present what you think you have discovered in a thousand different ways, each with its own advantages and disadvantages in producing insights and obfuscations. What remains interesting, I think, and what I hope always remains interesting, are the lives of people who are different in some revealing way. In the case here, this means the lives of Berber-speaking Muslim farmers in a valley that is a little remote and changing fast. The people of Tadrar have a very different kind of day than those of us reading English-language books in warm houses in what we have self-identified as the "first" world. An underlying premise of this book is that such differences can be illuminating, even transformative.

This is partly a matter of faith, an odd faith that it is salutary to try and empathetically engage what seem curious ways of thinking, working, dressing, eating, loving, and fighting, even if our understandings are ineluctably imperfect, idiosyncratic, "biased," as my students relentlessly opine in their essays. I believe that it is particularly useful to try and understand people who seem the most different and, on the surface at least, most odd. So this is what I am up to: first off, I hope to render a portrait of a few remarkable people I am lucky to know, to add their way of being to the "consultable record" of what we are doing on the planet these days, and then to make the case that we can learn from them.[14] This last bit will be the toughest, and will require that readers follow me across a tightrope between romanticization (happy villagers living sustainably and communally) and condescension (stupid villagers who cannot seem to grasp the lessons of science and progress). Beyond such stereotypes, what can obscure Moroccan farmers offer the rest of us? What can we offer them?

Finally, it is worth specifically addressing the fact that the people portrayed in this book are Muslims, and often pious ones, too. In an age when Islam is sometimes asseverated as an enemy of freedom and other times held up as the *only* path to true freedom, when "experts" paint the Qur'an as antithetical to modernity and preachers offer it as a solution to modernity's ills, when revolutionaries use Islam as an excuse for reactionary politics while powerful states wield it as thin provocation for imperial slaughter, some readers will find it odd that I do not have a chapter on religion. This is not an accident. I have chosen to include religion when and where it occurs in daily life in the mountains. In Tadrar the practices central to being Muslim are so deeply embedded in daily life that they do not constitute a separable category of experience. I hope that readers can see this, can see how Islam is a crucial background to rural life without being an extractable "cause" for anything. In the mountains, Islam is indeed sometimes put to work for political purposes, but no more than any other religion might be, and almost always in the name of fair play, responsibility, and compassion for the luckless. Islam here is not, as one international "expert" recently intoned, "At a point that Christianity was during medieval times."[15] Islam in Tadrar is contemporary, like the people who profess it, like the social dynamics it informs, and the practices through which it is expressed.

Traditional and modern ways of organizing time are interrelated and interdependent—in Tadrar and everywhere else—and exist contemporaneously to one another. Islam is not on one side or the other, it is not going a different direction than Christianity or Judaism. All societies form households and raise children; we all hope to protect our babies, nurture them,

14. I take this notion of adding others' behavior, and the meanings that motivate it, to the scholarly or "consultable record" from a classic essay by Clifford Geertz (Geertz 1973, 30).

15. I heard this on Radio NZ in New Zealand in late 2005, but it has been stated many times by many people. In the case of rural Morocco, Mikesell wrote in 1973 that, "The economic and social environment of tribal Morocco more closely resembles that in northern Europe at the time of earliest Roman conquest. In recent years Morocco has been struggling with problems that were resolved in the West more than a thousand years ago" (1973, 415).

allow them to stay alive, and to lead meaningful, fulfilling lives. I do not see that Islam is any better or worse at providing the means to make a sensible world than Christianity, Judaism, or any other religion. For my purposes here, I confess that I have my own convictions about the surest paths to damnation, but I lack the requisite longitudinal data to prove anything, and thus cannot confidently recommend my beliefs. Meanwhile, I hope I can reveal my Muslim friends and neighbors as sensitive, sane, deeply caring people with reasonable desires and recognizable fears. I do not believe this is at odds with anthropology's longstanding "passion for difference" (Moore 1994).

The villagers of Tadrar are no threat to anyone's national security (despite the fact that they are Muslim), they do not have anything valuable to sell (except for their sweat, a few bags of almonds, or an occasional goat), and they possess almost no hope of buying any valuables we might (by proxy) produce. Still, despite their failure to be politically intimidating or economically alluring, the people of Tadrar are very much worth knowing. They may help us to better grasp the relationship between individual and collective action, and their inventive use of social forms for the common good offers hope for the future of their country, and beyond.[16] Not a dying branch of our human family tree, these Moroccans living high in the mountains afford a distinctive vantage into some dramatic variation in our contemporary world. Understanding the social logics operative in Tadrar can provide a critical counterpoint to typically Western ways of doing things, to our pervasive assumptions about the world, and how such assumptions shape our actions. My hope is that this modest illustration of an obscure place may help us to tread more compassionately through the angry world we have inherited, and allow us to leave it a more humane place for those who follow. In this sense, then, this book is written for my children, and the children of Tadrar.

16. See Rachik (1992) and Berque (1967, 218).

I

A Place in Time

From the air, Marrakech seems to throb in the summer haze of the brown Haouz Plain like an agitated neuron, thin asphalt tendrils winding out from it. Oddly shaped turquoise splotches ring the better suburbs of the city: the swimming pools of the rich and fortified tourist resorts hemmed in by high walls, palm trees, bougainvillea, and armed guards. Thin sheep graze outside the walls in dirt lots strewn with wisps of plastic bags. The streets are wide here, smooth black asphalt quiet but for the few hours a day when the commuters leave and return, or when busloads of sunburned tourists rumble past on the way to their compounds. Other suburbs are less elegant: mile after mile of rickety cement-block apartments, with rows of stores on the ground floor.

Folded within these suburbs is the medina, the old city center. It remains the core of Marrakech, with imposing red walls erected a thousand years ago and the venerable Koutoubia minaret rising as a sad reminder of spent imperial glory. In the poorer quarters of the medina laundry dries on every rooftop, stirring like Buddhist prayer flags when a breeze wends through the city. Below the jumble of roofs, in the raucous streets of the old urban center, smoke-spewing buses jostle with bicycles and trucks, cars and horse-drawn cabs, donkey carts, pushcarts, pedestrians, and swarms of whining, careening, soot-belching mopeds. At its core Marrakech is a city alive, one of the fastest growing in Morocco, popular with tourists from Kansas to Korea who come seeking heat, sun, and a dose of exotic, "timeless" culture.

The city is particularly popular with Europeans, and an international airport pipes great floods of them in for holidays. The rich retreat to their fortresses while the middle class sprawls into the streets to gorge on the cheap wares produced for them: carpets, scarves, brass bowls, pottery, T-shirts, turbans, thuya wood carvings, lamps, argan oil, ancient doors (and doors weathered to look ancient), and pot after pot of sweet mint tea. Marrakech is professionally exotic now. Tourism is big business, and the stalls of the famous outdoor carnival at Djeema El Fna have been numbered, electrified, and aligned on a grid. Since the end of the French protectorate in 1956, the city's estimated twenty-seven thousand colonial-era prostitutes have been dispersed or driven underground. The medina is now half living city and half folklore-for-sale, a slick and sometimes sad parody of itself. Marrakech remains alluring even in her dotage, however: a busy hive of humanity on a sweltering plain.

South of the city the massive Atlas Mountains stand silent against the sky. Snowcapped from November through July, the core of the range is anchored by a cluster of peaks over four thousand meters (thirteen thousand feet) high. Rivers of snowmelt plunge out of steep valleys, dissipating on their way down until they flow thinly on to the plains. To the north these waters slake Marrakech's growing thirst for daily showers and swimming pools. To the south, what streams escape the mountains are captured in cement dams, or seep into rocky alluvial fans that lose themselves in the desert. Beyond the Atlas is the immense expanse of the Sahara, and beyond that the rest of Africa.

From the perspective of Marrakech, the Atlas Mountains stand as solemn, unfriendly guardians between the modern, civilized world—anchored by the city—and the great desert beyond. The mountains are a place of the past, where cultural practices survive not because they are for sale, but because people evidently cannot, or do not want to, escape, because people labor hard to reproduce themselves and their way of being. Many urbanites are recent migrants themselves, but the children and grandchildren of mountain people do not dwell on this past, do not usually romanticize it. Most urban young people think of the mountains as dirty, old-fashioned, ignorant, laborious, forgettable. This is perhaps changing as the government begins to promote (rather than repress) the Berber heritage of the nation, but the stereotypical picture of a mountain Berber is still a bumpkin.

Marrakech is a city of migrants, a city built of migrant labor that flows out of the mountains like the melting snow. Some migrants stay and become urban. Some are here to seek their fortune and return to their mountain homes. Some have only physically left the mountains—they remain socially ensconced in their rural households and are still working for and within those households. From the perspective of the people who retain their links to the highlands, the forbidding Atlas look very different. There are no generic peaks, valleys, or rivers, no categorical villages, but instead specific named places, routes to, from, and among them, and warm known people in those places that bring them to life. To mountain people the mountains are "home," with all the particularity that such a word evokes. What might look traditional or old-fashioned or static in the flatlands can feel quite novel and even vibrant up in the thinner air; changes in the rural world are not easy to detect from without, and cannot be simply deduced from a television in a mud-walled house, or a cigarette wrapper in the dung by a shepherd's hut. If Marrakech hovers luminous and exotic on the periphery of the Western imagination, the Atlas are an imaginary beyond, a periphery of a periphery, even from the perspective of many Moroccans. This is a hard land of Berber (rather than Arabic) speaking farmers and herders, of insular mud-walled villages clinging to hillsides above the life-sustaining water of the rivers.

I first visited the village of Tadrar in 1995 while lost, wandering up the Agoundis River from the paved road at Ijoukak, searching for a Ph.D. dissertation topic and a place out of the heat. I had no map, no food, and no real plan. At that time there was no running water in the Agoundis, except

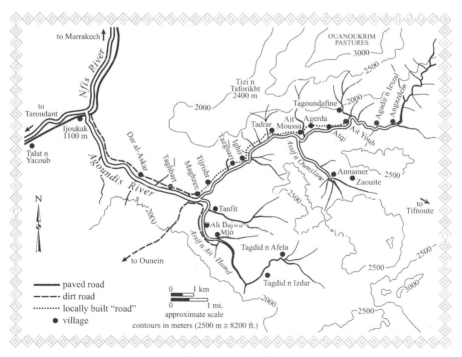

The Agoundis valley

for the river, no electricity, solar or otherwise, no toilets. Indeed, there was no road. The only way into the upper Agoundis Valley, and to Tadrar, was a series of narrow mule paths chiseled into the hillsides.

From the main path, looking down, you would see massive walnut trees crowding the boulders of the riverbed. Fields of maize (in late summer) and barley (in spring) grow in carefully built terraces above the spring flood level. Almonds are planted throughout the fields and even higher, on ledges beyond irrigation where they grow thin and dry in hopes of rain. Rock and mud houses are terraced above the trees, clustered together in places that least frequently suffer rock slides. Grapes, pomegranates, figs, blackberries, squash, mint, potatoes, and tomatoes grow where space can be found in the dizzying patchwork of fields, trails, mud dams, and irrigation ditches. Olives, carob trees, and prickly pear cactus are scattered around the lower elevations. On the highest slopes above the village there are a few remaining Atlas cedar, some juniper and oak trees that the women use for firewood, and clumps of overeaten grass for the herds of goats and sheep. These public resources are ever scarcer, however, and are protected by sporadically enforced government laws.

The fields in the valley bottom are watered year-round by the ever-melting snow of the great Ouanoukrim Massif. Water is captured in temporary dams in the river that feed seven main *targas,* or canals, and many hundreds of minor channels and ditches. Each of these waterways has a particular name, as does each of the 1,411 fields of Tadrar, and so people are able to discuss space and movement through space at a level of detail sure to baffle any outsider. The *targas* are operated in rotation by the twenty-eight households of the village, and each canal has either a nine-day or ten-day cycle, with different households owning different sections of the days. Sometimes a wealthier household will own a whole day's worth of irrigation water on a given canal, or even two days in a ten-day cycle. Poorer families can sometimes lay claim to no more than a few hours every ten days, and for them it is a long wait until they again have access to the precious water. The order of the rotations is decided by lottery at the beginning of the dry season, but the quantity of time is determined by inheritance, by the quantity of land owned.

The majority of the land in Tadrar is given over to grain, though some fields are too shady, especially those deep in the canyon beneath the walnut trees. These fields are used to grow *tooga,* fodder for the animals. The trails are too steep and narrow to drive the cows to the *tooga,* however, so the women bring the fodder to the cows. They cut it down near the riverbed until it runs out. When this is gone (as it is all winter long) women harvest bushes and shrubs from the mountains above the village and haul loads larger than themselves back to the lowing cows invisible in dark pens under the houses. The songs of the young women and girls echo through the valley as they carry fodder and water, collect wood for the bread ovens, or wash clothes, milk cows, and lug babies around in slings on their backs. Men and older boys work the irrigation system, plow, plant, and care for the sheep and goats in pastures both near and far. Younger boys mostly throw rocks at each other.

For those lucky enough to own flocks, there are more fertile, distant pastures, a day's strenuous hike up at nearly three thousand meters above sea level, beneath the ridges of the Ouanoukrim Massif, a cluster of peaks at the center of what tourists know as the Jebel Toubkal National Park. These pastures are comparatively lush, but terribly cold and wind-swept. They can only be used during a few months of summer. The shepherds bring the animals down to their winter grazing area just above the village in October, before the heavy snows. Other less hardy animals, especially sheep, are kept in these local winter pastures year-round.

Partly because of the availability of these extensive pastures above the villages, partly because of the availability of water combined with the scarcity of flat land, this is one of the most densely populated areas of Morocco in terms of people per arable land unit (Bencherifa 1983, 274). In other words, these Berbers make more human bodies out of less dirt than almost anyone. This is part of the reason that the mountains function as a demographic pump—constantly generating surplus bodies that seep into the larger economy. Bodies are necessary for the intense labor needs of highland farming, but these bodies can only be built slowly, over time, and it is hard to plan well in a constantly changing world. Babies are insurance for the parents, but babies, too, must grow up and find a place in the crowded fields of the village. With a finite land base, there is always emigration. The intensive productivity of its mountain agro-pastoral system gives Tadrar a lush, Shangri-La feel: it is a dense thicket of green bursting from the crevasses of dry, impossibly rugged mountains. But it is a hard place, no paradise. There is little to sell, and thus no cash for doctors or dentists, books, paper, medicine, or, sometimes, even shoes. "*Ishqa*," people said to me again and again, "*toudert n'idrarn ishqa*." Life in the mountains is hard.

◈ ◈ ◈

The body of Tadrar, the village itself, appears as a single mud and rock structure, a tumble of uneven blocks piled up the side of a steep ravine, or *talat,* that slices down the cliff face and empties into the river. Strewn with massive boulders and usually dry, this streambed plunges from a fracture in the rock wall above the village and falls through a progressively greener, thicker cover of walnuts, figs, and almonds. Tadrar is stacked up just outside the trees, above the irrigated terraces next to the *talat.* The village is a jumble of roofs and walls, a seemingly ad hoc set of straight lines that somehow form the right angles and odd rectangles that make buildings and indicate "home." Some houses stand apart from the main village—solitary, squat, earthen structures with flat rooftop patios and small windows inset with metal screens and wooden shutters. But most of the village houses are wound together into a central knot that rises precipitously fifty meters above the road in a three-dimensional labyrinth of packed earth and precariously balanced rock. Invisible from outside the village, there is a cramped plaza open to the sky at the core of Tadrar, an *assarag.* Three dark passageways provide access to it, and go out from it on to the trails that lead to the surrounding animal pens, fields, orchards, storehouses, streams, and pastures.

On one side of the *assarag,* with a view out of the village over the road and river, is the mosque. It is indistinguishable from any other building. No plaque, special entrance, inscription, or directions tell you that this is the religious heart of the community. Inside the low door is a small antechamber: a bench runs along one wall along with an open window giving out on a view of the river; the wooden bier for the dead is propped in the corner. Just beyond this room is a long, narrow chamber with a series of taps running along the wall and another bench. Here the village men wash before praying and also do their more thorough bathing. The water is heated by a wood furnace invisible beyond the walls, or was until solar hot water was installed in 2004. Past this room is the actual mosque where men pray, a room empty but for reed mats on the floor, one high window, and a niche in the wall facing east.

The village is not set in two-dimensional space, and few visitors will be able to ignore what scholar Jacques Berque called the "audacious verticality" of the region (1955, 29). One never moves simply in or out from the village core, but always up or down, usually up *and* down along with much winding and turning. On the ground nothing is straight, nothing flat. Movement can be a general vector, but progress is a sensuously uneven route inscribed in the dirt, with a named destination at the end of it; destinations always involve travel past named places, around places and through them, and always moving up or down in addition to out or back. The paths unwind from the core of the buildings along the contours of the mountains like nerves to the extremities of the body. In one sense Tadrar, the mud and rock of the village, the physical structure itself, appears part of the land, a convoluted reconfiguration of the mountains themselves. But it *is* reconfigured. The ragged peaks seem to have been coaxed into recognizable order only in this one unusual spot. The stately, upright mien of the village states emphatically that here, within precisely built walls and perfectly smooth roofs, live *people*. Consistent angles and straight lines exist nowhere else in the mountains but for the tightly structured enclaves where people labor to set things straight. As in other areas of Morocco, the common word here for trustworthy, honest, or reliable is *nishan,* straight. To be *nishan* is to be—notably and in the best sense—human; it is to behave humanely.

This overview might give the reader some sense of how it feels to dwell in Tadrar, but is not, of course, how a villager comes to know her place. Imagine a baby born here. She enters the social world as she did the biological: through her mother. Babies come first to a small, dark room, maybe near the kitchen, certainly away from the door. From the world outside this room there are sounds—lowing cattle, chickens clucking, barking dogs, a crackling radio, the gentle rhythm of the call to prayer. Babies are born in the darkness on the carpets they will live on for years to come, blankets hand woven by mothers and grandmothers from wool sheared from sheep raised on the mountainsides above them, blankets that growing children will sleep under, fold, wash, stack, and shake out for themselves or guests countless times. But at first the world will be dark, the window, if there is one, shuttered. Neighbors and family visit, voices in the gloom. There will be eating and talking, the smell of mint tea and henna, wood smoke, women's sweat, warm bread and boiled eggs, women's voices mostly, and whispered prayers rolling from individuals and small clusters of the pious, submitting themselves to the will of God in the lambent poetry destined to form the soundtrack of every major life transition to come. As the week progresses more light is let in, and after seven days, if the child has survived, groups of women will come with gifts of food or firewood and the new villager will receive a name. Blessings given, blessings received, the new baby will be strapped with a shawl to her mother's back and venture out from the room where she entered this world. The mother returns to work, and the child comes to sense the places that matter to women's work.

Preeminent among these is the kitchen, the *anwal.* These exist in all sorts of formations, but most are simply an empty room with two or more conical ovens built into the floor, the *tikatin* (singular, *takat*)—the hearth of the home. It is constructed of mud packed around a specially designed clay pot, set upright and scored such that one longitudinal section can be taken out. Daily fires harden the mud to what feels like concrete. The slit up one side allows for kindling the fire and adding wood. They are open on the top, where pots of soup may be set to boil. *Takat* means "oven," "hearth," and also "household." This hearth is the heart of the home, the primordial origin of all new villagers. Here, warm against mother's back, eyes closed against the acrid smoke, babies are bathed in the scent of women, spiced coffee, boiling barley, and bread baking slowly in the ovens.

Most families eat on the roof in summer, or in an open terrace called a *hneet,* where they gather around the *tajine. Tajine* is the word for the peaked clay pots in which meals are simmered, and the word for the meals themselves. Cooked over coals scooped out of the *takat* and placed in a brazier, the *tajine* is filled with vegetables, a little oil, maybe some pepper or cumin, maybe a small piece of meat. It is placed on a low, round table, around which everyone sits on the floor. New babies suckle while mothers eat, or make many trips back and forth from the kitchen to the table with mother if there are no younger boys and girls to fetch the food. The patriarch (usually) reaches into a straw basket covered by a cloth and tears the rough, bowl-shaped *tanoort,* the bread distinctive to this region, into pieces. He scatters them around the table and announces the beginning of the meal with the name of God. Each person repeats *bismillah* before his or her first move to eat. The lid is removed from the *tajine,* and people tear their scraps of *tanoort* into smaller, bite-sized pieces, then dip them in the oil and vegetables of the *tajine,* and savor what the grace of God and the labor of women have delivered.

If there is meat, it is removed and placed in the lid until everyone is finished. Anyone who stops is encouraged to continue, and the conversation around the table is continually punctuated by the command, *shta,* eat. You draw only from the section of the dish in front of you, and to be polite you might press particularly delicious bits away from your section into a neighbor's, who, usually, will subtly flick them back. When everyone is done, or almost done, the patriarch divides the meat, rarely more than a bite per person and usually not even that. In lean times there may be no vegetables or meat, but there is always bread. Bread is provided by God through the fertility of the fields or, failing that, by God through the properly Muslim generosity of more fortunate family and neighbors. Nobody goes hungry.

After dinner the table and the *tajine* are removed, uneaten *tanoort* goes back in the basket and is taken to the cows or chickens, and someone young brings around a kettle of warm water and a bowl to wash in. Then there is the extended ceremony of drinking tea, and while the young clean up, the older people rise to get back to work. There is no local category of "work," however, except for relatively rare paid labor. Carrying babies, preparing food, tilling fields, threshing barley: these have their own verbs, but in general people are "making," "doing," or "busying" themselves. People are always busy, always doing, but they do not necessarily think of it as "work."[1]

The fields are terraced up the steep mountainsides and strung together with a dense arterial network of canals and ditches that must be constantly maintained. As the river bites steadily into the bottom of the valley, scratching incrementally deeper into the history of the mountains, back in time, men struggle upward, pushing against gravity, against time, hoisting stone, moving rock, carrying dirt, transporting the animal dung that will render the land productive, that will allow the women to harvest the grain comprising the subsistence economy of the mountains—an economic mode coupled to a set of values (Michel 1997, 3). Every field has been wrenched from the mountainside, constructed and reconstructed, repaired, watered, and cared for by a long series of nameable persons. Each field has come into existence through human labor and survives (and remains fertile) only through continuous, coordinated work. This is the most "constructed" rural landscape in all of North Africa (Berque 1955, 24), and the construction is entirely accomplished through the sweat of humans and their animals.

Each field has a name and a history. The *egran n tamghart,* or "fields of a woman," were a set of plots a long-dead father graciously gave to his son so the son could marry; the *egr n akshoodn,* or field of wood, was passed between families one particularly cold winter when "the snow was above our hips" and a man traded it for firewood. Sometimes fields are spoken of as families, such that a small field next to a larger one will be known as "the

---

1. For an Algerian example of the same sort of thing, see Bourdieu (1973, 83).

son of" that larger one, the medium-sized one beside it the "wife." These families of fields support the human generations and flow through them, separating and coming together in ever-novel combinations as households arrange and rearrange themselves, accommodating death, incorporating migrations, births, and marriages.

Trees, too, are sometimes named, especially the giant, venerable walnut trees dominating sunnier areas down near the river. Young walnuts are planted in the middle of fields, in full sun. They grow quickly, shooting out bright green new leaves, but are said to be "girls" or "virgins" until they are moved. When they reach the age when they are too large for their natal field, young walnuts are dug up and transported to the spot where they will reach adulthood, where they will grow to become reproductive. The area to which a tree moves will be more steadily watered but shadier than the field of its birth, an appropriate place for the needs of an adult tree. The new place will probably be near the river or at least near the beginning of one of the larger canals so that the deep roots can drink through the heat of summer. Here the girl tree becomes a woman, a *tamghart,* and begins to produce walnuts. Like women, it is believed a tree will not be fertile unless she leaves the place of her birth and goes to reach maturity someplace else.

A boy child comes to understand his house as the house of his father, his grandfather, and his grandfather's father before him. The household—the people who operate the house, stay alive within it and through it—are all assembled around the social skeleton provided by a line of men. Girl children, too, belong to this line of men, the father's family, but girls come to understand that the house that they are born and grow in will not be the house in which they grow old. A girl will move to marry, will live among other men and women. To become a woman a girl must move as her mother has, as her mother's mother and her father's mother have also. If men provide the bones—the *ighsan,* or lineages—that are used to organize everything from male labor to property devolution and the politics of the village, women are the blood of rural life, flowing between families and villages, and sometimes down to the city, nurturing the bones and connecting the village body into a broadly reticulated social order.

Beneath large walnut trees the earth is too shady for grain and grows only *tooga,* grass for the animals. Bound to their mothers, babies move first to the places where *tooga* is gathered, as it must be collected twice a day if the family is lucky enough to have a cow. Babies may go with aunts or sisters or cousins, too, but they move *through* the vast majority of village territory, *past* most of the trees and most of the fields, and only move *to* the small, scattered parts of it that the household owns. "Land" is not a general thing, but a collection of a few highly familiar places nestled among the less familiar. All places are associated with people, individuals who own them, groups who work them, and the relationships between places reflect relationships between people. The fields and their sustaining canals connect people. Women are likely to gather *tooga* with other women whose household fields are near to theirs. Boys are likely to cooperate in cleaning canals or irrigating with neighbors who have fields nearby, or who have irrigation rights on the same day of rotation. Sometimes these rights and properties are held by larger family groupings, clusters of households, sometimes the fields of related households are coextensive because they were inherited from the same person, and the work can be shared among relatives. But not always. The lands of Tadrar are enormously complex, as particular as the social relations deployed to render them productive. There is much give and take, borrowing and loaning, gifts of labor and time, the occasional theft of water or crops, and a constant assessment of who is working with whom, for whom, against whom, and why.

As her back grows strong and her hands calloused, a girl comes to know the forests where she cuts wood, and how to avoid the government rangers. She will milk the cow on her own, and gather fodder for the cows with her girlfriends and cousins rather than her mother; she will help the older women pound clothes clean in the river and spread them to dry in the trees or on warm rocks, and she will squat in the kitchen learning to cook, listening to stories, assessing opinions, gathering news. From being scrubbed in the *hamam,* or steam bath, along with the other children, a girl learns to scrub younger children. And at the end of the day, if the men have yet to return from the mosque, women will sit together on rooftops or in dining rooms, or at one special spot on one covered lane just off the open *assarag* at the center of the village. Here they rest briefly between the work of the day and the work of the evening, as the sun sinks beneath the peaks. At this time the wind settles and you can hear the faint bleating of the flocks become louder as the shepherds return to the village. The sunset call to prayer echoes from the roof of the mosque deep into the canyon. Come to pray. God is great. There is no God but God. God is great. Come to pray.

People eat, then drink tea, some go for a final prayer, dishes are cleaned, blankets unfolded, then most lay down on the carpets they have eaten on and drift into sleep. The shepherds up in their *azuab,* or huts by the pastures, douse their small fires. They have the flocks corralled and turn them over to the care of the dogs. Down in the village, mothers suckle crying babies and shush them to sleep, a few people listen to cassette players until the cheap batteries fade. Propane lanterns blink off, glow orange for a minute, then die, one by one. If there is no moon, the men with night rotations on the canals leave to irrigate with lanterns or flashlights, often in groups of two or three, talking softly, walking surely down the treacherous paths their feet know well from a lifetime's experience. The sky swims with stars, fireflies swarm in the dark pockets beneath the walnuts; a million frogs croak madly for mates above the susurrus of the river. A dog barks, then yelps and is silent. And the village is quiet.

This was how I came to see Tadrar when I lived there for part of 1998 and 1999, but I did not come to these impressions all at once. Like anyone else, I was introduced to Tadrar along a specific route, a set of pathways that came to structure what I knew. In fact, when I passed through the village the first time I did not stop. It was 1995, and I was trekking with a Moroccan friend. We were lost and paused only long enough to chat with a man who invited me to stay; I did not write down his name, but said I'd be back. I am sure Abdurrahman was surprised when I returned.

When I staggered into Tadrar the second time, I felt nearly dead. It was July of 1998. I was a nervous Ph.D. candidate with a backpack crammed with the paraphernalia of fieldwork, from cooking pots to tape recorders, a camera and water filter, antibiotics and a sleeping pad. The village now boasted a Peace Corps volunteer, and a few tourists wandered through, so I was not the novelty I had been only a few years before. There was a dirt road now, but I was still walking. The backpack weighed more than me, or seemed to, and I had been traveling since 4:00 A.M. by bus, crowded group taxis, and then by foot. It was nearly dark when I got to the final incline below Tadrar; I doffed my pack, collapsed by the side of the road, and prayed for a mule, a truck, a miracle.

Instead, to my horror, a group of women rounded the bend below me, chattering and laughing. When they came nearer, I saw they were not just returning from the fields but were traveling resplendent in their best clothes, with sequins, bangles, and scarves of every hue, from luminous lime green and yellow to crimson, purple, gold, and orange. They wore jangling tin jewelry, beads, and twittered all at once, musically, singing and joking. Their hands and feet were stained the burnt rust color of henna. I wrote that night in my journal that they appeared to me like a flock of tropical birds, or bright reef fish. I thought I might be hallucinating. They belonged anywhere but on this dusty mountain road.

The women were coming from a *moussem,* they said, a kind of fair held around the tomb of a saint, and they gathered in a circle to examine me. At first only the older women would speak, but my obvious helplessness and their festive mood soon had everyone peppering me with questions. I could not understand most of them, especially with the younger girls giggling hysterically, literally crying with laughter behind the skirts of their elders. They wanted to know where I was going, if I meant to go to Tadrar, if I was looking for Abdurrahman (since I was obviously going to Tadrar, and he was the only one there likely to know foreigners), and, most of all, what in God's name was in that huge pack. My *Tashelhit* (Berber) was worse than shaky. I said, "I'm tired," which sent them into paroxysms of laughter. "My pack is very big" also sent them into convulsions, and inspired one brazen lady to lift it single-handedly and declare loudly that it was not heavy at all. She strolled off insouciantly with the pack over one shoulder, and I was forced to stumble after her to take up my ridiculous parcel myself. Thus humiliated, shaking my head confusedly to the questions that kept coming, I shouldered the pack and dragged myself up the road, prodded by the women like a decrepit mule.

Thus I arrived at Abdurrahman's door, the man who had invited me three years before. It was the first door of the first house next to the road, at the base of the village. By this point the women had run silent, melted into the village pathways, slid inside houses and disappeared into stables, their ebullience muffled by the weight of village propriety. I was bidden to enter Abdurrahman's small, irregular door and passed into a dark hallway, then through a second door, then a third. I dropped my pack to the floor. Abdurrahman laid thick carpets on top of the plastic mat, a red one, an orange one, and a striped white and black blanket, too. I writhed out of my boots and collapsed. He asked, "Would you like some tea?"

"Yes," I stammered. "And some water." He left me there lying flat on my back in the room that every outsider visiting Tadrar seems to come through. It is the only room most guests ever see.

Abdurrahman's reception room is just over two meters wide and five long. The walls are rock and mud covered by smooth cement, the faded blue and red paint wearing off. The low roof beams are painted with geometric designs in red, yellow, and green. They are patched, like the cracks in the walls, with gashes of white plaster. A stern old print of Abdurrahman's father, Ali, hangs high on one wall, above an elaborate calligraphic rendering of a verse from the Qur'an and a small calendar with both the Muslim and Christian dates. One tiny window looks out over the *agrur*, or stable, and has a shred of screen tacked over it to deter the flies. Another window looks out over the road and the valley southward. There is no glass in the windows here or, in 1998, anywhere in the village, rendering all rooms permanently dark in the winter. Both small windows contain metal arabesque screens that keep children from tumbling out of them; both close only with small wooden shutters. The evening light through the open window fills the room with a wonderfully warm, lemony light, and I lay there that first day staring at the designs on the roof beams, rapturously thankful for the sugary tea seeping into my veins.

This was the first place I came to know—Abdurrahman's reception room—and through the end of my fieldwork it remained the room I knew best. Even as I am writing, in distant New Zealand, a year after I last sat with Abdurrahman, I can still imagine every crack in the walls of that room, every chip of paint. I know the design of every carpet stacked in the corner waiting to be unfurled. I spent hours there eating and talking, listening to tapes of the Qur'an and Tashelhit music, making tapes of English words for Abdurrahman to learn, asking questions about kinship and property and writing down the answers, watching Abdurrahman entertain guests and dignitaries, listening to him expound on village history and family relations. For the first six months I lived in the village this was the only room in Abdurrahman's house I ever saw. It was nearly three months before I ever had a meal with his family as a whole. Before that it was always Abdurrahman and me, alone or joined by the Peace Corps volunteer, Ryan, or by senior men visiting from other households or other villages or, sometimes, Abdurrahman's eldest son, Mohammed. Even when the whole family did come to eat together, there were always two tables, clearly separated by status. I was stranded at the elite one. Khadija, Abdurrahman's wife, would barely make eye contact with me and plainly preferred that I talk to her husband, her sons, anyone but her. She remained at the far table for the duration of my initial stay in Tadrar.

Abdurrahman has, in short, a fairly formal household. What I call the reception room was used for other things when I was not there. But my presence transformed this room into a formal space, and to some degree this remained the case all the while I lived in the village. I saw the kitchen once in fourteen months, when I was asked to translate its contents for an older, female tourist who had asked Khadija to see it. I saw their bathroom from time to time (the only one in the village in 1998, installed to meet the requirements of Abdurrahman's occasional tourist guests). And I spent one night sleeping on their roof. A few times in winter I packed into a small windowless room they have along with all the family to stay warm. This was during Ramadan, when Abdurrahman would awaken me early for the *sahour*, the pre-dawn meal that would sustain us through the day's fast. As time went on, Khadija and Abdurrahman stated plainly many times—together and apart—that I was always welcome, that I was one of the family, that I should walk in and not knock. But I was a friend of the patriarch, not a member of the family. Even warm summer evenings on the roof, Abdurrahman and I tended to gravitate to one end, the women and children to the other, with Mohammed and the older boys in the middle. This house, and this household, was my first portal, my first path, into understanding Tadrar.

The second came with my neighbors, the Lukstaf family. Within a day of arriving in Tadrar to begin my research I rented a room in a house owned by Hamad Lukstaf, who had moved to the city. His brother Mohammed lived next door, but the brothers were not on good terms and so I was not especially welcomed by the Lukstaf family in the early days of my village life. It did not matter to me, since my language skills were too poor to talk much anyway; I was happy to spend time alone studying in my room. But I was always observed, never really alone.

Omar Lukstaf was Mohammed's grandson, and he was about eight or nine years old. He didn't know exactly. When I met him, he wore a threadbare "Superbowl" T-shirt almost daily, with a faded Joe Montana dropping back for a pass, but of course he had no idea what football was, much less "a pass." At first Omar would just sit furtively in my doorway, his big brown eyes watching me write or read. But I soon gave him a notebook of his own to draw in, and we began to practice writing Arabic letters and Berber words for things; we became friends. There was no government school then, and Omar had only studied at the mosque. He was not very good at writing or drawing and in fact could barely make out his name. He wanted to learn, though, and filled his pages with written lines of "Omar" and the names of his brothers and sisters. He began to bring his younger siblings, and they would cluster together to examine magazines my mother had sent me from home—*Sports Illustrated, Surfer,* and *National Geographic* were what she supposed I might read. The children tried to guess what the pictures meant.

(They had a particularly hard time with surfing pictures, and they assessed Tiger Woods golfing as an imam leading a prayer.) I also had a book with me that had pictures of household objects with the Tamazight (Berber) words spelled next to them. Once I had memorized it, I gave the book to Omar to practice reading; later his grandmother Aisha, Mohammed Lukstaf's wife, came over to thank me and invite me to dinner.

The Lukstaf family is much poorer than Abdurrahman's. Their house was twenty meters or so from mine, a freestanding structure away from the core of the village. It presented what might generously be called a casual appearance. You enter from the uphill side, on the second floor. As in most houses, there is only one door. Upon entering, immediately on your right is a small storage room with a tattered cloth to hide it; there is little stored there, just some pans and a bit of crockery. On the left is the *anwal,* the kitchen, a cramped, dark room with a few clay bowls, wooden spoons, a stack of branches and kindling, and the two ovens continuously belching smoke. There is a small hole in the upper part of the far wall, but often as not the smoke pours out the low doorway. The whole room is black with soot, and the floor is packed earth. A step beyond the kitchen is the *hneet,* a large room with a sort of bench running along one side, open with a view out over the road and the river. It has cement-covered floors and walls, and a tree trunk in the middle to support the roof made of sticks, roughly hewn branches, and packed dirt. To the right of the *hneet* is the only other room the family uses for living quarters. Small children are put down for naps here, to keep them out of the way, and in the winter the whole family squeezes in to stay warm. There are storage rooms down below, and a stable, accessible only from outside. Upstairs, where the people live, there is only the open-air *hneet,* the kitchen, and this one other small room for sleeping. There is no concept of "dining room" or "bedroom." All rooms are multipurpose except kitchens. Unlike Western houses, rooms here do not so plainly prescribe their contents and the processes appropriate to them. The way people use the space in the rooms, however, is highly prescribed by gender, and the position of the individual within the composition of the family.

After that first meal I generally ate at least once every day with the Lukstaf family. At first the patriarch, Aisha's husband, Mohammed, ate alone with me. The Lukstaf house, though, does not have a separate room to serve guests, so Mohammed's teenaged granddaughter Khadija would either have to crouch on the other side of the room waiting to serve us, or pretend to busy herself in the smoky kitchen and wait to be called. It was similar with the other women: Fatima, Mohammed's oldest son's wife, Mohammed's own wife, Aisha, and the little granddaughter Fatima. The boys, too, would want to see their grandfather talk to the odd foreigner, and so Omar and his brothers, Mohammed, Hassan, and Hussein, were always lurking around, hunched in corners, watching me with suppressed giggles. All were kept away for the first few meals, but slowly people started to creep in, first listening in on the conversation, but soon joining it from across the room. Little by little people started to join old Mohammed and me on the carpets around the low table. First his son Ali, on the infrequent occasions he was down from the pastures. Then grandmother Aisha, always jolly, always laughing. Then the older grandsons, Mohammed Jr. and eventually Omar. The little ones would climb on, too, until at the end of six months there would be thirteen of us pressed around a wooden table only a meter across trying to eat out of one common bowl. The Lukstaf family was still careful to outfit me with a comfortable carpet to sit on, and a warm wool blanket with which to wrap myself when it was cold. They were always extravagantly hospitable, presenting me with too large a share of any meat that might be available, and beseeching me to eat more long after I was stuffed. *Ar timiyartik,* they would say, you are "used to" or "comfortable" here. If I had not exactly become one of the family, I was assuredly a different kind of guest.

The structure of the Lukstaf house allowed for little formality. In the summer everybody slept together in the *hneet.* In the winter all were crammed into the one small, warm room next to the *hneet.* Grandfather Mohammed certainly ruled with an iron hand, but this was guided by a soft heart. It was far from uncommon toward the end of a meal for the grandchildren to run quickly out the door and disappear as the old man started to delegate work assignments. Old Mohammed would thunder fiercely for their return, but when thunder broke without effect, and even the mischievous giggling of the grandsons had faded, he would chuckle. Mohammed would open his eyes with mock incredulity and ask, "Did you see that? They went! They just *went!*" And he'd laugh quietly and get up to busy himself in his fields.

The third household through which I came to know Tadrar was that of Mohammed Belaid and his wife, Fatima Id Baj, who were my neighbors on the other side of my house from the Lukstafs. I met Fatima before I came to know her husband. One morning in the first few days of my stay, when I knew little of who was who, and people still did not know me, Fatima called at my door. She stood with a pot of coffee and a big bowl-shaped loaf of bread wrapped in a scarf. I don't remember what I had been doing. What I do remember is that I was experiencing a lack-of-caffeine crisis alone in my room, and that I had nothing but canned sardines to eat and nothing to eat them on, and that there could have been no more welcome sight in the whole universe than a pot of coffee and a folded slab of freshly baked *tanoort*.

Our communication was poor because I had not yet mastered even the simplest Tashelhit. But Fatima had lived for a short time in Rabat and could thus make sense of the Moroccan Arabic that at that time I could still remember. This was sufficient to make our way through the formal conversation that all people everywhere seem to have when they first meet. It was clear enough that she was welcoming me, her bright smile alone said that. The bread and coffee were for me; that seemed clear, too. I was thrilled. I was stumbling around trying to thank her, trying to figure out how to invite her in for coffee, sardines, and bread without appearing to ask anything inappropriate. It did not seem wise to invite a married woman into what was effectively my bedroom, but it did not seem right to just retreat inside with the coffee and food to consume it alone. More delicacy was required than I could verbally manage, and in the midst of my stammering and stalling my landlord's voice came booming from the inside of the main part of the house.

"Get out of here with that coffee," Hamad yelled at Fatima. His tone suggested that she was supremely ignorant. "Don't you know Christians don't drink coffee!?" Fatima apologized in a flurry, thrust the bread into my hand, and sped off with the coffee. I nearly wept. The other "Christian" in the village, the Peace Corps volunteer Ryan, or "Khalid," was Mormon and indeed did not drink coffee, and through limited contact with him my landlord had, in his inimitable way, become as much an expert on Christian practices as he was on all else. Thus began the first of many explanations I was to give about the different kinds of "Christians," explanations that never failed to perplex the villagers.

Fatima was not altogether convinced by Hamad, probably because she saw me so obviously crestfallen when she retracted her coffeepot, and also because it simply did not make sense to her that a person would be offended by an offer of coffee. In any case, it was not long before I began to eat meals at Fatima and Belaid's house, and not long after that that Fatima started to care for me, bringing me small cups of fresh milk each morning and checking on me at night to make sure I had eaten, that I had a candle for light, that all was okay. She and her husband loaned me carpets to sleep on, dishes, sugar, bread, and good will. I eventually hired them to help with laundry, and Fatima always broke up my bricks of sugar because I tended to smash my fingers when I tried to do it. Fatima became something like a sister, while Aisha o Hussein (Mohammed Lukstaf's wife, or Granny Aisha as I came to call her) was a kind of mother. I admit that I did little to dissuade them of my utter dependency. After those first days I never again ate alone. Fatima's house came to be the most comfortable place in the village for me, at least when Belaid was present to dampen any suspicion of impropriety.

Fatima and Belaid's house sits just below the window of the antechamber of the mosque, where the old men gather to pass the time and look down over the few houses below the main part of the village. Belaid's front door is very small, less than a meter and a half high and more suitable for hobbits than men. This gives into a dark, cramped hallway about four meters long and a head or two shorter than me. I nearly knocked myself unconscious here at least a half a dozen times. This cramped hall in turn gives on to the only room in the upstairs part of the house. It is low and narrow, not quite two meters high, and just over two meters wide by about four meters long. There is a doorway leading outside to the *akfaf*, the rooftop of the stable below, where the family sleeps and meals are served on the hottest nights of the summer. This *akfaf* is protected from public view by the house, and so is a cozy, private outdoor space. Some of my best nights in the village were spent here. With the children asleep on the blankets around us, Fatima, Belaid, and I looked up at the night sky talking about everything from comparative parenting techniques to the virtues and drawbacks of city life, from the mysteries of walnut pollination to the origin of starlight.

The very structure of Fatima and Belaid's home could not support the sort of formality that Abdurrahman manages, or the sheer number of people in the Lukstaf household. Partly this is what made my interactions with them so intimate. Certainly, too, they were approximately my age, and in 1999 they had only two children, who in the evenings would fall asleep in our laps and allow us to speak privately. Privacy can only exist in a place like Abdurrahman's, where a room is specifically defined for it, or in a place like Fatima and Belaid's, where the small number of people in the house virtually ensures it. But these seem to me different sorts of privacy, one self-conscious—a room preserved from family use—the other organic, a function of the space itself. The specified privacy of a reception room is different from what Belaid and Fatima offered. More than just allowing for privacy, the forced intimacy of sitting knee to knee in a small room does something to encourage a different, more personal or more expansive mode of conversation, as does reclining together drinking tea under an African sky alive with stars. This is not to propose a spatial determinism, but a small group of people (as opposed to a large group) conversing in a securely private space (as opposed to a public one) encourages intimacy of conversation. Also, in the winter the cramped quarters made it necessary to walk through the area where Fatima cooked in order to get to the place where we ate. This is how I, as a male, came to understand something of how women worked. Fatima was able to remain involved in the conversation while she went about preparing meals or baking bread. There was little, or at least less, separation by gender as compared with larger households, or wealthier households, and certainly households that were both larger and wealthier. Houses are "machines for living" (Bray 1998), and their spaces become what they are through practices—especially labor practices—which reflect gender and other inequalities of power.

In this chapter I have tried to conjure a sense of the relationship between physical space and social life in Tadrar. Through an overview of the spaces important to village life, and snapshots of the places through which I came to understand the village, I have tried to evoke the sensuous particularity of the village. I have emphasized that spaces are a product of human labor, while at the same time they shape the lives people undertake. My intention has been to suggest that such labor-produced spaces can help us think more deeply about social transformation. So far I have emphasized the way I observed Tadrar during my 1998–1999 fieldwork. However, when I returned for short trips in 2001, 2002, 2003, 2004, and 2006–2007 it appeared that much was changing.

Most striking for me—ironically, perhaps, given the mushrooming satellite dishes and new cement canal—was the disappearance of a particular trail. In the mountains southeast of Tadrar there is an area called Tikhfrin where women gather firewood and a small spring supports a stand of walnut trees. While hiking in the mountains in 2004, I tried to come back to Tadrar by the precipitous path down the cliff face from Tikhfrin but found the trail had completely disappeared. It was now just a treacherous slope of loose rock. Abdurrahman was with me, and I asked what had happened. Evidently there was no more wood in the region, or the area was now better patrolled by the government forestry agents, and thus for several years nobody had bothered to maintain the trail. It seemed ordinary enough to him, but it struck me powerfully that things that seem ancient and durable (a stone trail well-trod by women) are in fact quite fragile. Only a few years of disuse and trails cease to exist, fields wash away, houses collapse. Entropy erases human order from the world; only human labor can restore it.

This means that places that seem to remain are in fact constituted anew. This is evident in the many fields that had washed away and been rebuilt since my first visit. Detecting this is not very difficult. The oldest rock terraces are covered with ivy and brambles and the stones are weathered a deep black. New fields are easy to spot. The stones are different colors, look newly hewn, are perhaps still dusty, and the spaces between them are clear of rich soil, moss, and weeds. Fields that appeared eternal in 1995, I saw in 2004 as substantively brand new—if structurally identical to what I remembered. Stability is a product of labor as well as the product of the human mind: what is stable and what is changing is a matter of choosing not just particular elements to consider, but the temporality of the observation. I did not tend to notice the changes right before my eyes while I did my original fieldwork, but trips back to the village thrust issues of transformation and regeneration to the foreground of my attention. Change, in other words, is what I most noticed over the years I was absent, not the years I was present in the village. How much of this "noticing" is a product of the observer (changes in me and my life, my time away) and how much the observed? How much of the change was due do my new interest in change, and how much was due to the transformation of Tadrar itself?

I am not ready to accept that this is purely a matter of perception. Materially in 2004 the house above Abdurrahman's was abandoned, as were several others, while Abdurrahman's own house had nearly doubled in size, and included new cement quarters for tourists, a proper ceramic toilet, solar power, and even a shower. *Zound Marraksh,* he told me excitedly in Christmas of 2003 when visiting me in the city; it's "just like Marrakech." By 2004 Belaid and Fatima had done renovations, too, though not so dramatic. They had two more children (they now had three boys and a baby girl) and had removed and then raised their roof by half a meter, making it possible to enter their house without bending over.

Sadly, old Mohammed Lukstaf had died. Aisha was still mourning when I came up to the village, and we sat and held hands and cried quietly and talked about the loss of her "friend" (as she called him) and mine. Aisha's husband was dead, but her household was intact, and transformed by new babies born, a daughter leaving for marriage, and Aisha's son Ali taking over the role of patriarch. The Lukstafs had purchased Hamad's house that I had earlier rented, and installed a small solar panel and a television with a video disk player. They still lived in the old house, but they entertained in the big upstairs room of the new one.

In fact, while several houses in the village core were crumbling, a whole new set of houses was being built on an empty hillside next to the village, an area people now jokingly referred to as a suburb, "new Tadrar" or *Tadrar Jdid*. A main irrigation canal, *targa Taforikht,* had been rebuilt also, with cement and rebar replacing rock and mud. This is not a "new" canal, but it is built of new materials and operates in some new ways. Also in 2004 there were no more stone dams in the river (and thus no more complicated labor negotiations about who would build and maintain them) because there was plenty of water to go around. Potable water, too, was now delivered differently. Fetched by bucket from a spring in 1995, and then taken from a series of public taps in 1999, water was being piped directly into the majority of houses by 2004. This created new problems (the cheap plastic piping breaking constantly) and changed social dynamics (no more girls meeting at the well to gossip), and it illustrated new forms and new degrees of village inequality (from different amounts of female labor to fetch water to differential ability to afford plastic pipe). The mosque now had solar hot water and electricity (provided by grants I had obtained), there was a diesel-powered grain mill owned collectively by the village, and a new public bath for the women.

What happened? The people of Tadrar had labored mightily to keep some things the same and change others, to maintain some village spaces, reconstitute them in new forms or with new materials, erase some others or let them be erased, and create some entirely new places. How this happens, why and how this complicated reproduction and transformation is taking place, will take us the rest of the book to explore, but at the outset we should reflect on *kinds of change*—not just different processes but different ideas of what we mean by "change." Is a rebuilt house an example of change or continuity? What if it is rebuilt slightly differently, with new kinds of materials? What if it is owned by new people or new forms of collective ownership? These questions have no obvious answers, but should call us to abandon the simple "stability vs. change," "tradition vs. modernity" model that most of us use to understand the transformation of our world. Globalization is not about the elimination of traditional places, but about particular types and degrees of transformation inevitably coupled with forms of regeneration, especially, I will argue, in the organization of time.

So what kinds of transformations are driving change in Tadrar? We might begin with demography. Villagers depend on their children to keep them alive, and having children is both a central cultural ideal and a material necessity. Abdurrahman estimated that in his life infant mortality has dropped from 30 percent to 10 percent because of government health intervention efforts, which would explain the rising population. In my genealogical tables it is clear that over one hundred people today live on land that was owned by a single man four generations ago. In interviews women repeatedly emphasize the mortality of children as one of their greatest concerns. Changing numbers of people in a finite space requires dramatic reorganization of social relations. It certainly requires a reorganization of space.

By 2004 an eight-year drought ended. I had not appreciated before that these farmers were going to extraordinary lengths to capture water for their fields, not simply following ancient patterns that their culture dictated. This is an area of the world where the climate is famously erratic, but from the perspective of the men of Tadrar there used to be one dry year in eight, while now there is one wet year in every eight dry seasons. In Tadrar, 2003 was this wet year, and so in 2004 I got to see for the first time what the village "normally" looked like from the perspective of the older men. There was far more grass for the herds, and it took far less work to irrigate the fields. Women's labor did not seem to have changed much, but men's work was dramatically easier in wet years because they did not have to build and rebuild dams on the river to capture diminishing levels of water. Thus men had much more time on their hands to coordinate changes they desired, to work with development agents, or to send men and boys off for wage labor outside the mountains.

Exogenous development exploded between 1995 and 2004. Through the efforts of two Peace Corps volunteers and a World Bank scheme to improve the environment and tourism capacity of Toubkal National Park, Tadrar had become a major recipient of outside assistance. Thus cement and money flowed into the village and corruption—at least the predatory exactions of outside officials—largely stopped. The Moroccan government added an official school and teachers, even if it failed to pay them, and gave one man (Abdurrahman) the materials to build his new tourist hostel. The government even offered support in getting guides to bring troops of tourists to stay there. If development was uneven and supported new kinds of inequalities, there was also some trickle down effect, some ways in which all villagers benefited, and certainly ways in which all of the villagers' lives were transformed.

Most significantly, perhaps, I found that more villagers than ever worked outside the village. My 2004 census showed that eleven households out of twenty-eight now had at least one member working in the city, and some had as many as three. Only by such outside cash remittances can villagers afford televisions, cement, gas stoves (and the gas to power them), indeed anything that requires money. The village itself only produces almonds, walnuts, and goats in amounts barely sufficient in most cases to handle the costs of clothes, shoes, and medicine. Goods beyond this require money from outside, and these funds are coming to be available by sending household members to work in the plains and cities. The use of the cash economy for local purposes is arguably the most important spur to local social and spatial transformation.

Given these sorts of integration, what makes "the village" a social unit worth considering? If some villagers live in the city, and urban and international goods flow in, why situate our study in so fusty and seemingly over-determined a locale as "a village"? My response to this is simply that the people of Tadrar see themselves as a being from a place, as being connected to a particular collection of named, built places that only a person from Tadrar can name. While the membranes of the community are porous, elastic, stretched out in space to new places, and individuals may belong to more than one community, the canals, fields, pastures, and buildings of Tadrar are solid emblems of a carefully nurtured village identity; a deep sense of belonging to a place comes from knowing its secrets. Amin Maalouf begins one of his novels with the line, "In my native village, the rocks have names." I do not think this is uncommon, and the "native-ness" of the village is related to knowing the proper names of things—the rocks, people, trees, and history.

The buildings, terraces, trails, and canals of Tadrar are an apotheosis of the dead: a slow-moving monument to the generations of villagers who have bent their backs to the building and rebuilding of this place. Identifiable people have constructed these fields and canals slowly, incrementally, over many hundreds of years, but the built environment itself has worked on the builders, too, calling them into certain pathways, pressing them into relations within a small part of the range of all possible interaction. People have made and continue to make their lives from the materials available, and "in this sense the most important work that technologies do is to produce people: the makers are shaped by the making, and the users shaped by the using" (Bray 1997, 16). The homes, canals, fields, threshing areas, and pastures comprise a fabulously intricate technology for living that requires constant care. But Tadrar is now in the hands of the living, and the men and women who continue to live there are operating their patrimony in a novel global economy. To understand how this changes the nature of their social operations, we move now to examine the most basic, most important set of relationships in Tadrar, the household.

2

Intimate Matrices

This chapter moves from an evocation of the spaces of Tadrar to a discussion of households, the fundamental social units that build, rebuild, and live within those spaces. Households are not the same as houses, and in Tadrar households are not the social realm of leisure, people with whom you relax after work. Instead, in Tadrar households are the primary locus of work, the social bodies that coordinate where and when a person labors, what she or he does over the course of a day, and what becomes of her or his productive efforts. It is this involvement with who does what, day in and day out over many years, that makes households "fundamental," and fundamental in a different way than in urban areas.

In most households in urbanized, modern societies production is partially or wholly separated from reproduction, which means simply that making money is spatially and conceptually separated from making babies. There are exceptions, but generally adults go "off to work" and children are either cared for at home or sent elsewhere to be trained or educated. In the words of David Graeber, "one of the most striking things about capitalism is that is the only mode of production to systematically divide homes and workplaces: that is to say that the making of people and the manufacture of things should properly operate by an entirely different logic in places that have nothing to do with each other" (2006, 62). We even say in the United States that women or men who stay home to do the difficult job of raising children are "not working." Americans think very differently about work in the home—"housework" and "homework"—than they do about paying jobs. For most Americans, work in the home is not really work.

Not so in Tadrar. As in many rural societies, and almost all traditional ones, the distinction between production and reproduction makes little sense. Young people labor for their parents in their homes, pastures, and fields, then marry and produce the children who will in turn work for them. Girls work alongside their mother until they marry and join other households. Boys work for their father, then bring their brides to live and work in the father's household. Only upon a father's death do most boys fully become men by establishing their own independent households. In Tadrar productive labor is not recruited through contingent, short-term contracts and the allure of a Friday paycheck. It is instead generated, disciplined, trained, and rewarded in a long-term process that does not sharply distinguish between "household" and "labor," or the exigencies of production and reproduction.

In some ways these conceptual distinctions in Tadrar are unusual even among rural societies. For the agricultural Maale of Ethiopia, for instance, there are several different kinds of labor groups and ways of trading labor back and forth, but a clear distinction is made between work in the home and work without (Donham 1985, 264). By contrast, in Tadrar the key distinction is between work *within the household* and outside of it, and we should not confuse the social unit "household" with domestic space, the house. Household labor—whether undertaken within the actual house, outside in the fields, or off in distant pastures or the city is subject to a strict hierarchy of age and gender; work organized between households is far more egalitarian.

Households in Tadrar are strongly patriarchal and gerontocratic, meaning the father or eldest male rules more or less absolutely, at least in theory. Patriarchs rarely have much to say about women's labor, however, so in practice the eldest woman (often the wife, sometimes the mother of the patriarch) manages the feminine labor of the household. Thus there are parallel lines of age-based authority, one among women and one among men, with each person dominating the next youngest, but these lines converge in the patriarch. Intriguingly, some villagers imagine the broader Moroccan political system to operate analogously, with the king acting as patriarch of the nation.

If household labor is organized hierarchically, labor organization between households is marked by negotiation, consensus, and a concern for fairness rather than authoritarianism, both among women's labor groups and men's. (This is explored specifically in chapter 4.) This is not to say that age-based authority is absent in interhousehold labor exchanges, but that in villagewide negotiations gerontocracy accommodates other, consciously equitable organizational models. In some sense this might be seen to reflect a widespread cultural pattern in the Muslim world—an emphasis on total submission in some domains (the term *Muslim* means "one who submits to the will of God") coupled to a powerful ideal of equality (all believers are equal before God). I would not want to push such an argument too far, but there would seem a conceptual tension between authoritarianism and egalitarianism in the religious sphere and a refraction of this in the prosaic world of village labor organization. Such an integration of contradictory values is certainly not unique to Tadrar or the Muslim world, and ought to make us cautious about general claims that this (or any) culture "is" authoritarian, egalitarian, or anything else. In societies, and for individual members of societies, the real-time drama of life involves action, the more or less thoughtful deployment of contradictory principles in ever-novel contexts. Nowhere is social life pre-scripted, even if the materials for writing it are often quite limited.

For now, we need emphasize that most villagers make their lives through the social context of households, a set of interwoven, asymmetrical relationships where people are not paid money for their time, but are instead provided food, shelter, love, and security. Each villager will labor for most of his or her days and will only develop some measure of personal freedom and control over others relatively late in life. This contrasts with wage laborers, who might be seen as slaving absolutely all of their working days, as never having control of their labor, but who do at least go home at the end of the day. Urban laborers may never get away from the need to sell their labor, but they do manage to avoid their boss for some hours of the day. Household members almost never escape the household. They can only abandon it and start their own. There is no vacation, no days or nights off, because the dynamics of household authority permeate household life and thus, in a village, life itself. The key distinction between laboring in a village and working in a capitalist factory or farm is not between good or bad work, not between easy or difficult, or even between more or less control or creativity. It is about the type of domination and the temporality of its expression.

Neither system is obviously desirable in all circumstances for all people; being poor involves having few good options. Given the precariousness of life for the rural poor, taking the short-term benefits of urban labor may make sense. But it may also be that the village way of trading labor over the long haul seems best, or that different modes seem better at different times, or, as we will see, integrating the two modes might work to the best advantage for some people. Those who reap the advantages may not be the ones doing the actual laboring, of course. What the village has to offer is some guarantee of long-term reciprocity and some potential for dignity in old age. To be part of a *takat* is to feel rooted, bound to the world by being bound to *a* world. Such roots come with fearsome responsibilities, a lifelong requirement to put others above oneself, to sacrifice one's desires for the benefit of other, usually older people, to labor year after year waiting to be rewarded by still younger people who may not live long enough to serve, who may, these days, abandon you for urban opportunity. We will return to this scenario in the concluding chapter.

The wait is not easy. The long-term "cycle of domestic development" does not churn happily along generation after generation; it is not a frictionless machine. Each household has a unique history: its own traumas and triumphs, its own variously empowered members with different ideas about who owes whom what, when, and where (Conley 2004). Households are not just the fundamental economic associations in rural Morocco, and they are not only fundamental to understanding larger social processes, they are also fractiously political. Domestic politics is knotty, elusive business, very difficult for outsiders to fathom—as readers probably know from their own families, networks of friends, and roommates. But in a place where production and reproduction are the right and left hand of survival, and where survival is based first of all in households, we cannot hope to appreciate how life happens unless we at least attempt to fathom the travails of household life, principally the reproduction of a new generation of laborers to support the declining members of the household.

A commitment to organization by household in Tadrar should not be confused with a valuation of family. Family (*'aila* or *famila,* as they say in the village) is a very important cultural category in Morocco, perhaps the most important concept of sodality to cut across social classes and linguistic groups, from the most isolated rural areas to the country's large cities. But "family" is a malleable concept, a notion put to work to concretize the elusive connectedness of extensive networks of people more than it is a thing, or even a clearly bounded social unit. Households can be variously built from family connections because "family" is a vague, inclusive notion open to negotiation. Households are clearly demarcated economic associations. One is or is not part of a particular household because being *of a household* is to be economically obligated—you either work for and receive sustenance from a particular household or you do not. It is not an affective cultural category, or not just an affective category, but an economic one.

All households in Tadrar are centered in a house, a *tigemmi,* but a *tigemmi* without an oven is only a cold building, a storeroom or a hut. It is an oven that warms a *tigemmi* into a home, and it is women who make and use ovens. The word for oven is in fact *takat* (plural, *tikatin*), which is also the word for household. This association is not arbitrary. There were twenty-eight *tikatin* in Tadrar in 2004. Each person belongs to one, and only one at any given time, and many people will only be part of two households over the course of a lifetime—the one they are born into, and the one they join at marriage (for women) or form after a father's death (for men). Though there are exceptions, most *tikatin* are nominally headed by a patriarch; all, however, are culturally and materially constituted by women. One can conceive of a household without men, but a *takat* without an oven, and a woman to feed it, is unimaginable. A hearth is the center of a household.

For the rest of this chapter I will sketch the features of particular households, focusing on the one I know best, and to the degree I am able I will try to show *tikatin* in motion. I will describe the daily activities, the social practices that make households what they are, but also the trajectories inherent to social bodies plagued by the finite lives of humans. No household lasts forever, and while they endure longer than at least some of the individuals who comprise them, households are not immortal. The growth and decline of households will figure prominently in our analyses of broader political economic dynamics discussed later in the book. To prepare us for this I will show how households operate, how they change in time, and how these transformations reflect and inflect the lives passed in and through *tikatin*. We will only be able to make sense of how the village is connected to global processes by examining the social context of the household.

A DAY IN THE LIFE

The next section is my reconstruction of a day in the life of Abdurrahman and Khadija's household. It is a composite picture of their domestic world in June of 1999, based on my fieldnotes, but does not represent any specific "real" day, and it was not written in the village. My intention is to catch the feeling of a day unfolding, what Malinowski called the "imponderabilia of actual life" (Malinowski 1984 [1922], 18). By this I mean to illuminate the quotidian regularities of this social world—the rhythm of sleeping and waking, cooking and eating, planning and undertaking the work of the household. However, I hope it is clear that even regular days are situated in

particular times. Events that might be "typical" for a village are always specific to an instance, so, for the people evoked below, this is (or was) a particular moment when their children were young, the season busy, the watermill broken, and an anthropologist was around writing everything down.

Khadija is up early, stoking the oven. She tosses a handful of small
twigs on the coals and pumps the old bellows until the twigs crackle
and a small flame jumps to life, splashing the soot-black room with
yellow light. Another couple of sticks in the *takat,* then a bigger
branch, and she leaves the fire to burn and turns to do her prayers.

Fatime is up, too. She has been sleeping in a side room, barely
larger than a closet, with her husband, Mohammed, and their three
small girls, Fadma, Aisha, and Malika. All the girls are under five
years old, and the baby is sick and wakes often to nurse, and so they
try to sleep away from the main family area. Fatime mutters a greet-
ing to her mother-in-law. Khadija, still praying, doesn't answer, and
Fatime takes up a bundle of grass she had cut the day before and
stored in the corner and makes her way outside and down the path
to feed the cow. It is dark in the stable beneath the house, but the old
cow expects Fatime's visit. While the cow chews yesterday's grass,
Fatime squats beside it, reaches under, and wipes the udder with her
skirt, rubs her palms to warm them, and milks the cow into a small
tin pail. There is not much, only a couple of cups. Fatime takes the
milk back up to the kitchen and sets it by the oven.

Abdurrahman also wakes early. Each night he checks his cheap
digital watch and sets the time and the alarm on his wind-up clock.
The alarm plays the call to prayer in the whiny, Saudi Arabian style,
always before the *muezzin* has announced the morning prayer from
the roof of the mosque. Abdurrahman is proud of this, and proud of
the fact that he drags himself out into each cold predawn and up to the
mosque for the *sirowit* prayer. Not many men do. Over the years I have
known him, Abdurrahman has gradually developed a faint dark spot
at the center of his forehead—a callus he wears as proud testament to
the amount of time he spends praying. Khadija hears the door close
behind her husband, then open and close again as Fatime returns from
the stable. Khadija has finished her prayers and, as her daughter-in-
law enters the kitchen, says *sbah l'kher,* good morning, and asks after

the health of the baby. The chickens have begun to cluck and scratch. Khadija asks Fatime to return to the stable and feed the chickens with the previous evening's stale crusts. Fatime goes.

Mohammed is up next. He greets his mother in the kitchen and enters the family room to wake his younger brothers Hussein and Hassan; they let Brahim sleep as he is only about seven years old and is more trouble than he is worth in terms of work. Mohammed begins to heat water for tea, using a single propane burner kept in a small enclave next to the family room. Hussein and Hassan leave the house together, the sky still dark, Hussein turning down the path to the small kitchen garden to gather mint for the tea, and Hassan up the path, next door to wake his uncle, Khadija's brother, another Hussein. This Hussein suffered an accident when he was young—he fell off a roof—and now is mentally retarded. He sleeps in his own house, but eats and works with his sister's household; he is part of Abdurrahman's *takat*. Like everyone, he has slept in his clothes and so only needs to slip on his cheap plastic shoes to leave the house. Like everyone, Hussein discreetly makes his way outside to use the toilet, either in the stable or down in the boulders of the ravine.

Abdurrahman returns from prayers, sets his candle on the windowsill, folds the blankets of the main room, and rearranges the carpets to sit on. He carries Brahim, still sleeping, into a corner, and sits down in his customary spot with his back to the wall. Mohammed enters carrying a low metal table that he sets before his father, then leaves to bring in the propane burner with the water still heating on top of it, then the teapot, the sugar box, and a new box of loose leaf "gunpowder" tea from China. This one has a lion on the package, and is known by that symbol since few can make out any of the words in Chinese, Arabic, or French. Abdurrahman arranges everything on the table in front of him, unwraps the cellophane from the new box, and leans to throw it out the window, then asks Mohammed about mint. "Hussein went to get it," Mohammed replies, and both men sit in silence.

In the kitchen the fire is roaring. Khadija scoops coals out of the oven with a small tin shovel, places them in a brazier, and adds more wood to the fire. She looks over to where Fatime has begun to knead the dough, then pours most of the milk into a coffeepot and places it on the brazier to heat. She adds about a tablespoon of coffee and several sprigs of thyme. She pumps the coals with the bellows until they glow bright red. Little Fadma has awakened now and comes into the kitchen rubbing her eyes. Khadija greets her granddaughter, then sends her off to ask Abdurrahman for sugar for the coffee. Khadija turns to the sacks of wheat and barley flour, lifts one of barley, and says to Fatime, "It's almost empty." "Yes," replies the daughter-in-law, "someone will have to walk down to Maghzen and have more ground." This is a man's job, and the women will have to let Abdurrahman know so he can assign it. Khadija fills a pot with water from a plastic jug, then pours what there is of the barley flour into the water, stirring briskly to wet the flour and get it to mix. Fadma returns with the sugar box. Khadija opens it, surveys the contents, and dumps all of it into the coffee, then sets the pot again on the brazier to heat. She gives the box back to Fadma, tells her to take it back to Abdurrahman and then go to refill the plastic water jug at the public tap just beyond Uncle Hussein's house. Khadija takes the *askeef,* the barley flour soup she has been mixing, and sets it to heat on top of the oven. The pot is big enough that it fits across the whole top of the *takat.* She adds a bit of salt, a handful of rice, and stirs.

Hassan has returned with his uncle Hussein, and Hassan's brother Hussein has returned with the mint. All the men sit on the floor, backs against the walls; Mohammed and his younger brother Hussein are mumbling in disagreement, indistinctly arguing about something; the younger brother evidently gives up and turns to address the next youngest, Hassan, who gasps in protest and affects an air of wounded incredulity. The first hint of dawn is now in the sky.

Abdurrahman shakes a palm full of tea into his thick right hand, and then dumps it in the teapot. He glances around the room with the teapot lid up and growls sharply, "Hey!" Hassan sighs but rises quickly to pour the hot water, glaring at his smirking older brothers. His father offers no verbal instruction, just a slight wave of his hand when he wants the water to stop. Abdurrahman swishes the steaming water around the pot to wash the tea and pours the dirty water off into a glass. Then more water, more swishing, then into a second glass. Hassan then fills the teapot until Abdurrahman indicates that he stop, and the boy places it on the burner to heat. Fadma returns with the empty sugar box, and hands it tentatively to her grandfather, shrinking back even as she extends her hand. Hassan takes the two glasses of dirty water and empties them out the window. The tea is left to heat in the teapot on the burner. "Sugar?" Abdurrahman asks, looking around and weighing the empty sugar box in his hand. Mohammed mutters something while he stands up; Abdurrahman searches his pockets and hands Mohammed a small key to a locked cabinet hidden deep in the house. Mohammed leaves.

In the kitchen the thick *askeef* is bubbling like blonde lava, and Khadija stirs it gently but constantly to keep it from boiling over. The dough is ready, and Fatime has pinched it into loaf-sized portions. She has three of them on a tray and squats by the oven with a pan of water. She wets her hands and pats the dough flat, patting and turning it into the shape of a thick pizza. Khadija moves to the side of the oven to give Fatime room while she continues stirring the *askeef*. The baby starts crying, however, and Fatime looks at Khadija. "You go," says the older woman, "I'll make the bread." Khadija calls for her granddaughter, "Fadma!" Fadma comes in quickly. She has been lurking just beyond the door, enjoying the heat of the kitchen, and takes over stirring the *askeef* without being asked. Fatime scoops up the well-swaddled infant from the side room and takes her into the main family room, still crying. She sits in the corner by sleeping Brahim, removes her breast from the ragged, torn neck hole of her dress, and lets the baby nurse. The baby goes instantly silent except for the sound of avid sucking. Fatime sighs and pats baby Malika.

Khadija wets her hands and forearms, then takes the patty of dough and squashes it against the inner wall of the oven, pressing and spreading it until it is a bowl-shaped against the curved inner wall of the *takat*. She yanks her arm out to let it cool, wets her hands and arms again, and presses another loaf against the opposite wall of the oven. "Enough with that stirring," she says to her granddaughter. "Take the men their *askeef*." Little Fadma lifts the great pot to the hard dirt floor, using her skirt to protect her hands from burning. It comes nearly up to her thighs, and she has to almost drag it away from the oven. Fadma scoops out bowls of the glutinous soup, being careful to dip the ladle deep to the bottom of the pot each time, and stirring between scoops of the still bubbling goop. She arranges the six full bowls on a tray and struggles to lift it evenly. The cheap porcelain bowls rattle on the metal tray as Fadma takes them through the dark hallway and finds her way to the men.

Fadma pauses at the door to the family room as her father comes up behind her. "Go in," Mohammed says to his daughter. "Why do you wait?" Fadma crosses the threshold gingerly, shyly. "Help her," Abdurrahman barks, and Hassan springs up to take the tray from his niece and set it beside his father. Mohammed enters and Fadma skips out to fetch the water that her grandmother had earlier commanded. Mohammed returns the key to Abdurrahman and hands him a loaf of sugar wrapped in blue paper along with a short iron bar. Mohammed then goes to the corner and kisses his baby Malika on the head, stroking it. "Any better?" he asks his wife. "A little," she answers, and Mohammed sits looking down at his daughter.

Abdurrahman orders Hassan to carry bowls of *askeef* around the room, and he begins with his oldest brother, Mohammed. Mohammed tries to give it to his wife. "No," Fatime says, "drink." "No, you," Mohammed says. "No, drink," Fatime replies sternly. From across the room Abdurrahman says "Drink!" "No," Fatime lies, "I had mine in the kitchen." She pauses, then says almost inaudibly, "we're out of barley flour." "Huh?" says Abdurrahman, and Mohammed answers, "We need to grind a sack of barley." Mohammed and Abdurrahman discuss who will take the donkey and a sack of barley and walk down four villages to Maghzen, where there is a diesel-powered grain mill. They lament the fact that the river is too low to use the watermill in Tadrar. They consider walking one village up to use the still functional water mill at Ait Moussa. "It will be cheaper in Ait Moussa," says Abdurrahman. "If it works," replies Mohammed. The water mill in Ait Moussa has been broken lately and there is disagreement about who will put up the money to fix it. It seems wiser to go down and use the diesel mill at Maghzen.

Fadma has fetched the water for her grandmother and appears at the door again, this time with a conical basket containing the bowl shaped loaves of *tanoort*. She sets it down and returns with a small tray of shallow dishes of olive oil and butter. The butter smells strong, like cows. "Where's the jam?" asks Abdurrahman. Khadija enters and answers as she sits, "It's gone." She places the coffee she has carried in on the tray in front of her husband.

The tea is hot, boiling over, and Khadija takes it from the burner and sets it on the floor next to Abdurrahman. She then takes a seat on the opposite side of the room. Little Fadma collects the *askeef* bowls and leaves to wash them in a flat plastic basin in the kitchen. She will dump the dirty water out the window. Abdurrahman spreads a towel over his lap and takes the loaf of sugar—a large, smooth thing the shape of an artillery shell—and raps it crosswise sharply with the iron bar. The sugar breaks off into disks like large hockey pucks. Abdurrahman then crushes each of these into smaller chunks, dumps most of them into the sugar box, and puts half a dozen large clumps in the teapot. He takes the coffee, which is mostly milk, and pours a glass, then pours the glass back into the pot. He does this three times, to mix the sugar. He then pours a small amount in a cup and tastes it. Satisfied, he pours it into the six glasses on the table. "We need more glasses," he says, and everyone looks to Hassan to go get them.

Fadma returns with more bowls of *askeef,* and now her mother takes one. Khadija tries to get the others to take a second bowl, but when they will not she takes one and slurps at it. Only then will her sons agree to take a second bowl. "Coffee?" asks Abdurrahman. Khadija declines, but others drink.

Once Hassan has returned with more glasses, Abdurrahman arranges them in a semi-circle on the tray before him, counting to make sure there is one for everyone. "Brahim," he shouts, "get Brahim up," and Fatime rousts him roughly. She then hands the baby to Khadija and leaves to get her other girl, Aisha. Aisha is moaning and sleepily rubbing her eyes when Fatime returns, and is placed on the carpet next to Brahim, who still will not get up.

Fatime leaves again and returns with a low wooden table. Meanwhile Abdurrahman is pouring the tea. He begins as he did with the coffee, pouring it into a glass from high up, aerating the tea and mixing the sugar, then pouring the glassful back into the pot. Then he tastes it. Then he pours each of the glasses before him a third of the way up, then starting over he pours the next third, then tops each of them off. *Bismillah,* in the name of God, he says and hands the first cup to Hassan, who takes it to Mohammed. Hassan returns to his father to pass each of the glasses, including one for little Aisha and the reluctantly semi-vertical Brahim. Each person says *bismillah* before drinking. They finish quickly and pass their cups back to the tray when done. There is a second cup of tea for everyone, and the pot is refilled with water and set back on the burner.

Fatime has set the wooden table in the center of the room and taken up the baby from her mother-in-law. Abdurrahman scoots up to the table, removes the conical lid of the bread basket, and tears a *tanoort* into pieces and scatters them around the table. People gather around, knee to knee on the floor. Each says *bismillah,* dips bits of bread in the oil or butter, and eats. Most of the discussion concerns the day's work. It is a busy season. Today Uncle Hussein will take the small herd of sheep and goats—maybe twenty or so—from the stone enclosure in the village up to a grazing area above the village, Agouni n Ait Anou. Hassan will help him, as they have to pass a number of fields with almond trees and they do not want the goats to get at the trees and anger the neighbors. It will take two men throwing rocks at the goats to keep them on the trail and out of trouble.

Fatime and little Fadma will go to the kitchen garden and get vegetables for the midmorning meal, then Fatime will take a shortcut through the fields to catch up to Hassan and Hussein and climb up to the fields at Agouni n Ait Anou. She will finish cutting the rest of the barley there. These are the last fields to harvest. It will take her most of the day, though once the herds have reached the pastures Uncle Hussein will shepherd and Hassan will leave to help Fatime. Other women will be working in the fields around Abdurrahman's, but Hassan is likely to be the only male. Khadija is too old to climb up the precipitous path to Agouni, and Fatime is the only other woman in the household, so some of the boys have to take on women's labor. Some of the older boys might indeed enjoy this, as they get a chance to work near the younger girls and flirt out of sight of their fathers and mothers, but Abdurrahman sends Hassan, who is too young to appreciate the opportunity.

Khadija will be busy cooking, preparing the dough and making the *tajines,* and washing clothes for the children. She will have Fadma to help her. Fadma is only five and cannot be left alone in charge of the younger Aisha, at least not for long, but she can be useful carrying laundry and water. Khadija will cut *tooga* for the cow while she is down at the river, too, and little Fadma will carry the fodder up the hill. If Brahim is not learning his prayers at the mosque or hiding out with his friends, perhaps he will help, too, but most likely his younger aunt Fadma will get the job. Baby Malika will go with her mother, tied to Fatime's back while she cuts the barley, ties it into sheaves, and ties the sheaves into great bundles that she and Hassan will carry down to the village threshing area. At the end of the day, when he brings the herd back to their corral, Uncle Hussein will carry a bundle of barley back, too. It is unusual to see men carrying barley, but this household has many men and few women.

Some of the lower fields, below the house, have already been plowed, but others have not even had manure delivered to them yet. The stable has been dug out and the manure left to aerate in the sun, but this June most of it still has to be carried to the fields. Mohammed and the two Husseins have already worked together to fill baskets, load them on the donkey, and then take them to aerate. They left the manure to cure, but now must scoop it again into baskets using hoes, then dump the baskets into larger, stronger baskets on the back of the donkey, and drive the animal to the fields. Piles of manure are left there a while longer, and then are plowed into the soil along with the maize seeds. After plowing, men take a *tamadirt,* a short-handled hoe, and divide the fields into small sections two or three meters across with low, thirty-centimeter ridges between them. These ridges are cut open to form "keys" which let water in, then are closed. Water must not be allowed to flow around the field, carrying the seed to any low spots or, worse, flowing off the terrace and taking the precious soil with it.

Today Mohammed and Hussein will have to carry manure to the fields, plow some fields, prepare some to be watered, and irrigate others. They have irrigation time on two different canals today, Taforikht and Issreran, and Abdurrahman does not have to remind them to check with their cousins and neighbors so as not to miss their turn on each canal. If Mohammed is plowing when the turn is likely to come, Hussein will help one of the other people with their fields in exchange for help irrigating his own household's fields. It usually takes two men at least, in case any of the keys break and need to be rebuilt quickly to keep from washing a field down the mountainside.

Meanwhile, now that most of the barley has been carried to the threshing floor, it is time to arrange a group of men and a team of mules to help with the hot, dirty work of processing the grain. Mohammed, Hussein, Hassan, and Uncle Hussein have all been periodically "loaned" to other households by Abdurrahman to help thresh, and it is time for these other households to provide men or mules to Abdurrahman. A man or a mule counts the same in terms of threshing negotiations, so some richer households simply loan their mule out continuously to incur a team of men to help them. Mules eat a great deal, however. Not many households can afford to keep one. Donkeys are cheaper, much smaller, but also do much less work. Many households cannot even afford donkeys and have nothing but the labor of their men to trade.

The teams of men who do the threshing must be provided with tea, *tanoort,* and *askeef* while they're working, and are given a big meal—with a meat *tajine*—when they're done. This means that women's labor must be organized, too. It is no small feat to cook for fifteen or twenty men on an open fire, so once Khadija knows when the threshing will take place, she will begin to arrange for relatives, neighbors, and friends to come help her, to loan her wood and maybe bread. Of course, she will also need to schedule time to help her helpers, or to send Fatime in exchange, as labor given between households ought to be reciprocated.

It is a busy season. The women sweat in the hot sun, hurrying to get the grain cut and hauled to the threshing areas. The men break their backs to dig the manure out of the stables and the shepherds' huts and haul it to the fields, get it plowed into the earth, and get fields seeded, sculpted into irrigable sections, and watered. Men and women move from within the house, out to the fields, back to the house, out to threshing areas, back to the house, out to the mill, to the river to wash clothes or children, to other houses where they will contribute the labor necessary to secure the assistance of neighbors, friends, and relatives. And back to the house. The household works through synchronized, stochastic pulses, with bodies moving out to the extremities of the village and beyond, then returning with whatever the household needs to sustain itself, like blood in the veins of a giant body.

At the end of the day Abdurrahman's household foregathers cross-legged on the floor, knees touching, pressed in around the table and the single round clay bowl that will feed them, the *tajine*. Abdurrahman will tear the bread and spread the scraps around the bowl, he will divide the meat, and he is responsible to do this fairly, to do it in the name of God. Everyone has worked to provide the *tajine,* and everyone will eat from it—and eat until they are full. Nobody chews hurriedly. There may not be enough meat or vegetables or oil, some may lack shoes, the household may run out of sugar or tea if times are really dire, and there may not be enough hours to finish all the work. But there is always sufficient barley. If the land does not provide it, Muslim decency will. Nobody goes hungry in Tadrar, no matter how poor. Thus every household eats steadily and confidently in its inter-dependent rhythm, confident that however unequal the work, however short or long anyone's life, however onerous the labor, nobody is alone, nobody is left behind.

Abdurrahman is a lucky man. He has more land than most people (we will see why in the next chapter) and more sons to work it. Abdurrahman is also an ambitious man, and his fortunate position with regard to land and labor means that he has the most precious resource of ambitious men everywhere: time. Abdurrahman himself does not have to physically labor, at least not very often. In fact, lurking invisibly within the household labor scheme is Abdurrahman's second son, Lahcen, who in 1999 worked northeast of Marrakech on a dairy farm near Demnat. Abdurrahman traveled to Demnat once a month, received Lahcen's wages, left the boy an allowance, and returned to Tadrar. Abdurrahman not only has enough labor to operate his land productively, but can send sons out for wages, too. We will explore some consequences of this in subsequent chapters.

Because of his sons, Abdurrahman has some atypical opportunities. In planning the *zerda,* or meal, for the threshing party, Abdurrahman has money to buy meat and vegetables at market, extra tea and sugar, and extra *tajines* in which to cook the meal. He can afford to buy extra grain at market and feed it to his donkey, and then loan this donkey out to other threshing parties and receive the labor of men, mules, and donkeys in return. Abdurrahman will even invite a number of the *fuaqih,* or religious teachers, to his *zerda* from nearby villages and have them chant from the Qur'an before and after the meal. Abdurrahman's *zerda* will be larger, with more people, more meat, and a good deal more religious formality than most others. He will seek to have a meal appropriate to an important man.

Abdurrahman will also have time to be on hand when the village men meet to elect the *amshardo,* or guard, for this season. Each year the households of the village contribute money and hire one man to guard the walnuts and almonds when they near harvest. This man's job is to roam quietly around and try to catch people eating almonds from each other's trees on the way to or from the fields, or, more seriously, people harvesting walnuts early. All the village walnuts must be harvested on the same day, as the falling nuts tend to bounce down the mountain; all want to be present at the harvest to argue over what belongs to whom. It is important to be available to elect an *amshardo* that you trust, as he can levy significant fines—up to five U.S. dollars, or what amounts to almost a tenth of the poorest families' yearly incomes.

As the river is low in 1999, and water is scarce, Abdurrahman will be present for the lottery to decide the order of the necessary irrigation rotations. The percentage of time each man gets on each canal each day is fixed by the amount of property owned, but as the river level drops and the new maize fields come to require more water, a rotation is necessary to determine what order the days go in. Having a convenient rotation can save yet more time. As we will discuss in detail in the next chapter, the village assembly, or *jemaa,* also must decide how labor will be contributed for communal projects like making new, temporary dams in the river to channel more of the water into the canals. Such decisions do not only happen during the actual meeting of the *jemaa.* Much politicking occurs before the meeting is ever convened, and such politicking takes time. In short, Abdurrahman is lucky to have the labor and land to allow him to do political work. Luck facilitates certain capacities for Abdurrahman, but what he does with the opportunities is certainly not dictated by culture, social structure, or simple economic rationale.

Consider some of my other neighbors. My old friend Mohammed Lukstaf, for instance, had many sons to work his fields, but I almost never saw him sitting with the older men of the village in the mosque. I never saw him politicking, and he rarely visited other villages or even the weekly market. He even spent a portion of his time high in the mountains shepherding, I think more because he enjoyed it than because he lacked sons that could be made to do the job. One of the things I most cherished about Mohammed was how happy he seemed in his fields. Mohammed *wanted* to farm, wanted to work with his grandsons rebuilding fields, irrigating, thinning his maize plants, harvesting his walnuts. In my favorite picture of him Mohammed is standing amid his maize, working alone, smiling up at the camera.

Or take Belaid. He and his wife, Fatima Id Baj, had only two small boys in 1999, and Fatima was forever foisting her kids off on her mother or her sister Aisha so that she could get out to the fields and forests to cut the barley and gather fodder or wood. To support her household Fatima had share-cropped a cow from a wealthy man in another village, a cow she had to feed every day but from which she could keep the milk and half of all calves born. Fatima was trying to make a better future for herself and her children by taking on the job of raising a cow. Since Belaid had few fields devoted to fodder, Fatima needed to go often to the mountains to gather shrubs and oak branches for her cow to eat. Even with the help of her sister, Fatima could not hope to keep up with the feminine tasks of a household by herself, so Belaid sometimes cooked, sometimes washed clothes, and occasionally gathered wood. Since Belaid was busy with his fields and helping Fatima, he was rarely present when political decisions were being made, at least if they occurred during the busy season. Abdurrahman and Mohammed Luk-staf could choose how to spend their time; the former is interested in poli-tics, the latter not. But Belaid can only choose between allowing his wife to be completely overwhelmed by the labor necessary to sustain a household or not. Belaid is constrained by demography, by the current position of his domestic cycle. When his boys are older, Belaid's life will be easier; Fatima's will still be difficult, however, unless she gives birth to girls or until one of the boys is old enough to marry.

Other households exhibit other aspects of household dynamics, of exi-gency and strategy. Fatima's sister Aisha (the one tapped for babysitting) was married to a young man named Mohammed from the Ait Hussein branch of the Ben Ouchen lineage. (Lineages will be discussed in the next chapter.) Mohammed and Aisha had broken away from Mohammed's fa-ther, and in 1998 they had their own house and ate by themselves. But Mo-hammed had no fields of his own because his father was still alive, and he was still called to work on his father's property, especially at peak seasons. Mohammed's solution was to maintain his wife and younger children in the village and go to the city and work in the off seasons, but he also sent his older daughters there to work full-time. Mohammed had no sons in 1999, but he had three teenaged or pre-teen daughters working in the city, two in Marrakech and one in Casablanca, and the wages of these daughters allowed him to subsist as an independent household in the mountains. Few would find this arrangement ideal. It is well known that girls sent to the city to work as nannies are sometimes abused in horrific ways, and that in any case they make precious little money. But Mohammed and Aisha had determined that for them this was preferable to continuing to be part of Mohammed's father's household.

Mohammed and Aisha's neighbor, Omar Idzdo, shows another way that personal choices influence household dynamics. Omar is old, his wife is dead, his only son still in the village is married to one of Abdurrahman's daughters, and the two of them have a baby boy. Omar is very poor, has too few fields to live on, and relies on his goats to earn him enough to stay alive. The goats must be taken up to the pastures of the Ouanoukrim each summer—a difficult journey. I accompanied him once, and our borrowed donkey (Abdurrahman's, in fact) dropped to its knees in exhaustion several times trying to carry Omar's meager supplies up the mountain. We had to literally lift the struggling animal through the most painfully steep stretches. One would expect that Omar would stay in the village to irrigate his few fields and send his strong, adult son up to do the difficult job of shepherding. But he does not. Omar shepherds in a ten days on/ten days off rotation with a nephew, and this allows Omar's son to stay home in the village with his wife and baby. It seems to me a tremendous sacrifice. Needless to say, this means Omar is often away when village decisions are made. Even as an old man, Omar has not given himself any rest. He continues to do the hard work of a much younger body.

Finally, consider Fatima o Haj. Fatima was married to a man named Ohomo, and in 1998 and 1999 they ran their household remarkably independently; they had no children and Ohomo was the last person in his whole extended family left alive, so he had no obvious relatives with whom to share labor, and no younger people to labor for him. Belaid and others helped Ohomo with plowing and other difficult tasks because, as they told me, "he is tired," but in general the old man and his wife managed to collaborate to make a small household of two. In 2003 Ohomo died. I expected Fatima o Haj would go to live with one of her brothers, but instead she took the property she inherited from her husband and ran the household on her own. She sought out one of her sisters, who had married to another village, and this sister sent one of her unmarried grand-nieces to live with Fatima to do the cooking, and in general to handle Fatima's feminine household labor. Then Fatima arranged to hire a young man from this same village (another distant relative) to come periodically and do her plowing and other male labor. She paid him the standard rate of 30 dirhams, about three U.S. dollars, per day. Instead of joining one of her brother's households in Tadrar, or moving in with one of her sisters in a different village, Fatima continued to manifest her own *takat* by incorporating one distant female relative and by hiring what male labor she needed. She still lived in a household of only two, but it was now two women.[1]

Fatima's example illustrates a centrally important point about households: they move. Nobody lives in the same household forever. The constitution of each household changes as people come and go and the capacity of household members evolves. To update the examples just given, by 2004 Abdurrahman had welcomed more babies to his household (Mohammed and Fatime had their fourth and fifth girls) and Abdurrahman had married his son Lahcen to a young woman from Tadrar, Zahra, and brought her to live in the house to help Fatime and Khadija. This lessened the feminine labor that the boys had to undertake. Abdurrahman also helped Lahcen find a new job in Marrakech, so that the young man could come home more often to visit his new wife, and he sent his third son, Hussein, out to work full-time in Marrakech. Abdurrahman was able to send his oldest son, Mohammed, to work part-time in the city, too, as his younger boys Brahim and Hassan became more responsible. These shifts in labor responsibilities, especially the addition of an able-bodied woman to help Fatime and Khadija, allowed Abdurrahman to more effectively run his newly built, government-sponsored tourist hostel.

By 2004 Mohammed Lukstaf had died. His son Ali took over the position as head of household, which he ran with his mother, Aisha. They bought Ali's paternal uncle's house, the one I had rented when I lived in the village, and Ali and his wife had another new baby, their eighth. When I left at the end of the summer of 2004 they were preparing to marry Ali's oldest daughter, Khadija, to a man from a distant village near Imlil, and to bring in a girl from another village family to marry Aisha's oldest grandson.

In 2004 Belaid and Fatima were still struggling with caring for babies and trying to farm, and had even added two more children—another boy and, finally, a blessing for Fatima, a girl named Sumaiya. Fatima's sister Aisha and her husband, Mohammed, added a baby boy, too, one who someday will help his father till fields, at least once his household inherits fields to till. They still had three daughters working in the city, but their oldest daughter still in the village was now responsible enough to care for the younger children, and even to help out her aunt Fatima.

1. For more on women's role in constituting households, see Crawford (2007b).

And in 2004 Omar Idzdo was still working in the distant Ouanoukrim pastures. Every other household had ceased using them because it was simply too difficult. More changes were afoot by 2007, but we will address those at the end of the book.

In this chapter I have made a series of claims about households and their importance in Tadrar. I have sought to evoke a sense of power relations within households, to show some of the subtlety of patriarchal, gerontocratic hierarchy, and to suggest how it changes over time. An ethnographic portrayal of all household dynamics and all households would require much more than a chapter, but I hope to have at least sketched a number of crucial points.

To recapitulate, I have argued that households are economic organizations, and indeed are the central locus of production, reproduction, and consumption in the village. Households are not simply "family," but are generally built from family connections. Households change in time, both in terms of the changing capacities of the members (children take on more responsibility as they get older, old people gradually lose their ability to labor) and in terms of household members leaving (for marriage or to strike out on their own or by dying) or arriving (marrying in or for other reasons conjoining their economic fate to a particular household or by being born). Household labor is gendered, though for practical purposes the boundaries of many gendered tasks are flexible. Women typically work harder than men, and girls start working younger and work harder than boys, but who does what in a household depends upon who else is available. Households with lopsided ratios of men to women or children to adults must make accommodations, and sometimes these accommodations involve swapping labor with other households. Men have formal systems for this (as we will see in chapter 4), while women's labor exchanges are less formal, more ad hoc, but no less important.

As I will detail in the next chapter, households are not equal. Some have significantly more property than others, and some have significantly more labor. Within households authority is based primarily on age and gender, and while in general we can characterize governance within households as "authoritarian," how power is exercised varies across time, between social contexts, and from household to household. Much depends upon the personality of the patriarch. Power and resistance are complicated topics in any context, and are particularly hard to research within households.

Finally, I should say that not all labor exchange is straightforwardly calculated, or is "calculated" at all in the sense normally employed in economics. Sometimes people help one another just because, as they tell me, someone needs help. Combined with the Islamic requirement for assisting the poor (a portion of each household's harvest goes to the poorest in the village, for instance), households both care for their members and, to a lesser degree, take care of neighboring households. The people of Tadrar are boisterously litigious, but also deeply compassionate, exorbitantly generous, and kind. Selfless love and carefully calibrated labor exchanges coexist in the household economy of the village.

3

HOUSEHOLD INEQUALITY

In the previous chapter I made the case that households are configured in many different ways, travel different trajectories, and are embedded in an array of larger social dramas and dynamics. Households within a village are not, in other words, like so many potatoes in a sack (Donham 1999, 34); households are interrelated, indeed interdependent, and while their capabilities evolve over time, I argue here that in Tadrar they are significantly unequal.

My specific focus in this chapter will be household property. All households are dependent on productive property—fields, pastures, trees, threshing floors, stables, kitchens—and to understand the linkages between specific household economies requires that we examine the social life of their productive resources. Land is obviously critical to farmers, and in Tadrar land does not statically or simply exist. Fields must be built and rebuilt, nurtured and maintained. Acquiring the right to build and rebuild is, in Tadrar as elsewhere, a critical and contentious process. Life in the mountains is produced through a delicate dialectic of scarce land and hard labor, and to understand the labor we have to attend to rights over land.

Irrigated land is the paramount, most consistently productive local resource, and is the most important property controlled by a household. Non-irrigable fields might prove a boon in rainy years, herds of goats might grow rapidly and provide income when the grass grows well, but such resources will not keep children growing through bad years. Irrigated land depends on the reliable snowmelt of the high peaks rather than fickle local rainfall. Irrigated land feeds households when the rains do not come, when herds dwindle and die, when trees fall victim to disease, when corrupt officials demand more walnuts than you can pay, when there is no wage labor available in the plains or cities, or when the beehives go silent from the predations of mites. Pastures are held in common, but irrigated agricultural land is vested in jealously protected private ownership regimes of various kinds. From a long-term perspective land is strikingly vibrant. It is made and remade over seasons, but it also moves in a deeper rhythm of human generations. Land is divided and consolidated as people come and go, as new villagers are born and old ones die. Inheritance is the main way land moves between households in the long term, and inheritance is skewed to favor men.

Inheritance laws are outlined in some detail in the Qur'an, and local understanding of these passages provides the basic schemata for longitudinal land transfer in Tadrar. The ancient law is not always followed to the letter, however, and even when it is there are a number of ways to move land laterally, between people alive at the same time. Land can be loaned, it can be sharecropped (through what is called an *amshrek* agreement), it can be donated, and in extraordinary circumstances it can even be sold. Selling irrigated land is problematic, however, because all private land is dependent upon contested public property—canals. Here, as elsewhere, the reconciliation of water rights—and the dependence of "private" household productivity upon a "public" villagewide resource—is a continual source of tension. In the one instance when land was sold to outsiders, people from the next village downstream, continual complications have ensued.

Canals are somewhat fragile. Like fields, they do not just hum along doing their job, but need the care of human hands. Built onto the sides of steep mountains, and traditionally made of only rock and mud, canals easily wash away. I was nearly killed in the summer of 2004 while walking along a canal called Issreran that simply dropped out from under me, sending rock and a torrent of water crashing dozens of meters down to the boulders above the river. I was terrified, hanging from a tree branch, and once I had climbed back to relatively safe ground, I ran gasping all the way back to the village screaming for help to fix the canal. I banged on three doors in a row, but could not get anybody to do anything more than ask whether I was alright. Evidently canals break all the time. As long as they do not break above a field, and thus are not washing away anyone's property, a broken canal is no cause for worry, and certainly no cause for screaming like a lunatic.

Canals are cause for much complicated work, however. Canals not only have to be rebuilt after clumsy anthropologists wreck them, but in drought years especially new dams must be constructed in the river to capture more water for the canals. While I was doing my 1998–1999 research, the river level was very low and teams of men were commonly found building and rebuilding dams in the river to capture the dwindling water. Clearly this sort of work subtracts men from their regular household labor equations, and thus who must labor on such village projects is another contentious matter. It is thus clear why development agents who visited Tadrar consistently found that cement for the canals was a top village priority. Sturdy cement canals do not break or leak, thus new dams are not required and men can focus on their own fields and avoid dealing with larger labor organizations, particularly the lineage-based organizations that I will detail in the next chapter. Cooperation is itself hard work, work to be avoided if possible. By 2004 the villagers were proud that they had managed to garner the resources to cement one of the canals. This was their first major development effort after the potable water system was constructed in 1998. This canal arrived with some illuminating problems, as we will see in chapter 5.

For now, this chapter will explore inheritance, how households come to possess their necessary productive property. Beginning with inheritance through men, I will show how dramatic inequalities are built into households (*tikatin*), then how this inequality is inflected, sometimes counteracted, and often exacerbated by the dynamics of women's inheritance. The end result is that households are significantly unequal in terms of the property they control. These productive inequalities condition (but do not strictly determine) the capacity for households to produce children to labor, and this in turn influences the kind of lives lived within particular households, the amount of leisure, the quality of food, the availability of medicine, the political potential of the patriarch. Inequalities between households influence (and are influenced by) inequalities within particular households, and they influence (and are influenced by) inequalities at the broader lineage and village levels, too. While these different social levels articulate complicatedly, to explain them I am choosing to isolate each level, freeze the fluid dialectics among them, and press multidimensional social process into the linear confines of text—one letter, one word, one paragraph at a time. After all this I will try to reanimate the whole, but this may be easier if readers understand that the "things" considered here are not inherently inert, only made that way by my attempt to explain them.

Villagers are too often conceptualized as undifferentiated individuals slugging their way through simple, stupefying labor with little concern for the past or future. In fact, there are salient differences in the conditions villagers face, and the creativity of their responses to these different conditions varies as widely as it might in any group of diverse individuals. And while villagers respond by drawing on what we might call a common "culture," they do not draw upon the same cultural principles in the same ways at the same time. Doing something culturally does not mean culture wills it to be done (Sahlins 1999).

Diversity in property ownership is only one kind of diversity within the village, and one of the easier ones to document; its significance ramifies up and down the levels of social integration. Understanding how inequalities between households emerge in Tadrar will allow us to explore how the village relates to the Moroccan state and international development agencies, and ultimately the different ways households engage the constraints and potential of the global economy.

INTERVIEW WITH ABDURRAHMAN AIT BEN OUCHEN
October 30, 1998

David: First I would like to hear the history of the Ait Ben Ouchen, the old history. When did the Ait Ben Ouchen come to the Agoundis Valley?

Abdurrahman: When did the Ait Ben Ouchen first come to the Agoundis? Rahamna [between Marrakech and Casablanca] was their homeland; they were Arabs. They came to the Agoundis in the time of Mahdi Ibn Tumart, [the twelfth century A.D.] and the white mosque [Tin Mal], the capital of Morocco before the Alouine [the present ruling dynasty]. But the Mahdi Ibn Tumart, I have no idea who belongs to his family. Ibn Tumart was the Imam al-Mahdi of Islam. They came in his time, they came, the Ait Ben Ouchen. The man who came, the original Ait Ben Ouchen, his name is Abd al-Haq Rahamnani from Rahamna. His homeland was Rahamna in the region of Ben Grir, that was his homeland, then he came to Agoundis. What else?

David: After Abd al-Haq, what were the names of the other men who came to the Agoundis?

Abdurrahman: Haj Abd al-Haq al-Rahamna came and lived [here], and had his son Mohammed. He died, this son Mohammed, and he left his son Mansour. He lived for a period and left

his son Abdurrahman. Abdurrahman died; his son was
Lahcen. Lahcen died and his son was Ouahman. Ouahman died and he left Mohammed. Mohammed died and he
left Ali. Ali died and left Abdurrahman, me. I am Abdurrahman son of Ali Ait Ben Ouchen. The old family name
of Abd al-Haq was Yousfi, they say Yousef, Yousef. Mohammad ben Ouahman was *amghar* [local leader], he was
amghar in the area of Agoundis. He was with the Goundafi
caid [the regional leader]. The Goundafi *caid* named him
"*Ouchen*" [jackal]. After Mohammad was *amghar*, he had a
son Ali Ben Ouchen. Me, I am Abderrahman Ben Ouchen.
Ait Ben Ouchen is our family name.

It is clear that Abdurrahman understands himself as linked deep in time,
and while it seems a few links might be missing, Abdurrahman traces his
lineage back to the arrival of Islam in these mountains, the time of the fiery,
revivalist preacher Ibn Tumart, the twelfth century. Ibn Tumart founded a
political-religious movement that became the Almohad Empire, one of the
great Moorish dynasties that came to control all of Morocco and much of
the desert to the south, most of Spain, and much of what is now Algeria.
The Almohads started as obscure religious puritans but came to sponsor one
of the great courts of Islamic Spain.

Abdurrahman thus links himself through a line of men back to a time
before the present royal dynasty—the longest continuously ruling dynasty
in the world—back to a time when the base of the Agoundis Valley was, in
his words, the "capital of Morocco" and eventually much more. The Tin
Mal mosque is still there today, rebuilt by the government of Morocco as
an important historical landmark and now visited by tourists from all over
the world. From Abdurrahman's perspective, his family is associated with
major historical events that extend far beyond the mountains: the arrival
of Islam in Morocco, the founding of the Almohad Dynasty, and much later
the rise of the Goundafi *caid*, one of the great "Lords of the Atlas," in the
nineteenth century.[1]

We will pursue these connections between Tadrar and the outside world
and explain what they mean in chapter 5. Here I want to focus on the idea

1. The history of the Goundafa is interesting in its own right, but is beyond the scope of
this work. See Arrif (1985), Bidwell (1973), Crawford (2001), Cunninghame Graham (1997
[1898]), Doutté (1914), Justinard (1951), Montagne (1930a), Segonzac (1903).

of lineage, for while Abdurrahman takes a single line back into time (his father's father's father . . .), many of these fathers had brothers, and these brothers had sons, and Abdurrahman sees himself as related to these lines, too. In the classic view of the Moroccan mountains, these branching lineages would have formed the basic structure of political action. Men would be able to locate themselves socially and politically by finding a common ancestor with other men, and war parties could be organized by drawing on these ramifying ties of brotherhood. In other parts of Morocco, lineage associations have been claimed to have formed the political glue that allowed tribes to govern themselves without any permanent authority or the intervention of the state (Gellner 1969), and to marshal the military resources to resist French colonization (Hart 1981). In the region around the Agoundis, these sorts of genealogical orderings were split into two grand leagues, or *lfuf*, called the Ait Atman and the Ait Iraten. Most villages were associated with one or the other of the *lfuf*, but some, like Tadrar, had families representing each of the leagues.

However, this kind of tribal organization was destroyed by the mid-nineteenth century with the rise of "The Goundafi," the ascendancy of the Ait Lahcen family from Tagoundaft, near Tin Mal. The original "Goundafi" (as he came to be called) was named Mohammed. He seized power over both moieties and made himself, and later his son Tayeb, unquestioned lord of the mountains south of Marrakech. Abdurrahman's grandfather Moham-med Ait Yous was the Goundafi's agent—his *amghar*—in the Agoundis Valley, and later, probably for his habit of surly independence, the Goundafi re-named his uppity *amghar* "the jackal." Thus Abdurrahman's patriline went from being the "people of Joseph" (Ait Yous or Ait Yousef) to the "people of the jackal" (Ait Ben Ouchen). The original jackal, Mohammed Ait Yous,

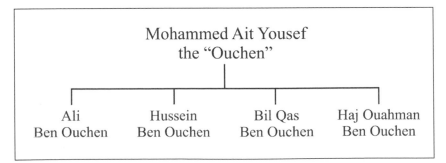

Fig. 1. The primary Ben Ouchen ancestors

had four sons, and these four sons are the patrilineal ancestors of all the Ait Ben Ouchen alive today, 114 of the 222 people living in Tadrar in 1999.

In the classic work on the operation of lineages in Morocco, a main theme is equality; we would expect each of these four lines of Ben Ouchen to be equal, and nominally, in local terms, they are. This presumption of equality bears upon village projects in various ways. Each of the four branches ought to contribute equally to any common endeavor. But people do not live in lineages, they live in households. Households are dependent upon property, so understanding the dynamics of lineages in Tadrar is impossible without understanding the households from which they are built, the property upon which households are based, and the social projects to which lineal related-ness is applied.

The Holy Qur'an states that upon his death a man's land should be divided among his heirs. In Tadrar this is believed to mean that one-eighth should go to a man's surviving wife (almost nobody has more than one wife) and the remainder to his sons and daughters (each son gets twice as much as each daughter).[2] A woman's property is inherited by her children equally; girls and boys receive the same shares. Of course, the Qur'an has much more than this to say about inheritance, but these simplified rules demonstrate one of the persistent problems of High Atlas farming: gaining enough land

2. What is important for these purposes is less what the Qur'an actually says than what it is understood to say. For details of the text itself, see especially Sura 4:11 and 4:12 (1993 trans. Taqi-ud Din Al-Hillali). The first reads, "Allah commands you as regards your children's (in-heritance); to the male, a portion equal to that of two females; if (there are) only daughters, two or more, their share is two thirds of the inheritance; if only one, her share is half. For parents, a sixth share of inheritance to each if the deceased left children; if no children, and the parents are the (only) heirs, the mother has a third; if the deceased left brothers or (sis-ters), the mother has a sixth. (The distribution of the cases is) after payment of legacies he may have bequeathed or debts. You know not which of them, whether your parents or your children, are nearest to you in benefit (these fixed shares) are ordained by Allah. And Allah is Ever All-Knower, All-Wise." Sura 4:12 reads, "In that which your wives leave, your share is half if they have no child; but if they leave a child, you get a fourth of that which they leave after payment of legacies they may have bequeathed or debts. In that which you leave, their (your wives) share is a fourth if you leave no child; but if you leave a child, they get an eighth of that which you leave after payment of legacies that you may have bequeathed or debts. If the man or woman whose inheritance is in question has left neither ascendants nor descen-dants, but has left a brother or a sister, each one of the two gets a sixth; but if more than two, they share in a third. After payment of legacies he (or she) may have bequeathed or debts, so that no loss is caused (to anyone). This is a Commandment from Allah; and Allah is Ever-All Knowing, Most-Forbearing."

to begin a household is not easy with a growing population. In each passing generation land is divided, and so each generation of young people is faced with the challenge of assembling the productive resources to support a household. The failure of many families to accomplish this is a major spur for migration out of the mountains.

In Figure 2, each numbered box represents a Ben Ouchen household in 1999; all four of the ancestral brothers have long since died, and the hatched boxes below refer to their sons who had households but now have died and passed on their property. I have assigned numbers to the households, beginning with Abdurrahman at "1" and continuing out to his brothers and cousins. Some men have managed to start their own households while their fathers are still alive (households 3, 6, and 10) using some combination of local trade and urban migration to make up for their lack of land. We will meet these landless patriarchs again. By 2004 the head of household 2 had died, releasing his property so that household 3 was less dependent on business, and household 10 had given up village life, abandoned his responsibilities to his father, and moved his family to Marrakech. These dynamics, and the relationship of inheritance and lineage-based labor organizations to them, are explored in later chapters.

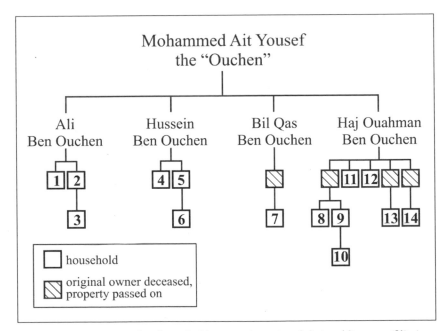

Fig. 2. Fourteen Ben Ouchen households extant in 1999 and their sublineage affiliations

Fortunately, the original Ouchen was a wealthy man, because the contemporary Ait Ali, Ait Hussein, Ait Bil Qas and Ait Haj Ouahman (usually shortened to Ait l'Haj) each must divide a quarter of his inheritance. Worse still, while the one Bil Qas household still retains what seems like a quarter of the entire Ouchen stake, the Ait l'Haj have divided their quarter seven ways! As I will show in a moment, things are not quite so simple, but at the outset we might guess that the Ait l'Haj may take cold comfort at being part of the most politically powerful lineage in Tadrar—the Ben Ouchen—as their stake in its property is, on a per- household basis, quite small. The boxes representing contemporary households are here drawn as exactly the same size. But this sort of nominal equality between branches of a lineage does not mean equality among households. It is striking that Moroccan Imazighen (or Berbers) have been labeled "egalitarian" by scholars. Clearly this is at best political equality among certain categories of men; the inequalities present in Tadrar suggest that any claim about things being equal in any society depends centrally on the specificity of the thing under consideration.

The situation is apparent if we look at an idealized property inheritance chart for the lineage of Abdurrahman's wife, Khadija Idzdo. Figure 3 depicts the relative property of the four contemporary Idzdo households by tracing their idealized property inheritance. We see that the Idzdo ancestor had two boys, each of whom received half of the land. These two (through their descendants) eventually bequeathed their property to five male heirs, five potential household heads by 1999. This original Idzdo was certainly less wealthy than the original Ouchen, so we can imagine that in general the Idzdo lineage has had less room to grow, and indeed has grown less. Here the boxes are proportional to their inheritance.

For simplicity's sake we look only at male inheritance. Half of all Idzdo irrigated land remains in the hands of one man (household 18), while three households split a quarter (19, 20, 21). One of these (19) belongs to my neighbor Omar Idzdo, who, as I wrote in the last chapter, continues to shepherd high in the Ouanoukrim despite the fact that he is quite old. The final quarter of the land has been taken to household 1, Abdurrahman's household, which is obviously not in the Idzdo lineage. We explore this curiosity in the next section. For now, the point is that while every man has an equal voice in the village *jemaa,* having property can dramatically impact how you spend your days—out working other people's fields in a sharecrop arrangement, or kibitzing at the mosque while your sons do the work. In terms of property—the basis of prosperity and the means by which men produce households, children, and the free time necessary for political work—male inheritance is quite unequal.

However, the inheritance of sons from fathers is only part of what turns out to be a very complicated and contentious story. Invisible on our chart of Ben Ouchen households (Figure 2), the four original Ouchen boys had a sister named Ija, who married into another branch of the Ait Yousef lineage in the distant village of Tizi Oussem. Ija does not have a household in Tadrar and is not on our chart, but her descendants still visit the village twice a

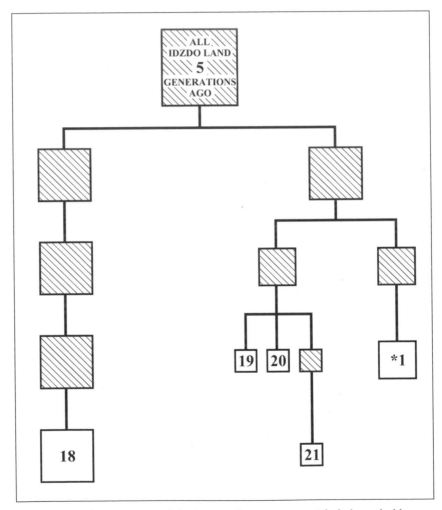

Fig. 3. Relative property inheritance of contemporary Idzdo households

year to receive some portion of the harvest. This amounts to one half of what each of the four Ait Ben Ouchen lineages began with—a considerable sum in this context. Not all sisters are so successful at claiming their rights, especially in villages they marry away from, and it is even rarer that they manage to establish rights in perpetuity. Still, the heirs of Ija illustrate one way that patrilineal connections significantly involve women. Ija's success was probably helped by the fact that she was a full sister to the two youngest brothers, Ali and Hussein, and they remained in Tadrar to argue on Ija's behalf. Ija's two brothers thus had some material interest in protecting their sister's rights against their half brothers. (Indeed, Ija's heirs are likely to *amshrek,* or sharecrop, her property with one or both of the brothers' descendants since they cannot possibly come and irrigate themselves.)

We can demonstrate more of the importance of women to the constitution of property by returning to the story of Abdurrahman's household. Abdurrahman's father, Ali, had children with three wives in succession: Yemna, Fatima, and Nejma. Ali married in succession and the timing of his marriages significantly impacts the lives of his sons. For instance, with his first wife, Yemna, the young Ali had his first son, Mohammed, another son, Lahcen, who survived long enough to be remembered but died before having any children, and three girls. When Yemna died, Ali took a new bride, Fatima, and built a new house for her two villages away in Tazguart, leaving the other children in Tadrar to live in the house they had grown up in. This allowed the oldest boy, Mohammed, married by this time, to be nominally in charge of a household while still dependent on his father's property.

Meanwhile, with his new bride Ali had another son, Hussein, who is not listed on our chart of the Ait Ali because his household is outside of Tadrar. He is, however, still involved in the village in some ways and he was fully included in the negotiations over inheritance. When Hussein's mother, Fatima, died, Ali left Hussein in charge of his property in this new village of Tazguart. It is very unusual for men to own property in more than one village. The Ben Ouchen do so only because their ancestor, Ali's father, Mohammed, was a powerful *amghar* and, as his grandson Abdurrahman claims, "bought" land from this other village. The people of Tazguart contest this claim, and have unsuccessfully attempted to sue the Ben Ouchen several times in Moroccan court to reclaim property they claim was taken generations ago by "the jackal." In any case, after the death of his second wife in Tazguart the aging Ali left his son Hussein there to run the house and moved back to Tadrar.

Here Ali married again. He built his new wife, Nejma, yet another house, and there they had a boy and a girl, my friend and colleague Abdurrahman and his sister, Fatime. At this point Ali had grown very old—he had two grown boys already—and he relied on his youngest boy, Abdurrahman, to help him move about. Thus Abdurrahman spent his formative years in an entirely different house from either of his two half brothers, in a very differently constituted household; he had a very different life. While the older boys worked the patriarch's land, Hussein down in Tazguart and Mohammed in Tadrar, Abdurrahman became a kind of aide to his father. As Ali had himself been the youngest son of Mohammed Ouchen, this was a kind of family dynamic repeating itself—the youngest son of the youngest wife again this generation became a kind of nurse and assistant, a repository of an old man's stories, family lore, and history. This is why Abdurrahman can recite so much local history, why he can name ancestors back eight hundred years, and why, despite being almost illiterate, he can talk confidently and accurately about much of the history of Morocco that you will find in books.

Ali died in the late 1960s at a reported age of one hundred. One-eighth of his property went to his wife, Nejma, and the rest was divided among the three boys, Mohammed, Hussein, and Abdurrahman, each of whom continued to live with their respective wives in the houses in which they had been born and raised. Contrary to what would seem the dictates of the Qur'an, none of Abdurrahman's sisters and half sisters received anything from Ali's death, although the one surviving wife got her share. When Ali's surviving wife, Nejma, died, too, Abdurrahman, as her only son, received all of her property. Thus, Abdurrahman received his mother's eighth of his father's inheritance, plus a third of what was left, or a total of 5/12ths of Ali's property (or 10/24ths, if we want to keep the denominators common for comparison). His brothers each got 7/24ths, leaving the youngest brother with the newest house, somewhat more property than his two older brothers, and a wealth of knowledge about the family's history and connections.

If that was not enough, Ali had also secured for his youngest son a very favorable marriage to Khadija Idzdo. Khadija's father had only one son, Hussein, who as I noted before is mentally retarded and is thus dependent on his sister. Since Abdurrahman controls (but does not technically own) Khadija's land, he also has her brother Hussein's property at his disposal. This is why the Idzdo genealogy, Figure 3, includes household 1—Abdurrahman's *takat*. If we look at the inheritance pattern of the Idzdo, it seems Abdurrahman has come to control as much land as three entire Idzdo households, a quarter of the entire Idzdo farmland.

Even more useful from Abdurrahman's perspective, Khadija's mother married into Tadrar after divorcing the then-*amghar* of the Agoundis, who lived three villages down in Tijrisht. This man made his son *amghar* after him, and he remains so today, and therefore Khadija is half-siblings with the most powerful man in the valley. When today the *amghar* visits the upper part of the valley, he always stops in at his sister's and enjoys tea and chats about politics with her husband—Abdurrahman. The *amghar* allows his brother-in-law Abdurrahman useful access to the Rabat-appointed *caid,* who still rules the region from Talat n Yacoub, twenty kilometers away. Even more usefully, since Abdurrahman's mother was from a village right by Talat n Yacoub, he has a place to stay and politick near the regional political center.

In sum, Abdurrahman is abundantly blessed with property (through his father, his mother, his wife, and her brother), and he has been lucky in terms of progeny to labor on that property (he has five sons). Abdurrahman has both the time to gather information and practice politics and the connections—though his patrilineage, but also through his wife and mother—to do so. In a world of equals, Abdurrahman is more equal than most.

Clearly the importance of women's property, and the way women move property between male patrilines, demonstrates that inheritance is about much more than "lineages." Still, property is *thought* to be related to lineage affiliation in a general sense. Other lineage members refer to "the" Ben Ouchen as being "rich," even though we can see there are dramatic differences among the Ben Ouchen as a whole, and significant differences even among the three brothers of the sublineage Ait Ali. Women's importance to the constitution of households is not normally considered by scholars or villagers to include property, only labor. When village men explained the relationships between households and household property there were no women mentioned, and in the classic scholarly work on Moroccan Berbers women are usually, at best, an afterthought. I came to understand women's contributions very slowly, and only because the changing nature of households—and their very different behavior—raised questions as to why reportedly equal men were clearly in such different economic situations. It is true that women only occasionally managed to gain their juridical rights to property, but it seems to me that these successful claims are important hidden factors explaining inequality in property in Tadrar, and thus tell us much about the differential fates of men within their idealized lineage scheme.

Evident differences among villagers prompted me to try and quantify the inequality we expect from these idealized diagrams. It is subjectively apparent who the wealthier men in the village are. Abdurrahman and a couple others in the village are universally acknowledged as being, in Abdurrahman's words, "a little big." The most desperate families are apparent, too, as everyone knows the few who have no land and the three or four households routinely given charity at the end of the year harvest. But how much difference is there? How big is a little big? In 2004, visible differentiation between villagers has become evident in terms of who does and does not own televisions and satellite dishes, toilets, and DVD players. This was not the case in 1998, however. The whole village looked to be roughly the same—very poor—and this impression was not lost on development agencies and on most branches of the Moroccan government. The villagers of Tadrar were thought to simply "be poor"; differences among them were imagined to be insignificant.

Disproving this was not easy. While it is certainly the case that everyone in Tadrar is poor, poverty is not a simple, singular category; living as a poor person does not mean living in the same way as other poor people, and we find among the poor as much diversity, creativity, and differentiation as we do in other classes. Some villagers are, in my view, more significantly poor than others, and failing to account for this leads us to misunderstand how general village social dynamics work, and complicates efforts to make things better through development schemes. But, again, how to assess such a claim? Villagers do not like talking about their economic situations other than in the most evasive terms, and while most presented their conditions to me as dire (probably because I am a potential conduit of aid), a few clearly exaggerated their wealth and power, and are said to exaggerate it by their neighbors.

I tried different ways to overcome the problems of subjective interpretations of rich and poor. For instance, I first attempted to discover who owned which animals, since animals are an important form of wealth, at least in good years. This turned out to be ill advised; I seemed only to start arguments, as most men claimed that other men had vast numbers of goats and sheep while they themselves had none or few. It became clear that certain officials in power at the time had sought payment in animals, and thus everybody wanted to be able to claim they had none, and nobody wanted me hanging around the pastures counting the herds. Indeed, an official had recently done just such a count, and nobody locally found much advantage in the exercise.

I faced similar problems counting walnut and almond production (also good targets for expropriation), but even with barley there was obvious resistance to me calculating how much grain was in anyone's larder. My first day sitting at the threshing floor counting bags, measuring how much fit in a bag, and adding up total harvests was concluded by some people swearing I had counted too high by a factor of four, while others, presumably hoping to seem wealthy, asserted that I had counted far too low. It is true that I am no whiz at math, but I am not *that* bad. The villagers did not want animals, grain, walnuts, or almonds calculated, and they certainly did not want such calculations written down. In deference to their wishes I gave up.

Or mostly gave up. My compromise method was to try and assess wealth by field ownership. Fields are immovable, people do not deny that they own them, and they cannot be confiscated by government officials. Presumably corrupt officials could assess fines based on field ownership, but owning a field did not necessarily mean it was productive in a given year, and this gave people an "out" if grain was demanded as a bribe. Villagers did not seem to mind me spending days wandering around asking who owned which field, perhaps because this left the question of how to assess the value of fields. With, as I discovered, over 1,100 plots of irrigated land varying in size from a few square meters to over thirty, and varying also in how much sun they received, soil quality, proximity to a canal, and more, how could I know who really had more valuable property, or how much they had? The ambiguity of field productivity protected the villagers' sense that their wealth would not be accurately known, but complicated my interest in knowing the relative distinctions in wealth.

I designed a rough method, beginning with a simple field count and distinguishing irrigated from rain-fed fields. This took a surprisingly long time and much effort wandering to and fro, but produced dramatic results. The top three households in Tadrar in 1999 had 105, 90, and 85 fields respectively. The bottom three households had only 19, 18, and 17 irrigated fields (disregarding four others that had no land at all). While it is possible that the people with few fields have really large, sunny, fertile, and well-watered locations, this did not seem to be the case. Some people had better, larger fields, but if anything these better, bigger fields tended to be owned by the people who also had the most fields. Field size seemed randomly distributed, but I did not have the time to calculate the size of the irregular terraced fields, and so this is only a guess. Still, it seems reasonable to venture that there are fairly significant differences between households if some have five times as many fields as others. This is particularly salient if even the richest households are very poor in the wider Moroccan and global context.

To confirm these differences among households I calculated irrigation time, hypothesizing that water rights would be a measure of productivity, or at least would be a measure of predictable wealth. People with more total land but less water might do well on wet years; irrigation time was likely to provide a measure of how much productivity a household could count on in bad years.

This, too, was more work than I expected. There are seven main canals in Tadrar organized into four separate systems, two of nine days and two of ten days. Each day is divided into a daytime (dawn to dusk) and nighttime (dusk to dawn) rotation, and each half rotation can be split many ways into many different proportions. To facilitate the task of adding up rights to canal use, I first decided on a ninety-day common denominator, since that was the least common denominator for the nine- and ten-day cycles. (Every ninety days the ten-day cycles have made nine turns; the nine-day cycles have made ten.) I then set about discovering who had what rights on what days on what canals, and adding up these portions of days into a total. Figure 4 shows what households own what portion of each irrigation day.

This method is not exact. I was doing the research alone and was unable to observe all the canals at all times for all the rotations, and thus cannot gauge the difference between the ideal irrigation scheme I outline here and what really happened. I know from spot checks that sharecropping, for instance, is quite common and complicates the picture of wealth. That is, men with more land *amshrek* it with poorer family members who work it and return a portion of the harvest to the owner of the land. Whether seed and fertilizer are provided by the owner of the plot or the provider of the labor determines the proportion each gets of the final harvest. A very few plots were not farmed at all because the owner did not have enough sheep, goats, or cows to produce the fertilizer necessary to render the plot productive. A few fields were worked by neighbors of older people without descendants; in these cases men volunteered because, as they told me, "old men are tired" and simply need help. There is charity in addition to self-interested calcula-

day	Canal Ijaneten					Canal Issreran							
1	15		16		17	9	13	16	17	22	23	24	28
2	25		28		29	1				2			
3	18					26		22	23		24		12
4	19	20		21	1	22		23		24		12	
5	8		9		12 · 2	9		11	12		13		14
6	5	20		17 · 1	2	7						8	
7	Owned by the village of Ighir					4		5			6		
8	Owned by the village of Ighir					16		17	15		18		20
9	26		18		20	25		28			29		
10	15		16		17	1	2	4	5	6	7	9	25

day	Canal Taforikht						Canal Agouni n Ait Anou						
1	7			8	13		7				8		
2	18	19	20	21	1		9	11		12		14	
3	25	15		16	17		1				2		
4	2	1		4 · 5	6		22	23	24	9	12	13	25
5	7	11	12	14	8		4	25	28	29	15	16	
6	22	23		24	26		18					12	13
7	4	5		6			18		1		7		
8	1			2			19		20	21		1	
9	12	9	11	25	14 · 19		4		5			6	

Fig. 4. Household rights to irrigation time for the
four main canal systems of Tadrar

tion, as evidenced by the photograph included in this book of Mohammed Belaid plowing the field of his aged neighbor Ohomo.

Still, the thrust of the calculations are clear. In a 90-day irrigation cycle for the four main canal systems, the top three households had totals of 38.8, 28.3, and 28.1 days worth of irrigation time. The bottom three households that had any irrigation time (again, not including those with no time at all) had 7.1, 6.8, and 4.6 days (see Table 1). From this it seems that, roughly speaking, the richest owners of water have about five times as much as the poorest. Bearing in mind that the "richest" in this context are people who fit very comfortably within the World Bank definition of "absolute poverty,"

Table 1. Irrigation time, rank of irrigation time, and number of fields by household

Household no.	Irrigation days/90	Irrigation time rank	No. irrigated fields rank
No. 1	38.8	1	1
No. 7	28.3	2	19
No. 18	28.1	3	3
No. 2	17.5	4	4
No. 12	16.7	5	10
No. 17	15.5	6	2
No. 5	15.2	7	16
No. 25	14.7	8	8
No. 16	12.9	9	7
No. 8	12.3	10	15
No. 6	12.0	11	20
No. 4	12.0	12	21
No. 26	11.8	13	12
No. 9	11.5	14	17
No. 15	11.5	15	5
No. 11	9.8	16	13
No. 20	9.6	17	9
No. 22	9.5	18	14
No. 23	9.5	19	16
No. 24	9.5	20	22
No. 28	8.8	21	23
No. 29	7.7	22	6
No. 19	7.3	23	19
No. 14	7.1	24	15
No. 21	6.8	25	11
No. 13	4.6	26	18

Note: Households 3, 10, and 27 have no property and manage to support themselves through commerce, wage labor, and sharecropping.

this would seem to indicate that there are striking differences among villagers in terms of quality of life—not to mention political potential.

To confirm that these two ways of assessing wealth were not entirely unrelated, I ranked the households in terms of number of fields, ranked them in terms of irrigation time, and compared the rankings. For those with an understanding of statistics, the Spearman's rank correlation coefficient for this data is: $r = 0.42$, $p = .032$, $n = 26$.[3] In simple terms this means that if we

3. I thank Edward Hagen of the Humbolt Institute in Berlin for calculating these statistics.

know how comparatively wealthy someone is in terms of the number of fields he owns (i.e., his rank in the village in terms of field ownership), we have about a 40 percent chance of guessing how wealthy he is in terms of irrigation time. This is certainly not absolute proof that I am right, much less that I can confidently state exactly who is wealthy and who is not, but it is another part of what I think is a compelling argument: in Tadrar some households are considerably better off than others.

In this chapter I have examined differences among households in terms of property ownership. Irrigated land is the most important local productive resource, and thus for the purpose of assessing inequality between households I have focused mainly on irrigated land and on rights over water to irrigate land. Since property moves through the generations mainly along male lines (i.e., it is inherited from father to son), irrigated land in particular is locally understood to approximate patrilineal connections.

To have land is to have the means to run a household, thus to be married, to have sex and children, to be a man in Tadrar. However, some households lack any land at all, and keep themselves alive by migrating, through local businesses, by sharecropping with land-rich but labor-poor households, or by sending children out to work. In general, however, to be a man is to control property, particularly irrigable land. Women produce households (*tikatin*) through their hearths (*tikatin* also), their nourishing productive and reproductive labor, but men must provide the soil to grow grain for the women to make the *tanoort* (bread) and *askeef* (barley soup). This is why productive property is conceived as a masculine domain, and why patrilineal relatedness is basic to how males become men. It is a matter of fathers not only begetting sons, but rendering these sons productive in their own right by bequeathing the ancestral patrimony.

Complicating this, women also own property. As Jack Goody has written, "Though descent groups are always unilineal, kinship is everywhere bilateral" (1983, 16), and in Tadrar as elsewhere in the Muslim world women have definite rights to property. In chapter 6, I will argue that these bilateral ties are far more important than has been recognized. For the present chapter it is enough to demonstrate that women's inheritance—as prescribed by the Qur'an and as occasionally actualized in social life—is very significant to manifest inequalities in property ownership. If productive property is the base resource that allows men to produce sons, and thus laborers, and if sons working land allows patriarchs the time to politick, we can say that in some cases women's rights to property have in fact produced *imazighen,* a Berber word for "free men," and the general word for all Berbers across North Africa and beyond.[4] A man is only free when he has the time to exercise his will, when somebody else is doing the work of keeping him alive. Women not only produce all men through their bodies, breast milk, and bread, but women also control some of the property that allows males to become, socially speaking, men.

All of this bears on broad arguments about equality among Berbers (a venerable theme) as well as how households are ultimately situated to deal with the transformations wrought by the global economy. In terms of equality it has been said that "a constant preoccupation of all Berbers is never to let one head rise above the rest" (Hart 1981, 77), that "the system is egalitarian" (Gellner 1969, 143). This is argued to have been so in the past, and even today, "as traditional economic structures did not undergo radical changes during the protectorate period from 1933 until 1956 or the subsequent period of Moroccan national independence" (Kraus 1998, 6). Ernest Gellner most succinctly describes the operation of lineages in the mountains: "The condition is timeless" (1969, 60).

My argument, by contrast, is that the condition is necessarily *timeful.* The temporal dynamics of households—especially, in this chapter, the long-term transfer of land—are crucial to understanding what is in reality significant inequality. Lineages are important because they help us see how the people of Tadrar conceptualize households as being linked together through time, how they understand social responsibility, which groups of households should help which others. But we must recognize that this sort of sodality, and the formal equality between lineage branches, does not mean there is anything like real economic or, as we will see, political equality between households. As Robert Montagne observed dryly in 1930: in the High Atlas, "despite the respect paid to egalitarian institutions—to such an extent that the rich have houses that are no finer than those of the poor—one finds that it is the rich who exercise power behind the scenes" (1973 [1930], 59). In Tadrar all men—as men—are free and equal. But some are significantly more equal than others, and therefore more free.

4. See Crawford (2007b) on the "production of free men."

The village of Tadrar in 1998

Abdurrahman Ait Ben Ouchen and Khadija Idzdo with
three of their sons and two granddaughters

"Granny" Aisha working with her grandchildren

Mohammed Lukstaf thinning his maize field

Left to right: Four Ben Ouchen patriarchs: Mohammed Ben Salah (household 7), Mohammed "Azoomzoom" Ait l'Haj (household 13), Mohammed Ali (household 2), and Hamad ben Mohammed Ali (household 3)

Mohammed Belaid plowing a neighbor's field

The winter pastures and the terraces of Agouni n Ait Anou
Courtesy Bart Deseyn

4

ARRANGING THE BONES

At this point I hope to have established that households are the most significant social unit operative in Tadrar. It should be clear that there are marked inequalities of authority within households, and significant inequalities between households in terms of property. Property is seen to approximate patrilineage, which is to say that lines of ancestors through men are the main way that patriarchs are believed to be connected, and the devolution of property through time is thought to mirror this. This ideal equality of branching trees of brothers is confounded by demographic imbalances (more children born into one line than another) and by women's inheritance. The fact that some women manage to claim the *de jural* rights to property guaranteed by the Qur'an means that when women marry between lineages they may take property from one line of male ancestors to another. Thus, over time productive resources do not devolve equally to the putatively equal patriarchs within a lineage. Despite an egalitarian ethic among lineages, material conditions vary. We now turn to a second way that lineages factor in the social dynamics of inequality in Tadrar: labor organization for collective projects. Forms of labor allocation are meant to be equal in specific, culturally sensible ways; in practice the arrangement of lineages into viable work groups ameliorates some kinds of inequality, but exacerbates others.

There is a rich literature on lineages in Morocco. Before discussing more of this literature and why it is important, I should note that patrilineal descent groups—converging lines of ancestors leading back in time through the patriarchs of each household—may be the main way that households are thought to be connected, but they are hardly the only way. In the village assembly, for instance, all men are said to be equal. Nobody is supposed to be excluded or silenced; it is an arena of formal equality that, like equality before God, should not have anything to do with lineages.

Also, all men have family connections through women, and these resources can be socially, politically, and economically important. Relations through one's mother's lineage and her relatives, a sister's or daughter's marriage, one's father's sisters, and so forth all give men and women a wide range of social resources to cultivate for pleasure or advantage. About 80 percent of women in Tadrar marry outside of the village (Crawford 2001), forging new family connections wherever they go. Such connections through women tend to be extensive, leading out in space to other villages, or the plains and cities, and can be enormously important. This is especially true now that villagers are more interested in inserting themselves into the larger wage labor economy. Male lineage relations are by contrast intensive; they typically matter only within the context of Tadrar. This is somewhat different than the way lineages are said to operate in other areas of Morocco, especially the Eastern High Atlas, where ethnographers have argued that lineages allow large groups of men to organize themselves over large areas for different, especially military, purposes (Hart 1981, 1996).

As they grow, lineages branch because each brother begins a new line of ancestors. The branches leading down from these brothers are thought to be affiliated, to owe aid and solidarity to one another vis-à-vis more distant branches. Clearly, the further back in time you go, the more branches or lines you encompass under one lineage, so when we talk about the "distance" between two branches we are really discussing how long ago they have a common ancestor, how proximately they are related in time. The fact that you can imagine a lineage from the standpoint of any node or segment in the branching structure has led scholars to call this kind of organization "segmentary." In Tadrar such segmentary, lineal relatedness can be flexibly applied to include anything from a father and his children to hundreds of people alive and dead. Crucially, any group at the same level (as descended from the same link in the chain, the same node in the branches) is seen as ideally equal. Brothers should be equal with brothers, groups of cousins with cousins, and so on up the line of ancestors; as groups get bigger they are seen to be equal with other, bigger groups. The principle of forming the groups remains the same whatever their size, and the principle of equality between groups remains whatever their size.

While these basic organizational ideas are easy enough to grasp, fierce debates have arisen over the salience of lineages in the Moroccan context.

Some argue that lineages are the only organizing principle active in the mountains (Gellner 1969, 42; 1996, 649), others that they are an important principle, but are subsumed at the highest levels into moieties, grand leagues called *lfuf*, and are subject to other social dynamics (Montagne 1930a). Some scholars believe that lineages are but one among many organizing ideas (Berque 1938, 1953, 1978; Combs-Schilling 1985; Rachik 1993, 2004), and still others suggest that lineages have no real consequence at all, that the focus on descent groups has taken us away from the actor-centered, culturally informed process of negotiating social connections (Geertz 1979; Rabinow 1975; Rosen 1984).[1] Over time these debates seem to have become less about lineages and more about the proper object of anthropological investigation.

Here I will be concerned mostly with valuations of equality, and how the formal equality between lineage segments fits with *de facto* inequality in terms of household property and labor. This is a somewhat hybrid position in that I am not arguing that social inequality is reducible to cultural ideas of what counts as equal, but neither will I suggest that social reality can be explained without reference to these cultural ideals. Social reality is dependent upon how people understand, and thus act, in that reality—an unstable situation that renders interpretations and explanations time-bound, subject to the time frame of the observation. My argument will be that inequalities at the household level concatenate up to the level of lineages, but also that inequalities in the dynamics of supposedly equal lineages reverberate back down to households, amplifying already stark inequalities between them. The key to understanding how this works is what I term the "temporality of inequality," the way inequalities are expressed in time.

Clearly, in scholarly terms I fall into the camp that finds lineages important in some ways. Their salience is complicated by the gulf between the ideal of tidily branching patrilines and the vagaries of demography and history, by the changing uses to which the concept of lineal relations is put, and by the ever-evolving nature of the underlying social unit, the household. Lineages, then, are not concrete things-in-the-world, but inchoate cultural models—mutable, multi-part models that are integrated and artfully applied in fluid social contexts.

Readers unfamiliar with academic writing on Morocco will probably wonder why there has been such a fuss about lineages, but they might not wonder

---

1. See also Amahan (1998), Eickelman (1985), Jamous (1982), and Mahdi (1999).

enough to want to wade through the arguments. While the main thrust of this chapter is on how lineages are made to operate in Tadrar, I will begin with the larger terms of the segmentary debate, a debate that in Morocco was launched thirty-five years ago by the late Ernest Gellner. In this next short section I focus on what Gellner had to say about segmentarity, and on what I take to be the core of his definition. This has far-reaching consequences for the way we understand the social world.[2]

Gellner did his fieldwork among "saintly" lineages of Ait 'Atta Berbers in a place called Ahansal, northeast of Marrakech. These saints were seen to have *baraka,* blessedness bestowed by God, which allowed them a kind of moral authority to litigate on the boundaries of segmentarily organized tribes. Supposedly these saints allowed High Atlas Berbers to operate in all other social realms tribally, using no other modality of social cohesion beyond genealogical reckoning. This meant tribes could constitute themselves at any social level, in very small but also very large groups—when necessary, and only when necessary. In Gellner's writing there seems little reason to coalesce except warfare, particularly to deflect the incursions of the central state.

Gellner writes, "In . . . segmentary society, similarity [in the form of the segments] is not merely lateral but also vertical: it is not simply that groups resemble their neighbors at the same level of size, but it is also the case that groups resemble, organisationally, the sub-groups of which they are composed, and the larger groups of which they are members" (Gellner 1987, 31). The assertion is that segmentary society is fractal, that social units are similarly structured whatever their size and, thus, there is a single, exclusive logic by which all of a segmentary society is organized. In other words, "What defines a segmentary society is not that [segmentation] does occur, *but that this is very nearly all that occurs*" (Gellner 1969, 42, emphasis added).[3] While conceptually attractive, this last statement is ethnographically unsupportable, as Hammoudi (1980), Munson (1996), and I myself have shown (2003). A great deal occurs in High Atlas society that cannot be called seg-

---

2. See Addi (2003), Berque (1978), Combs-Schilling (1985), Dresch (1986), Hammoudi (1980), Hart (1981, 1989), Kraus (1998), Munson (1991, 1993, 1997), Pascon (1979), Perishetti (2004), Pouillon (2005), Rachik (1992, 2004), Roberts (2002), and Waterbury (1991), among others. See Gellner (1996) for a response to some of his critics. In contrast to the work on segmentarity, Ensel (1999) and Ilahiane (1996, 1998) offer very interesting portraits of institutionalized inequality in the Moroccan context.

3. In his more recent "Reply to Critics," Gellner still maintains that what "makes a society segmentary" is the "*near*-total absence of *any other* institution" (1996, 649).

mentary, which is why Jacques Berque's classic account of the matter is definitively plural: *Structures sociales du Haut-Atlas* (1978). The singularity of Gellner's argument is clearly wrong.

A more important aspect of Gellner's claim—and a part that gained it enthusiastic opponents—is that it seems to define an archetypal "Other," a way of being that is entirely unlike European society. Gellner writes, "In complex societies, the state or the city are quite unlike the family. In a segmentary tribe [by contrast] there is a resemblance between the tribe or clan on the one hand and the family on the other, not merely in terminology, but also in reality" (1969, 49). This distinction between segmentary and complex societies is founded, Gellner says, on Émile Durkheim's opposition between mechanical and organic solidarity, an opposition that Durkheim based on his idiosyncratic reading of the ethnography of Kabyle Berbers in Algeria (see Fanny Colonna in Masqueray 1983; Roberts 2002). Because Durkheim is today read as one of the founders of contemporary social theory, and is required background knowledge in most sociology and anthropology departments, Berbers and their lineages have long been quietly important to the way scholars understand the social world.

As Durkheim writes, "Thus, among the Kabyles [Berbers of Algeria], the political unity is the clan, constituted in the form of a village (djemmaa or thaddart); several djemmaa form a tribe (arch'), and several tribes form the confederation (thak'ebilt), the highest political society that the Kabyles know. The same is true among the Hebrews. . . . These societies are such typical examples of mechanical solidarity that their principal physiological characteristics come from it" (1964 [1893], 178).[4]

Durkheim summarizes his position by writing, "these societies . . . are segmental in . . . their formation by the repetition of like aggregates in them, analogous to the rings of an earthworm, and we say of this elementary aggregate that it is a clan, because this word well expresses its mixed nature, at once familial and political" (Durkheim 1964 [1893], 175).[5] Despite the inclusion of "familial" here, there is no serious consideration of household organization. We have seen that the hierarchical relations within households contrast sharply with the egalitarian relations between them,

4. This insight is taken from Roberts (2002).

5. As Fanny Colonna suggests in the introduction to the reissue of Masqueray (1983 [1886]), and as Roberts demonstrates at length (2002, 119), Kabyle villages are not comprised of a single clan, and in any case there seems to be no evidence that "clans" of sedentary Kabyle farmers are socially detachable—from each other or from the land.

and that the specific dynamics within households influence the dynamics of the larger social forms and vice versa. The relations are dialectic—they move both ways—and they are not at all simple to understand or explain. The organization of households and those of lineages and villages are *not* similarly structured, contra what Gellner and Durkheim had to say. Attention to the difference between household dynamics and lineages will make this clear.

Yet Durkheim's simple ramifying formulation fit conveniently with the prejudices of social evolution, as in "The Hebrews remained in [a segmental social condition] to a late date, and the Kabyles never passed beyond it (Durkheim 1964 [1893], 177), or in Gellner's review of the matter, "Durkheim used [Masqueray's Kabyle] material to highlight not the mechanisms of cohesion operative in nineteenth-century European societies, but the mechanism we have left behind, and which illuminates our condition only by contrast" (1987, 41). Clearly Gellner was in no way addressing Moroccan or a wider Muslim intelligentsia, or contrasting rural to urban Morocco; the "we" and the "our" refer to "European societies," and much like contemporary globalization theory, the "traditional" (in this case Berber) realm is seen as a thing of the European past, as a time the Europeans have left behind. Combining Orientalist *and* Darwinian themes to make the case for segmentarity guaranteed rejection by a wide variety of postcolonial scholars. This framing has led many to reject the idea of segmentarity *tout court*—as a cultural model or as social reality.

There are, however, a couple of broader and more interesting theoretical points. Durkheim suggests an irony in the emergence of what Norbert Elias (1994 [1939]) and others call "civilization," which is that an increasing specialization of labor gives rise to deeper and more binding ties between people. Even if Berbers cannot be considered Europe's contemporary ancestors, it makes some sense to imagine that societies with less specialization of labor may be less densely dependent (parts can survive independently, like polyps of coral rather than like the limbs of a mammal) while the individual is also less free to pursue her or his particular calling (because there are fewer callings available in a non-specialized society). From this perspective, a compelling interdependence is the price of our contemporary freedom. This is a Rousseauian twist to the social evolutionary model. It echoes Freud (1930), Foucault (1975, 1983, 1994), and others in that it is modern society and its fine-grained divisions of labor and status that smothers the soul with surveillance, with a pervasive discipline required of extreme interconnectedness.

Unsurprisingly, contemporary theorists of globalization have taken up this thread also, arguing that "the qualitative difference between traditional and modern life-stories is not, as many assume, that in older corporate agrarian societies various suffocating controls and guidelines restricted the individual's say in his or her own life to a minimum, whereas today hardly any restrictions are left. It is, in fact, in the bureaucratic and institutional jungle of modernity that life is most securely bound into networks of guidelines and regulations" (Beck 2000, 166). Whether globalization represents progress (from traditional to modern) or degeneration (from freedom to a perniciously subtle enslavement) depends on the position of the globalization theorist. What both positions have in common is an assertion that the two modes are incompatible and that one precedes the other.

My case here is different. In my view there are "suffocating controls" in Tadrar, in urban Morocco, in Europe, Cuba, the United States, and elsewhere. These are *qualitatively different sorts of suffocation,* however, not simple contrasts. Different modalities of inequality can be and are integrated. In chapter 6, I pursue this further, and argue that on one hand patriarchy is endemic to the wage labor economy, but on the other it is becoming ever more common for patriarchal agricultural households to take advantage of the urban wage labor economy. The temporalities of their dynamics of inequalities are different, but subsistence agriculture and wage labor are contemporaneous systems of production, and appear perfectly compatible. The point for the consideration of lineages, however, is that Gellner was not simply commenting on the obscure customs of North African agropastoralists and the saints who litigate on their tribal borders. He was addressing fundamental questions of social order that have global relevance today.

And there is more. While Durkheim, as the title *De la division du travail social* suggests, used the Berber case primarily in his discussion of the division of labor, Gellner restricted his concern to political organization. Durkheim writes, "We do not have to show the analogies between the type which replaces the preceding one and that of organic societies. *In one case as in the other, the structure derives from the division of labor and its solidarity*" (1964 [1893], 192, emphasis added). Gellner's contribution was to transfer Durkheim's model for the general social division of labor specifically to political organization, or at least to explicitly connect Evans-Pritchard's political model of segmentarity (1940) to the broader Durkheimian thesis.[6] Gellner makes strong claims for his political model, too, writing that among Berbers in the Moroccan mountains "a separation of powers is not merely a check on tyranny, as intended in classical political theory, but also a check on inequality. The inegalitarian potential of society is as it were drained by the saints. Here, at least, equality and liberty go together" (1969, 64).

This is a venerable theme. While few anthropologists today tackle large questions of equality and liberty, Gellner was writing at the end of the 1960s. Universities were boisterous, theories were wildly imaginative, and many scholars were less pessimistic, or at least less tired. Gellner's promise to have ethnographically located a contemporary social order of free men and balanced power imprinted itself on a generation of scholars—even as the framing of it excited explosive opposition. Thus, since the 1970s the notion of segmentarity has staggered on in the writings on Morocco and the Middle East in general, even if the larger audience has largely grown bored.

For the purpose of understanding life in Tadrar, all of this matters on several levels, beginning with the all-important canals and the need to maintain them to sustain the fields that feed the village. In 2004 most of the irrigation infrastructure of the village remained constructed of mud and rock, and demanded much labor from the villagers. In Tadrar there is a custom of dividing labor responsibilities for public projects like dam building or canal repair into five work groups—groups based on the ideal of equal lineage segments. However, it is not possible to follow biological lineages and have anything like an equality of labor obligations because village demography has not produced anything close to fair and balanced segments. Lineages in Tadrar are called *ighsan* (singular, *ighs*), or "bones," and indeed they are in some sense the skeleton of the village. Unlike real bones, however, the *ighsan* have to be arranged to meet the cultural requirements of particular kinds of justice. Thus, the question is not whether lineages do or do not exist in Berber society, but instead what villagers *do* with the idea of segmenting lineages. In Tadrar what people do with lineage affiliation is organize public labor.

The villagers of Tadrar organize their collective labor by putting a contradictory set of cultural concepts to work, by employing what they see as the natural basis of gerontocracy and patriarchal authority within house-

6. See Gellner (1987, 31), where he comments on the similarity between his notion of segmentarity and Durkheim's. Durkheim is absent from Evans-Pritchard's bibliography, though the latter is credited by Gellner with importing Durkheim's ideas into anthropology.

holds to preserve an egalitarian ideal between household heads. In schematic terms, this involves arranging the village households into five groups and charging each with providing four men for the duration of any communal project.[7] The word for "five" in Arabic is *khamsa,* and the system of dividing the village into fifths is called *l'khams.* Villagers stressed the importance of the number five to Islam (five daily prayers, five pillars of the faith), though five has no absolute authority, as other scholars have shown lineages assembled into three groups, or *atlat,* in an area very near Tadrar (Mahdi 1999, 47). Why the people of Tadrar use the Arabic word rather than the Berber *semous* for five is also unclear.[8]

The particular men representing any fifth may come and go during a day or over the duration of a project, but the fifth as a whole must provide four adult men for the job until the work is completed. The negotiations over which men will represent each fifth (and who will do what job) are conducted within each fifth. The main complicating factor is thus who is grouped with whom in a fifth.

Ideally, each fifth would comprise an *ighs* (plural, *ighsan*), a bone or lineage, and the patriarch of the lineage could decide which of his sons and grandsons was going to work on any given day: which man to send shepherding or to irrigate, and who would attend to communal canal maintenance. In this way the *khams* would free patriarchs from having to compel fellow patriarchs to work— an unacceptable and largely impossible task— and allow each man to lord over his own descendants, a perfectly legitimate exercise of authority. Unfortunately, as I noted above, biology and history have not cooperated. As Table 2 shows, the three *ighsan* in Tadrar are so demographically unequal as to require significant rearranging for any practical purpose; while a simple division by *ighsan* would be fair in one way, it is grossly unfair in terms of number of households and number of total laborers within each of the three groups. This is a problem of gov-

7. As Fleuret notes, "it is convenient to distinguish between maintenance of the canal in frastructure and management of the water within it" (1985, 110). See Ilahiane (1996, 97) for references concerning the relationship between irrigation allocation and social organization in Morocco; Ilahiane (2005) also explores time and conflict over irrigation rights. See also Rachik (1990, 98) and, for Tunisia, Bédoucha (1987), especially chapter 7. The *khams* is employed exclusively for repair rather than use of infrastructure.

8. The importance of fifths to different forms of Berber social organization has achieved considerable ethnographic attention. See Hart (1981, 35), Mahdi (1999, 54), and the article and bibliography assembled by Camps in the *Encyclopédie Berbère* (International Union of Prehistoric and Protohistoric Sciences, et al. 1984, 1958–1960).

ernment everywhere. In the United States there is a senate where each state gets equal representation—and a house of representatives where representation is proportional to the population of the state. The two kinds of fairness are different, and both are meant to be incorporated into a single political scheme. Other kinds of fairness are imaginable, too, both fanciful (representation by height or hair color) and serious (representation by age, race, income bracket, or sex, for instance). In Tadrar what is important is fairness between lineage segments, along with fairness in total labor obligation per household; lineage segments should be equal, but no family should be so overburdened that they cannot maintain themselves. We see below that to require the Idzdo to produce as many laborers as the Ait Yousef would likely be very burdensome for the former.

To achieve both kinds of fairness, the *ighsan* cannot be used to divide labor, but the *idea* of segmentation that underpins them is still used. The logic of the *khams* divisions is congruent with what is seen as the natural organization of the bones of the village—an arrangement aimed at realizing particular kinds of equality. The analytical issues raised are the extent of the match between the *ighsan* and the *khams* and the degree of fairness achieved in both realms (between lineage segments and between households). These outcomes do not depend purely on the structure of the logic itself, but also on its use. In other words, they depend on the political skill of the men negotiating the organization.

As we view Table 2, keeping in mind the goal of fairness among households in communal labor requirements, the issue seems to be what to do with the Ait Yousef. Dividing them into thirds would bring the average number of households in line with the other two *ighsan,* and would yield the five segments that are culturally desirable. But which Ait Yousef households should be grouped together? The question is partly mathematical, partly genealogical, and most centrally political. Today nobody in Tadrar readily describes himself or herself as being Ait Yousef. Most—but not all—of the Ait Yousef in Tadrar today are descendants of the former *amghar* Mohammed,

TABLE 2. Lineages (*ighsan,* or "bones") in Tadrar in 1999

Ighsan (singular, ighs)	No. of households
Ait Yousef	18
Id Hamad	5
Idzdo	4

the original "*Ouchen,*" or jackal. His male offspring and their children are now the Ben Ouchen. The two other branches of the Ait Yousef are the Lukstaf and Arbuz lineages. Nobody I questioned could specify the exact point of division between these three branches of the Ait Yousef, but all asserted that the three branches were part of the larger Ait Yousef *ighs.*[9] Only Abdurrahman Ait Ali Ait Ben Ouchen was interested enough in the connection to explain that the three lineages were in fact related, and to speculate how.

As Table 3 demonstrates, dividing the Ait Yousef into Ben Ouchen, Lukstaf, and Arbuz lineages would be culturally logical (it follows lineage segments, as locally understood), but does relatively little to achieve the separate cultural requirement of fairness between lineages. The three groupings remain manifestly unequal in terms of labor power. Even lumping the Lukstaf and Arbuz together and opposing them to the Ben Ouchen still leaves too many Ouchen for an equal division of labor. Somehow, to get the desired equalities in the *khams* labor groups, villagers need to do more than lump people together who may not feel immediately related (such as the Arbuz and Lukstaf families). They need to create a division *within* a group of people who *do* view themselves as related, people who can and do trace their ancestry to a single man only a few generations ago, and who all have the same last name stamped on their government identity cards.[10] Thus, for the purposes of collective labor, the villagers divide the Ben Ouchen.

The sublineages listed in Table 3 are the obvious choice for such divisions, but before examining how the people of Tadrar—and most especially the Ben Ouchen—actually divide themselves, it is worth acknowledging that the Id Hamad *ighs* is also conceptually partitioned. The Id Baj, Ohomo, and Belaid lineage members could not confidently explain their connection as Id Hamad, but they do accept themselves as related. The Id Hamad have the right basic demographic dimensions to form a fifth in the *khams* divisions, and so the question of the fairness of an internal division (or a larger association with another lineage) does not readily arise. The Id Hamad could be taken as one, or divided in three. There is no intermediate link since nobody knows how the three subsections are related to one another. A lineage that is conceptualized as such—as biologically integral, however vaguely—needs no justification in the minds of the people of Tadrar so long as it is

---

9. Technically, we should consider the *ighs* a clan since a relationship is assumed but cannot be specified, though I am not going to wade into the anthropological arguments about this.

10. These government identity cards are authoritative, but perhaps not very accurate. See Hoffman (2000a).

Table 3. *Ighsan,* lineage, and sublineage affiliations in 1999

Ighs	Contemporary lineage/ family name	Sublineage affiliation (if any)	No. of households
Ait Yousef	Ait Ben Ouchen	Ait Ali	3
Ait Yousef	Ait Ben Ouchen	Ait Hussein	3
Ait Yousef	Ait Ben Ouchen	Ait Bil Qas	1
Ait Yousef	Ait Ben Ouchen	Ait Haj Ouahman (l'Haj)	7
Ait Yousef	Lukstaf		1
Ait Yousef	Arbuz		3
Id Hamad	Id Baj		3
Id Hamad	Ohomo		1
Id Hamad	Belaid		1
Idzdo	Idzdo		4

demographically suitable for the job at hand. It is when known lineages are subdivided along lines that follow one branch of a genealogical tree rather than another that charges of unfairness and political opportunism arise. This will become clearer in a moment. For now, note that only the Idzdo remain both an undivided *ighs* with a known set of relations among lineage segments, and a viable *khams* group for the purposes of communal labor.

Table 4 illustrates the *khams* divisions that the men of Tadrar agreed upon in 1999 for most sorts of communal labor. There are other divisions for the ceremonial division of meat, for payment toward communal rituals, and for use in development work, indicating the flexibility of the concepts involved. In terms of labor organization for canal repair, however, we see that the five groups do not draw upon equal numbers of households. The first *khams* group has six households, the second eight, then four, five, and four households, respectively. Having one group with twice as many households as another would seem to indicate a breach of the main operating principle of fairness. However, this organization has advantages. First, it follows genealogical lines. The Ben Ouchen as a whole are bisected—two sublineages on each side seems an equal division—and none of the four Ben Ouchen sublineages are internally divided. Since each of these four sublineages descends from one of the four sons of the original *Ouchen,* each at least began with, and is thought to have, approximately one-fourth of the original *Ouchen* landholdings.[11] The dynamics of women's inheritance described in chapter 3

11. See chapter 3.

Table 4. The *Khams* divisions in 1999

Khams group	Lineage and sublineage	Total no. of households		Total no. of adult men
I	Ben Ouchen—Ait Ali		3	9
	Ben Ouchen—Ait Hussein		3	4
		Total	6	13
II	Ben Ouchen—Ait Bil Qas		1	2
	Ben Ouchen—Ait l'Haj		7	12
		Total	8	14
III	Lukstaf		1	4
	Arbuz		3	6
		Total	4	10
IV	Id Baj		3	7
	Ohomo		1	1
	Belaid		1	1
		Total	5	9
V	Idzdo		4	9
		Total	4	9

obviously complicates the reality of property flow through time, but in terms of how property is ideally imagined to devolve, the *khams* division approximates one understanding of equality, at least among the Ouchen.

Moreover, if we look at the total number of available adult men in each *khams* group, there seems more balance than at the level of households. This is primarily because the seven Ait Haj Ouahman (or simply Ait l'Haj) *tikatin* average fewer than two men per household. Since these seven households together have only as much land as the one Ait Bil Qas household, we see that the labor rich/property poor are joined with the property rich/labor poor. Since this division is for labor requirements, in practical terms the structure has to accommodate the labor reserves actually available. This puts pressure on the single "rich" Bil Qas household to come up with half of his *khams* group's labor, but we might expect that nobody feels terribly sorry for him.

In sum, the *khams* seems to achieve several kinds of fairness. *Khams* groups are formed so that smaller, weaker households can get help from patrilineal relatives, or relatives imagined to be patrilineal. Since there are clear lines of command within a patrilineage, the *khams* organizes labor groups in ways that make use of culturally satisfactory patriarchal and gerontocratic authority, and does not require patriarchs to try and compel one another to work. While retaining the logic of the bones, genealogical relatedness, *khams* groups are nevertheless formed so as to have approximately the same number of able-bodied men available in each of the five groups. This requires villagers to assemble some families into imagined lineages, and break the one large, biological lineage into two sets of two sublineages. In some cases, land-rich sublineages such as the Ait Bil Qas (a single household) are paired with fecund but resource-poor households in sublineages like the Ait l'Haj (seven households) to form a single *khams* group.

In all cases, *khams* groups allow for labor to be consolidated at levels beyond the household, and thus allow households at vulnerable points in their cycles to be assisted by "relatives," a category that in Tadrar begins (but does not end!) with agnatic relations on the father's side. Household capabilities change over time as members are born, mature, marry, sometimes migrate, and eventually die, and no household can be expected to contribute to the village equally over its entire domestic cycle. The *khams* provides a relatively stable structure—it has not changed during the time I have been working in Tadrar—to deal with the chronic instability of households. Thus it is long-term fairness between households that matters, not fairness at any particular moment. Many scholars have pointed out that any arrangement of social equality is faced with two major difficulties: the heterogeneity of human beings and the multiplicity of variables by which equality can be appraised (Sen 1992, 1). In grappling with this dilemma, Amartya Sen begins his classic book, *Inequality Reexamined,* by foregrounding the importance of values, of the preliminary issue of what a theorist or social system expects to be equal. Sen asks of any argument about equality, "equality of what?" The Tadrar case illustrates that an equally important question is "equality of when?"

The *khams* appears to ensure fairness over time, and in fact it does ameliorate some differences between weaker and more powerful households. However, this does not mean that we ought to categorize it as *essentially* fair or, based on this, characterize Berber culture or society as being "egalitarian" in anything other than a relative sense. Several forms of inequality remain embedded in the *khams* and, more interestingly, some forms of inequality are in fact exacerbated by it.

Perhaps the most obvious injustice concerns property ownership.[12] In the last chapter, I discussed the inequality of property ownership among households. These inequalities are also evident at the larger *khams* level—despite the fact that the *khams* is specifically meant to ensure equality. My neighbors in Tadrar admitted significant differences in the amount of land owned by different *khams* groups, assertions that seem born out by the data in Table 5. The parts of the Ait Yousef *ighs* that are not Ben Ouchen (the members of *Khams* III) seem to be worst off, with approximately half the number of fields and less than half the total time for irrigation as their fellow *ighs* members (the Ben Ouchen who comprise *Khams* I and II). This is better than the 5:1 ratio we saw between the richest and poorest households (in terms of irrigation time and field numbers), but such differences in the *khams* property is hardly what anyone in Tadrar or elsewhere could characterize as "equal."

TABLE 5. Comparative land ownership and irrigation time by *Khams* group

Khams	No. of fields	No. of irrigation days per cycle
I	252	95.48
II	215	90.30
III	122	40.23
IV	343	62.28
V	206	51.76

Clearly, as a whole, the division of the Ait Yousef into two Ben Ouchen parts and one non–Ben Ouchen part benefits the Ben Ouchen. The division does follow genealogical lines and is culturally logical because of this. It achieves equality between lineage segments (two each in the two Ben Ouchen divisions), and renders the five customarily required groups. In a strict material sense, however, the constituents of *Khams* III—the three Arbuz and one Lukstaf households—are significantly disadvantaged. They own much less than a fifth of the total village property, but are required to contribute a fifth of the labor to maintain the communal canal system. They are quite willing to expound on this inequality, too. The members of

12. Size, soil quality, proximity to a canal, shade from trees, and other factors make measuring productivity in terms of fields difficult. My methods for calculating property ownership were covered in chapter 3, and are explained in detail in my Ph.D. dissertation (Crawford 2001b). Here I rely only on a count of irrigated fields and, more usefully, the number of total irrigation days in a ninety-day cycle owned by each household, lineage, and *khams* group.

Khams III are not mystified by their position in the labor system. They might lack an idiom to effectively challenge this inequality, as the Ben Ouchen can counter that each lineage should contribute labor equally, and the division of the Ben Ouchen is in fact already subsidizing the Lukstaf and Arbuz lineages. From the Ben Ouchen perspective, the Lukstaf and Arbuz lineages not only have nothing to complain about, but should appreciate this subsidy as an act of generosity. From the Lukstaf/Arbuz perspective the system is unfair, and obviously so given the differences in labor and property contained in the different work groups of the *khams*. For my purposes here, the important thing is that the argument is made in contradictory terms: fairness differs between lineages, between household labor capabilities, and between amounts of property owned. All of these types of fairness cannot be achieved *at the same time*.

There are significant differences within *khams* groups, too. We will examine the case of *Khams* I in a moment, but it is worth noting first that within the Idzdo, who are the only intact *ighs* who comprise a single *khams* group (Number V in Table 4), the wealthiest household has eighty-five fields and over twenty-eight irrigation days, while the two poorest households have half as many fields and a quarter as much irrigation time. (Compare Figure 3 of the Idzdo lineage with households 18, 19, 20, and 21 in Table 1.) The integrity of an *ighs,* or lineage, is no guarantee of fairness in the *khams*. People with more land obviously benefit more from the canal system than people with less land, yet there is no attempt that I could discern to make social obligations congruent with property ownership. This is true in my own society, also. In Tadrar, as in the United States, the application of a value on fairness is limited to certain kinds of fairness. It is not employed in others, for instance matching labor contributions to canal upkeep with benefits from this essential piece of communal property.

A second seeming injustice lies in the fact that young men do a disproportionate amount of the male gendered work. This should be equitable over the long term if young men grow up to inherit the right to command the labor of the next generation, but this is demographically impossible. A rising population and a finite land base ensures emigration. Many young men will have to leave the village and thus will never be able to take advantage of the system they have supported with their labor. While each brother ostensibly has rights to a share of the father's property equal to all his male siblings, by the time a father dies the oldest son has often been acting as paterfamilias for some time. Second and third sons are often the ones sent out to work in the plains or cities to return money to the household. This is especially true once grandchildren are old enough to fulfill labor requirements in the village, and thus it is hard for all sons to claim rightful shares of property once their father dies.[13]

Often at the death of a father an arrangement is made by which one son (usually the oldest) agrees to pay his siblings for their parcels of land, or they sharecrop it. This arrangement to pay is complicated by the limited potential to generate cash in the subsistence-oriented economy of the village, and there are cases where disagreements over land payments between brothers have been litigated sporadically for the lifetimes of the brothers. Villagers find it shameful that seventy-year-old men—brothers especially!—take each other to court over land rights, but it is easy to see why this happens. Only a fraction of the young men will reap a reward later for the labor they invest in the canal system now.

Thus there are inequalities in the benefits of the *khams* between owners of more or less land, and between men who are able to stay in the village until they are old and the ones who will be forced to migrate. The *khams* division does nothing to address these, but neither does it create or very much worsen them. There are other ways this institution does exacerbate existing inequalities, however, and we will examine one of these in detail. This involves *Khams* group I in Table 4—the combined Ait Ali and Ait Hussein.

As I detailed in the previous chapter, the Ait Ali are the most powerful lineage in the village. By his own admission, Abdurrahman Ait Ali Ben Ouchen is well positioned in many ways. In general the sons of Ali seem to have done comparatively better than their cousins, the sons of Hussein. Some of the difference surely came about through Abdurrahman's acquisition of so much Idzdo property through his marriage. It is unclear whether some of the Ait Hussein have left the village and sold their property, or perhaps because Ali was the last Ouchen boy of his generation he managed to consolidate extra land during his lifetime, or garner his mother's portion of the original Ouchen patrimony.

What is clear is that as of 1999 the Ait Ali had three times as many fields, more irrigation time, and a total of nine adult male laborers to the four of the Ait Hussein. This is probably not a coincidence. Land requires laborers,

13. Note that this is precisely what happened in the Ait Ali Ben Ouchen, where Ali and then his son Abdurrahman each benefited from being the youngest son, not least in that they eventually inherited their mother's share of their father's inheritance.

but laborers require land to feed them. When it comes time to devote labor to communal work on the canals, however, the *khams* obligation is divided equally between the two unequal sublineages. Two men are called from the Ait Ali and two from the Ait Hussein.

Unsurprisingly, while the Ait Hussein acknowledge the genealogical sensibility of this, they grumble nonetheless about its fairness. The Ait Hussein lack a cultural idiom to directly challenge the labor allotment, but they do grouse that the Ait Ali are "rich." The Ait Ali, for their part, accuse the Ait Hussein of being lazy and attempting to shirk their responsibilities. It is easy to see how this would come about. Half of the total Ait Hussein male labor force is siphoned off during any communal project, putting a great deal of pressure on them in terms of maintaining their own fields, while the Ait Ali contribute less than a quarter of their male labor resources. This allows the two Ait Ali patriarchs to have one son spend his time working as a grocer and to send other sons to work for wages outside of the valley. This diversity of income is impossible or at least difficult for the Ait Hussein, who will need their male labor to irrigate their own fields and to meet what they see as an oppressive public demand for their labor. The more communal projects undertaken in the village, the more disproportionately the Ait Ali benefit. They have more land than anyone else, thus their total advantage from any village project is greater and their comparative labor input is much smaller. The Ait Ali tend to be proponents of development.

This is one example of how the *khams* system is unfair at a particular moment. Still, the *khams* means that no household is left alone. All households are small and labor-poor at some point, and such weak, single households with only one male worker are grouped together to allow them to survive, to serve their public responsibilities over the long term without missing their household obligation to irrigate today. This seems to make things more fair. My neighbor Belaid, for instance, cannot himself work on public projects very much of the time because he is the only man in his entire lineage. By grouping himself with Ohomo and the Id Baj (his wife's lineage), Belaid is able to keep his own irrigation going and meet some part of his public obligation. Presumably when his sons get older Belaid will send them to help the various Id Baj households who are helping him now. Belaid's relationship with the Id Baj is only fair over a very long period of time—the entire life cycle of a household or more. The people "paying back" debts are not necessarily the ones accruing them; each generation serves the one above.

Table 6. Inequality within *Khams* I: Ait Ali and Ait Hussein property and labor

Khams I	No. of fields	No. of irrigation days/90	No. of adult men	Men required for *Khams*/day
Ait Ali	188	56.20	9	2
Ait Hussein	64	39.28	4	2

But *khams* groups do not have to be assembled as they are; as Dresch notes, the use of segmentary concepts does not specify their application (1986, 312). It would be conceivable, for instance, to let the Ait Ali stand alone as a *khams* group and contribute four laborers from the nine they have available—a proportion of their labor in line with all other *khams* groups. Comparing the Ait Ali of Table 6 to the various *khams* levels in Table 5, we see that the Ait Ali by themselves have more fields than one complete *khams* (group III, the combined Lukstaf and Arbuz families), and more irrigation time than two *khams* groups (both III and V, the Idzdo). They have exactly the same number of laborers—nine—as two other integral *khams* groups, yet the Ait Ali *do not form a group on their own*. The Ait Ali are joined with the Ait Hussein, and thus split their labor obligations with them. The Ait Ali successfully maintain the tradition of generating five labor groups by using a genealogically sensible, segmentary division that is fair in some ways, and quite obviously unfair in others.

Lineages are a daunting topic to explain, but they are an important organizational concept in Tadrar. While lineages have a long and contentious academic history, they are hard to evoke ethnographically because, in Tadrar at least, they have no enduring corporal existence. Lineages do not work together as a whole, they do not eat or sleep together in the same room, they do not own herds in common, you cannot find their leader or ask what any one of them wants to do because lineages are an idea, a practically evolving idea about who is related to whom, who owes whom solidarity, and who has authority among the people connected by this sort of solidarity. Material groups of people—what we are normally discussing when we use the word "lineage"—can be constituted by invoking any node in their branching structure, at least ideally. But in practical terms the "branches" are broken, grafted together, sawn off, and simply set next to one another. The remains of biological lineages in Tadrar have no ready representatives. The connecting patriarchs are dead, and sometimes not even explicitly known. Still, the *idea* of lineage relatedness informs local understanding of how household property is linked together, and is centrally important to notions of fairness that inflect the way work groups are built. Whole lineages of actual men never materialize in this part of the High Atlas, and in all likelihood it has been a very long time since the concept was used for anything other than labor organization.

If lineages are used by men for practical purposes, these deployments have to be deduced by the outside observer. They are not self-evidently available for observation. I could actually sit down with households, watch them argue and negotiate in small darkened rooms, palpably experience their subtle gradations of authority and resistance. I could without too much difficulty figure out what sorts of material conditions households lived in. They allowed me to sit on their rooftops, count their fields, ask questions about irrigation time, watch people open and close canals, and see the size of their piles of barley at the end of the season. But for most of my research, lineages remained ethereal and ephemeral. I would glimpse them dimly, occasionally, when for instance I was making my way among the boulders of the riverbed and would stumble upon a group of men building a dam. Even here, however, what I saw was a work group built through the idea of genealogical relatedness and notions of fairness, not a lineage per se.

Some men would be digging, others watching, some commenting, others (invariably the younger men) carrying bags of sand and rock to and fro. As I sat with them I barely noticed new men show up, others leave, some busy themselves making tea for the workers, others quietly bickering. It took a very long time to realize that new men arriving on the scene and others shuffling away to attend to household obligations were conceptually inseparable actions. Men did not punch in or out on a time clock, there was no baton passed from one man to another, no lineage flags raised, whistles blown, or announcements made. These men have lived together their entire lives. They all know who is responsible for what and to whom, who is in what *khams* group, and thus how many of what group's men are present. It may look like an informal hardworking group of friends to me, but the men in the river turned out to be a finely organized set of five groups, four men each, with older and younger men "naturally" falling into complementary roles of organizing and being organized.

The difficulty of this chapter—the tangents and charts, the backtracking and asides in my writing of it—illustrates something beyond my limitations as an author. It shows, I think, the fact that very small scale societies with relatively simple technology are nonetheless dauntingly complex. My forced schemata and caveats about contexts should caution us against Durkheim's assumption that societies that employ kinship relations for productive purposes are "simple," while the dependence of lineage organization upon household dynamics undermines Gellner's notion that there is a single modality for social organization in the Moroccan mountains. We see that cooperation is not at all a simple thing, here or anywhere, and that social action is a tangle of cultural ideals and personal ambition, social skill and material forces. We may privilege one factor over another, but it is hard to ignore the inevitable intersections among them.

The arranging of the bones nicely illustrates the tormented relationship between equality and inequality, and thus speaks to issues of great social and theoretical import (Dahrendorf 1969; Phillips 1999; Sen 1992; Verdery 2001). All societies valorize certain kinds of fairness, to the degree that we may see "what counts as fair" as a central component of cultural competence. In the case of Tadrar, equality between lineage segments is valued, as is equality of all men before God; on the other hand, equality between men and women, or older and younger men, is not valued, or even considered something that might be valued. Tremendous social effort is expended to form collective work groups that are "fair" in some local senses, but once these "fair" groups are down in the river at work, the old men tend to sit back and tell the younger men what to do. Old men might be part of the labor group, but typically put themselves in charge, often by sitting in the shade making tea, or offering suggestions about how other, younger men might do a better job. Young men have nothing to say. In this context they are simple labor power and are expected to work carefully, energetically, and unquestioningly. The tone of conversation is not exactly dour and humorless, but it is respectful. The old men within each *khams* group decide in the first instance which men should be working from the group, which means that if there are old men "at work" in a *khams* group it is because they did not have sufficient labor to substitute for themselves. The powerful old men are elsewhere, engaged, at least sometimes, in far more wide-ranging forms of social and political labor.

Thus, you are unlikely to see Abdurrahman at work in the river. This can partly be explained by household inequalities (Abdurrahman has many sons), but partly because he has the time for politics. The "fair" construction of *khams* gives him an unfair advantage in public labor obligations. The Ait Ali comprise half a *khams* group, and so Abdurrahman and the two other

Ait Ali households in the village need only devote two men to a work party while it is in progress. As his brother and nephew need to supply their half of this responsibility, the most Abdurrahman could be expected to contribute to a public labor project would be one man. It would take an extraordinary convergence of irrigation requirements and outside wage labor agreements for Abdurrahman himself to be forced to physically labor on a new dam or do canal repair. He is thus very interested in expanding the number of public projects the village undertakes. He is, as we will see in the next chapter, a main proponent of village development. The strict hierarchy of authority within the household, inequalities in property and available labor between households, and the inequalities built into the *khams* organization all combine for a very fortunate situation for my friend Abdurrahman.

What Abdurrahman does with his time is political work. While other fortunate men might pass their free time working in their fields—Mohammed Lukstaf, for instance, would surely choose his fields over a debate of any sort—Abdurrahman seeks to capitalize on his advantages by visiting the market every week, whether or not he needs to buy anything. Weekly *souk* is a market in information as much as grain, soap, and agricultural implements, and Abdurrahman is an enthusiastic trader in news of all sorts. He travels up the valley most Fridays for prayers in the larger village of Agerda, or sometimes he walks three villages down to Tijrisht for Friday prayers. These are times to demonstrate piety—and Islamic ideals of equality among men—but also to gather information about important events in the valley, to sip tea and cement friendships, to trade gossip, to express political views, to comprehend and comment upon political dynamics beyond the village.

Between Fridays (when he travels to pray) and Thursdays (when he travels to market), Abdurrahman spends much of his time at the village mosque. Here, too, men gather to talk, to stop and rest if they are traveling through, or to chat with other men. Over the time I have known him, Abdurrahman has come to do less and less physical labor and more and more political work. Abdurrahman has gradually grown fatter (like me), and his hands have become less callused while on his forehead he boasts an expanding dark spot formed by his frequent and devoted prostrations. Piety, the equality espoused by the Qur'an, and the larger Muslim community come to matter more to Abdurrahman as he delegates the physical labor involved in keeping his household alive. Here, as elsewhere, those of us with the time to ponder, to think, to read, to write, and to politick: we all depend on the labor of the less fortunate.

◈ ◈ ◈

In Tadrar, the limited use of lineages for some kinds of communal labor stands in contrast to the centrality of household labor for everyday survival, and the forms of equality achieved by the *khams* groups should not blind us to the forms of inequality they exacerbate. Men like Abdurrahman, who are at the peak of their household labor cycle, who have multiple mature sons and the productive property for them to work, are able to put the egalitarian institutions of society to work for their own benefit. This is very common in many societies. The inequalities built into "fair" labor organizations in Tadrar may help us see more clearly the ways other putatively fair and just political systems are used in unfair ways—and how what counts as fair is among the deepest and most fundamental questions of culture.

We can learn from the case of Tadrar. It may prompt us to consider our accepted understandings of what ought to be equal in society, and imagine how we might protect the egalitarian institutions we value from the predations of the powerful. At some point in the past Abdurrahman was not the man we see today. He was once a young man, single, serving his elders; he had not yet inherited property or married, much less put his wife's property to productive use, and he was not powerful. There is an indisputable temporality to inequality. Men who live long enough in Tadrar will eventually gain some power, some control over the labor of others, though few will be able to orchestrate the success that Abdurrahman has managed.

What Abdurrahman's success illustrates is the way inequalities are built in time, the way social institutions are used to dampen or amplify different forms of inequality, and the way personal agency, ambition, and skill are put to work on impersonal social dynamics, cultural norms, and historical contexts. Inequality is produced by people over time, and reproduced in time in particular locales. Jacques Berque, among the most knowledgeable non-Berbers ever to study them, wrote in 1967 that he "came to view the North African tribe as a compromise between social groupings and contemporary history, between a certain form of logic and the data of the *milieu*. The same compromise can be seen . . . between agnatic ancestrality and relationship by marriage, between consanguinity and topography, status and contract" (1967, 112). These dynamics, and the local inequalities in which they are grounded, set the stage for how contemporary villagers in Tadrar variously engage the larger world.

5
SEEING AND BEING SEEN
BY THE STATE

In this chapter I address some of the ways that Tadrar is engaged with the world outside of the Agoundis Valley, especially the relationship between the village and the state. I begin with some examples of the ways villagers experienced the political world beyond their valley in the past—from the arrival of lineage ancestors at the dawn of the Almohad Dynasty in the twelfth century to the rise of the Great Lords of Tagoundaft in the 1900s. These historical episodes are meant to demonstrate that Tadrar has long been part of a larger political world, even if this world was not "the state" as we think about it today. I then move to contemporary understandings of state power, and how various actors aligned with governmental and nongovernmental agencies affect local life via development projects. The transformations under way to improve village life are rapid and profound; no account of life in Tadrar would be complete without them.

One of the persistent criticisms of village-level ethnography—the type I attempt in this book—is that it fails to take account of larger social forces. Eric Wolf's landmark *Europe and the People Without History* damned generations of social scientists, especially anthropologists, for being insufficiently interested in the political economic processes within which local culture is expressed, arguing that cultures everywhere have been impacted by forces beyond their boundaries—preeminently, the expansion of global capitalism over the past four hundred years. Wolf warned that "concepts like 'nation,' 'society,' and 'culture' name bits and threaten to turn names into things" (1982, 3). He suggested that the success of anthropological fieldwork as a way of producing knowledge has made it easy "to convert merely heuristic considerations of method into theoretical postulates about society and culture" (1982, 13). In other words, the short, intense time anthropologists tended to spend in villages overwhelmed anthropological analysis, erasing the history of villages prior to the arrival of the researcher, and obscuring the long-term trajectory of rural life. Villages seemed to have no history before or beyond the research period, and to be unconnected to the post-colonial states that governed them or the capitalist economy Wolf sees as transforming the globe.

This "isolated culture" critique seems particularly apposite in Morocco. In the early 1970s, for instance, Morocco was a center of anthropological debate—with Ernest Gellner arguing his theories of segmentary egalitarian tribes in the mountains, and Clifford Geertz exercising his symbolic, interpretive analyses on more urbane Moroccans. Their debate would capture the discipline's attention for years. During the same period, young anthropologists like Dale Eickelman, Paul Rabinow, and Vincent Crapanzano launched their careers exploring various aspects of Moroccan Islam in works that would be influential in anthropology and cultural studies. Vanessa Maher, Kevin Dwyer, Daisy Dwyer, Elaine Combs-Schilling, David Hart, and Kenneth Brown were also making important contributions to anthropological understandings with their work in and on Morocco. And there was much more, too, in English and in French, including an emerging cadre of Moroccan anthropologists like Abdelleh Hammoudi, Ali Amahan, and Hassan Rachik who would produce path-breaking analyses. Such was the intensity of scholarly writing on the region that anthropology students of the 1970s and 1980s almost certainly had some familiarity with the culture and society of Morocco. The anthropological fascination with the country was so pronounced that one historian commented to me dryly that if aliens came to Earth having read any anthropology at all, they would surely think Morocco was the center of the world. Indeed, in the 1970s Morocco was an anthropological fixation.

Meanwhile, the country itself was in protracted political crisis. After forcing the French out in 1956, traditional political elites in Morocco struggled to contain the embers of democracy fanned by the independence movement, and they struggled among themselves for dominance. A fifteen thousand-man national army was marched into the northern Rif mountains in 1958 to quell what some have called a tribal revolt, but which others have conceptualized as anti-government populism (Slyomovics 2005b, 145). The king himself was nearly assassinated in 1971, and subsequent state military incursions in 1972–1973 murdered and imprisoned tribesmen from the mountains very near where Gellner had been working. Over time a growing system of secret prisons and state repression maintained a tense peace, as well as a desirably stable tourist destination and research site (Edwards 2005; Howe 2005). Forty years of political repression facilitated amenable conditions for anthropological research and debate, but such conditions seem to have been largely invisible to the researchers, or to have been deemed irrelevant to the scholarly debates then current.

Prior to Wolf's influential critique, anthropologists seemed uninterested in the global implications of Morocco's strategic position, even the colossal shift from North African-dominated overland trade to corporately organized maritime trade in slaves, gold, and salt that put Europe on the path to global hegemony (Mojuetan 1995). The rise of Europe to world power was reciprocally related to the decline of the Moroccan empire, and the shriveling of the Moroccan state to a poor, provincial shadow of its former glory (Rosenberger 2001, 9). Moroccans have not forgotten that they were once Europe's equals, even if French domination in the twentieth century made acknowledging contemporary Christian power humiliatingly unavoidable.

It is no longer easy to ignore state-level Moroccan politics. As I write, a Moroccan justice and reconciliation commission is actively holding hearings in Morocco devoted to bringing the crimes of the state to public light, and to lay the groundwork for a more substantive democracy.[1] As Susan Slyomovics has argued—in some of the rare anthropological work on the topic in Morocco—endemic government corruption and repression has bled rivers of resentment and generated a long-term crisis of political faith (2001, 2003, 2005a, 2005b).[2] Given the tumultuousness of the 1970s in particular, and this decade's importance to the history of anthropology, the classic debates in, of, and around Morocco seem almost bizarrely divorced from the political reality of the country.

During the 1980s and 1990s the anthropological gaze shifted elsewhere. Still, in Morocco student demonstrations were quashed by the military; some young people were shot, while others disappeared. Bread riots erupted in various cities, hotels owned by the royal family were burned, Islamist, socialist, and Amazigh activists were harassed, tried, tortured, "erased," and

1. See http://www.ier.ma.

2. For example, Slyomovics cites "the infamous *dahir* or decree of 1935 (*dahir de mâ min sha'nihi*), a French protectorate law invoked as the legal cover to suppress Moroccan national aspirations during the colonial period (1912–1956) and carried over intact to imprison political dissidents in Morocco's post-independent era" (2005b, 142). See also Maghraoui (2001).

every local police station had (or still has?) its own special room for extracting information through the use of physical pain, threats against one's body and family, and fear. The collapse of the Soviet Union and a global expansion of politicized Islam have shifted the government's interests away from socialists and Amazigh cultural activists to Islamists, a shift that some see as vindicated by the May 16, 2000, Casablanca bombings, and the Moroccan origins of the perpetrators of the May 11, 2004, Madrid train attacks. But the persistently ruthless behavior of the Moroccan state cannot be considered a reaction to terrorism, a weird aberration, or "a few bad apples." Fear seems instead to have long been a deliberate government policy affirmed at the highest levels and intended to silence those perceived as enemies of the state. At the very least the state had, in effect, "criminalized all manifestations of political activity and thought during the thirty-eight year reign of King Hassan II (1961–1999)" (Slyomovics 2005b, 143).

After the death of Hassan II in 1999, his son and heir King Mohammed VI has struggled with the legacy his father bequeathed: a relatively stable country by regional standards, but a stability purchased at the high price of arbitrary justice, economic disparity, and restricted participation in the political process. The new king has sought to redress some wrongs, ventilate the taboo subjects of Moroccan history, expand rights for women, and attempt some neo-Liberal economic reforms, including free trade agreements with the United States; he also has worked to end the repression of Amazigh (Berber) cultural groups. While here as elsewhere political Islamists are under as much pressure as ever, the implementation of an Amazigh curriculum in schools has deflected some of the criticism of the state's anti-Berber policies (Silverstein and Crawford 2004; Crawford 2005). The government-led reconciliation process is slow, uneven, and to some unsatisfactory in that it does not seek to publicly name those directly responsible for torture and murder, but it does seem a positive step. Most importantly for our purposes, the state has become more interested in ameliorating rural poverty during the opening years of the twenty-first century.

The machinations of the Moroccan state and the politics of its urban areas have not necessarily been important to rural life. The urban elite never had control over the country's rural hinterlands in the typical, premodern European sense, and while it is probably overstating the case to say that tribal power extended to the city walls, the countryside has traditionally been somewhat autonomous (Valensi 1985, 157). Therefore, it is not clear that our anthropological blindness to the behavior of the Moroccan state is necessarily very relevant in the countryside. From the perspective of Tadrar, not all wider political or economic issues matter. The arrest and torture of activists, poets, and teachers in Rabat has little perceived relevance in the mountains, for instance. Nor are villagers particularly concerned with actions against Islamist groups, as in the countryside religion is a taken for granted aspect of daily life, and hence nothing a "group" could really be formed to promote. The few "Muslim brothers" I saw traveling through the mountains were distrusted as outsiders, and as young, sanctimonious men who did not properly respect their elders. It appeared to me that these young bearded men were simply on vacation, but they were scrutinized with an intensity that even European tourists are not. This general rural conservatism may account in some measure for the countryside being considered a well of support for the monarchy (Leveau 1985).

This does not mean that a general climate of fear does not radiate far beyond the urban centers of power and the secret prisons on the edge of the desert. Especially in the postprotectorate period, as the state has become more insinuated into the rural world, there is a sense that state agents can exercise their authority arbitrarily. But in the mountains, relations with the state are specifically identified with particular agencies and even more particular agents or officers—some good, some bad, some indifferent. Moreover, the people of Tadrar are not isolated individuals vis-à-vis their leviathan or its representatives, but are instead embedded members of households, lineages, and a village such that men negotiate with "the outside" from within locally dense thickets of alliances and animosities. Village relations with the named representatives of specific state agencies are colored by the local positions of the village men doing the relating, and local understandings of the origins of state power. The main, though certainly not the only, link between Tadrar and most agencies of the state is Abdurrahman Ait Ben Ouchen, whom we have met. His views and actions—and reactions to them—form much of our story about the interaction between "the state" and "the village."

Thus, while state policies clearly have local importance, this importance is mediated through a chain of nameable men and local frameworks of meaning. Few people seem to follow or much care about the distant apex of the government, or what newspapers might define as national interests, even very important ones. In this sense, some of the earlier anthropological disinterest in the state may be vindicated. It may be that the long history of anthropological disinterest in the role of the Moroccan state can be explained by the fact that the state does not operate everywhere in the same way, with the same arbitrary cruelty, severity, or consequence. While there is no need to pretend that the state power is ever absent in Morocco, neither should we assume that everything local is merely a refraction of more powerful exogenous interests, policies, and processes. When contemporary scholars write that "in Morocco . . . a conceptualization of power begins with the state" (Bourqia and Gilson Miller 1999, 5), they are reacting against earlier avoidance of the issue, and older arguments that "there is no such thing as the power of the State" (Radcliffe-Brown 1940, xxiii).

The issue is *how* the state matters. Crucially, in Tadrar, the actions of government reverberate through the local political economy and are made sensible in local cultural terms. A brief history of relations between Tadrar and the outside world will make this clearer and help set the stage to explain the ways that a groundswell of development—an important contemporary manifestation of "the outside" in the village—is now transforming rural life.

My specific argument will be that the state's ability to detain, imprison, and fine—with seemingly no recourse on the part of villagers—provides the backdrop for all relations between local farmers and representatives of the government. *Why* the state has power is not an issue. Still, the state rarely uses its power to punish, suggesting that some legitimacy is accorded by the citizens; the state does not run purely on fear, but plays on culturally sensible understandings of authority, an aesthetics of power. This is a much larger issue than I can fully address in one chapter, as there is no single way of understanding the complexity of state power in all parts of the country in all social classes. Nevertheless, I will make the curious suggestion that in Tadrar relations with the state are understood as something like a segmentary lineage. I am not the first to propose this sort of thing in Morocco or beyond (see Waterbury 1970, 1991; Eickelman 2002), but I believe that the view from Tadrar offers a different spin on the debate. Here the difference between the linked dyads that lead to the king and the linked sons and fathers that lead to lineage ancestors is that the chains of men who comprise the state are alive, unlike the ancestral genealogical links by which village men imagine themselves related to one another. The power fathers have over sons is seen as natural, and grandfathers have even more power over more people, and so on up the line. State agents are seen to exist in similar lines, from local officials up to the king, each lording over those below and owing fealty to the man above him. But the state agents are alive now, all at once. State agents are powerful like ancestors, but ancestors who have come alive; they must be treated with deference.

Again, this is not to say that there is a single enduring modality of power in the mountains. Relations with the regional economy and state power have clearly shifted over time, and take different forms in different places. Appreciating the current aesthetics of power in Tadrar requires some attention to the past.

The earliest recorded history generally available about the area around the Agoundis concerns the arrival of Ibn Tumart. A native speaker of Tashelhit[3], the language of the Moroccan south, Ibn Tumart was born in the Anti Atlas Mountains sometime between 1076 and 1091. He left these dry, low mountains on the edge of the Sahara for travels that took him to Cordoba, Tunisia, Alexandria, Baghdad, and perhaps Syria and Mecca (Bourouiba 1974, 11–13). These were more than mere wanderings, as the future *Mahdi,* or "rightly guided one," sought out celebrated Islamic thinkers, including the scholar al-Ghazzali, whose works had been banned by the Almoravid elite who controlled Morocco at that time (Laroui 1977, 175). Once he found his way back to his natal village in the Anti Atlas Mountains, and later among the tribes of the High Atlas near Tadrar, Ibn Tumart had the opportunity to deploy his eloquence and erudition in his native Berber language, on culturally familiar territory. What followed was a radical social upheaval, one that eventually would lead to a new empire stretching from the Pyrenees across Spain, Morocco, and the Sahara, and east to Libya.

Ibn Tumart's political philosophy drew on diverse threads, but emphasized personal moral reform and individual responsibility for communal standards—sometimes fanatical convictions that had him assaulting the sultan's sister for appearing in public without a veil.[4] Perhaps what appealed to his mountain converts, however, was Ibn Tumart's message of social justice. Half a century after the Almoravid Dynasty established Marrakech, the political philosophy and ascetic teachings they developed in their desert homeland no longer accorded with their wealthy, urbane lifestyle. Ibn Tu-

3. This is the form of Tamazight spoken in all of the Moroccan south, including the High Atlas today.

4. See Cornell 1987 for a review of Ibn Tumart's "doctrine of responsibility." Note also that among the Sanhaja (the desert Berber tribe from which the Almoravids descended) it is the men who veil, not the women (El Guindi 1999).

mart seems to have convinced the mountain peoples that they—the illiterate, non-Arabic speaking "outsiders"—were predestined to recapture and reju- venate the vast House of Islam. How exactly he accomplished this remains a mystery, but the firebrand Ibn Tumart managed to transform the remote valley of Tin Mal (just downstream from the Agoundis) into the political center of the Western Mediterranean and the *omphalos* of Islamic civiliza- tion at its height.

Or so it seems to Abdurrahman Ait Ben Ouchen, with whom I spoke of the *Mahdi* many times. This period in history represents to him a golden era when the area around the Agoundis was the center of the world, and when the lineal descendants of Tadrar came to the mountains. Two tape- recorded interviews hint at what I learned from Abdurrahman about this foundational period.

INTERVIEW WITH ABDURRAHMAN AIT BEN OUCHEN
October 5, 1998

Abdurrahman: Our origins were in Rahamna [between present-day Mar- rakech and Casablanca] but we came to Tadrar in the era of the *Mahdi* Ibn Tumart, the Imam, *Mahdi* of Tin Mal, the capital of Morocco. It was the white mosque in Tin Mal, the time of Ibn Tumart, when he [Abdurrahman's lineal ancestor Abd al-Haq] came.

David: How do you know this history?

Abdurrahman: My father told it to me. The *Mahdi* Ibn Tumart ruled in Tin Mal. Tin Mal was the capital of Morocco and Andalusia. After the Mahdi Ibn Tumart there followed Ibn Tashfin.[5] All of them made their capital Tin Mal, at Talat n Yaqoub. There followed Yaqoub al-Mansour, he was the one who named Talat n Yaqoub the capital, Yaqoub al-Mansour.

David: Do other people know the history?

Abdurrahman: There are old people who know it, they have the history, but a lot of the old people are dead. As for me, I had my fa- ther who was very old, he gave me knowledge of ancient

5. This does not necessarily follow orthodox timelines of Moroccan rulers.

history, of Ibn Tumart, Yaqoub al-Mansour, and Yousef
Ibn Tashfin . . . everything.

October 30, 1998

Abdurrahman: The *Mahdi* Ibn Tumart, his history is really old, older than
Goundafi's [the family of overlords who took regional
power in the mid-nineteenth century].

David: Yes, I understand.

Abdurrahman: Ibn Tumart is far [away in time].

David: When did the other people come to Tadrar. When did the
Idzdo family come?

Abdurrahman: The Idzdo were brought by Ibn Tumart. Because Ibn Tumart was the unifier of Islam. The Mahdi Ibn Tumart was
the Imam [leader] of Islam, he showed the people the religion of Islam, the commandments of Islam. He would
bring one man who knows prayers from one place to another. Whoever does not know how to pray, say in Agoundis
or Talat n Yaqoub or anywhere, he takes a man to another
place where he lives until he knows how people "do" [pre-
sumably how they perform their religious obligations].
Those of the other place who know, he brings him to this
land to show people how to do their prayers. The first thing
is Islam. The correct Islam.[6]

David: The *Mahdi,* he taught the people to pray. . . .

Abdurrahman: Second . . . you asked me about Idzdo, where is their home-
land. Where is the homeland of Idzdo? The homeland of
Idzdo, the Idzdo we have in Tadrar. But their homeland is
Ida Ouzdout, homeland of Ida Ouzdout [in the Anti Atlas,
near where Ibn Tumart was from]. Another family is Id
Baj. Id Baj, their homeland is in the area of Ouarzazate.
One tribe from the area of Ouarzazate, they call it Tagour-
out. In Tagourout there was a *wali* [saint] they called . . .

6. This emphasis on orthopraxy accords with Dale Eickelman's argument (2002, chapter 10).

Sidi Mhand ben Nasser, his homeland is that which the Id Baj came from. The Id Baj family.

David: The Id Baj came with the *Mahdi* like the Ait Ben Ouchen?

Abdurrahman: Yes, like the Idzdo, like the Ait Ben Ouchen. The Irbuzen [the plural of Arbuz], the other family, they are like the Ait Ben Ouchen, they are brothers of Ait Ben Ouchen. [They are a branch of the Ait Ben Ouchen.] Ait Belaid, their family are brothers of Id Baj. Ohomo is brothers with Id Baj, even though he is from a different family. Ibn Aissa is here only lately. How he came, his father came to Id Baj's to shepherd, he married a woman from Tadrar, they stayed here, had children, and they call them Ait Ben Aissa. They don't have a homeland [*tamazirt*].[7]

This considerable, early mobility is one important lesson from the history of Ibn Tumart. As Abdurrahman's oral history of the contemporary *ighsan*,[8] or lineages, of Tadrar makes clear, people who knew how to pray were systematically moved around, integrated with those who did not, spreading the *Mahdi*'s brand of Islam and mixing tribes[9] and linguistic groups from different areas of the country. This ought to serve as a caveat to those who conceptualize Berbers as timeless, generic, and on the margins of history. Berbers who came to the cities a millennium ago learned Arabic, as they do today, but Arabic speakers who came to the mountains learned Tashelhit, and eventually forgot Arabic to become, over the generations, Berbers. Abdurrahman understands the origins of the three main branches of the village as from the north (Id Yous), south (Idzdo) and southeast (Id Baj), thus placing Tadrar at the center of the world. Abdurrahman constitutes his out-of-the-way village as an amalgam of diverse peoples alloyed in the forge of Islam, people intimately intertwined with the *longue durée* of the nation. Importantly, this larger history is accessed by a line of ancestors, from Abdurrahman back to Abd al-Haq, the founder of the Ait Yous

7. This notion of "homeland" (*tamazirt*) is of importance, though I do not examine it in detail here. See Katherine Hoffman's work (2000b, 2002).

8. *Ighsan* means "bones" or lineages. See chapter 4.

9. There is some argument about the use of the term *tribe* in Morocco. See Berque (1953), Hoffman (2000a), Sabry (2004, 50).

lineage in the mountains, and from Abd al-Haq to the great *Mahdi* of Islam.

Much contemporary anthropology eschews old-fashioned work on villages, and is fascinated with movement, dislocation, transnational flows, migration, hybrid culture, borderlands, and the like.[10] And yet in terms of such movements and hybridity, the people of Tadrar seem to have long been more modern—even postmodern—than their observers. These mountain people have for a very long time lived in a multi-cultural, mutable social and linguistic environment (Hoffman 2000a, 2000b, 2002, 2008). They seem to have always moved between the mountains and the valleys for a variety of reasons—economic, political, religious—wandering and returning, learning and sharing, plundering and retreating. The old history, that of the time of Ibn Tumart, suggests this, as does much that came later. This geographic fluidity is not incompatible with a temporal organization that locates people and power through lines of men: sons, fathers, and grandfathers stretching back in time. Fluidity is not chaos; it is ordered conceptually through patrilineages, at least by men like Abdurrahman.

A second locally significant historical period is the rise of the Goundafi family in the mid-nineteenth century. If the story of Ibn Tumart sanctifies the bonding of different lineages through the arrival of the Prophet's message, the history of the Goundafi is a cautionary tale about unconstrained ambition, the operation of naked power in the mountain milieu.

Other areas of Morocco seem to have long maintained comparatively egalitarian, tribal democracies,[11] but the mountains south of Marrakech were, by 1860, under the control of three powerful men, the "Lords of the Atlas."[12] The direct route south from Marrakech to Taroudant was the undisputed territory of the Goundafi, whose origins lie with a man named Si Ahmed n Ait Lahcen, *amghar,* or local leader, of the area around Tagoundaft, about fifteen kilometers upriver from the confluence of the Agoundis and the Nfis rivers. This was 1855 (Montagne 1930b, 14). Si Ahmed had a son,

10. See Anzaldúa (1999), Appadurai (1996), Bhabha (1994), Hannerz (1996).

11. See Dunn (1977, 52–68) where both Arab and Berber forms of tribal democracy are practiced. See also Hart (1981).

12. Montagne calls them "petites chefs de l'Atlas," but most others call them the "Grand *Caid*s." According to Montagne, by 1860 the western passes from the Haouz Plain around Marrakech to the southern valleys were secured by the M'Touggi *caid* (1930b, 6), with "*caid*" being the older term for a leader answerable, in theory, only to the sultan. Those in the east were under the control of the famous Glaoui *caid,* who would later play such an important role in the French rule of the country.

the "energetic and ambitious" Si Mohammed, who rallied the Ait Iraten moiety (or *leff*) to war against their counterparts, the Ait Atman. The local *caid*, or representative of the sultan, supported the Ait Atman in an expedition against the Ait Iraten centered in Tagoundaft, but these forces were repulsed. Thus, those of Tagoundaft—the Goundafa—became in Montagne's words the "heroes of Berber liberty" and quickly set about the destruction of their hereditary Atman enemies, who were of course also Berbers, though presumably less heroic for allying themselves with the sultan. The Goundafi "tribe" was thus born of the Ait Lahcen family, who were originally from Tiznit, south of Agadir.

The Goundafa reinforced their defensive fortifications in Tagoundaft and from 1860 to 1875 constructed another fort lower in the valley at Talat n Yaqoub, the present-day administrative center for the Agoundis Valley. This new fort was largely destroyed in 1875 by a *harka*, an armed government incursion assembled by the sultan's *caid* in the Haouz Plain near Marrakech. However, through "adroitly provoked defections" the *harka* was defeated before it took Tagoundaft, and Si Mohammed's son Tayeb was made *caid* of the region around the Nfis and its tributaries (Montagne 1930b, 14). In 1885 Si Mohammed died and Tayeb el-Goundafi gained uncontested power over the Nfis Valley and the pass south to Taroudant. Thereafter, "the" Goundafi refers to Tayeb. He was recruited by the French along with his rivals, the Glaoui and the M'Touggi. In May 1917 the French made Si Tayeb the Pasha of Tiznit, near his family's ancestral home (Landau 1969, 164), and from Tiznit he ruled much of the Moroccan southwest, with a certain Colonel Justinard for assistance (Justinard 1951). Goundafi never gave up his control of the Nfis, however. In 1920 Marshal Lyautey awarded Tayeb Goundafi the rank of *Grand Officier de la Legion d'Honneur* for his services to France (Landau 1969, 165). He retired in 1924 and died on May 25, 1928.

For those in the Nfis basin, where Tagoundaft is located, Goundafi's rule seems to have been rapacious and brutal. Descendants of slaves retained to entertain the *caid* still occupy Tagoundaft, and remain impoverished if locally famous for their musical abilities. Even in the Agoundis there are young men who told me their grandfathers were slaves, owned by the Goundafi family into the twentieth century.[13] Stories of the horrors perpetrated by the *caid* or his immediate underlings include arbitrary murder, rape, confisca-

13. On slavery in Morocco, I found it interesting how many Tashelhit words are devoted to different kinds of slaves. I stumbled on these in a list of Tashelhit "stories"—transliterated by Lieutenant Antoene Jorden in Arabic characters in 1935—in the back of the Peace Corps train-

tion of property, and much else. In the Valley of the Agoundis, however, memories were more ambivalent than in Tagoundaft itself. One reason for this is the relative isolation of Tadrar and the Agoundis. Physical distance from the *caid* must have made his exactions less frequent and less intense.

Certainly more important, however, the local *amghar,* or lieutenant serving under the Goundafi in the Agoundis, was for a long time located in Tadrar. Members of the Ait Yousef, the "bone" of the village that includes the Arbuz, Lukstaf, and Ben Ouchen lineages, had for long periods acted as the local arm of Goundafi's power, and at least one of these men, the original *Ouchen,* grew fairly rich on the job. Some local men traveled with the *caid* when he went to join the French fighting the Spanish (and their Ait Bamaran allies) in the Moroccan south, and thus military service is one way that villagers participated in the larger world outside of their village.

One of those who went to fight was Abdurrahman's grandfather— Mohammed "the *Ouchen*"—and Abdurrahman owes his relatively privileged position partially to this grandfather, and by extension to Goundafi. Abdurrahman does not deny the horrific stories about the *caid*'s rule, and even recounts them himself, but these are couched in negative recollections about the political instability and lawlessness of the period before the *caid* took power, and the equally unpleasant demands of what Abdurrahman called the "French *caid*" who followed. Had I been located in one of the villages that had not benefited from the *caid*'s power, opinions of the *caid* would have been more purely negative, less skewed to a view that he did "what had to be done" to maintain order. Certainly if I would have been based in Tazguart, the population of which was reduced to vassals to the Ben Ouchen *amghar,* I would have culled an unvarnished view of the power of the *caid* in the Agoundis. The men of Tazguart are still litigating in Moroccan courts to try and reclaim land taken by the Ouchen under the patronage of the Goundafi. Such particulars of family history are key to understanding the role of "the outside" in a village like Tadrar. The Ben Ouchen family history illustrates that Tadrar has been importantly involved in larger political processes for a very long time, but that not all villagers were involved in the same ways.

Few understand this history like Abdurrahman. Most villagers, in fact, had little interest and almost no understanding of Ibn Tumart beyond some

---

ing manual for Tashelhit areas. I am not sure why contemporary Peace Corps volunteers need an elaborate vocabulary for types and qualities of slaves.

idea that he was associated with the mosque at Tin Mal. This was true of both women and men. Most villagers could talk in general terms about the horrors of the Goundafi, but did not have specific information and did not seem to think of themselves as the types of people who should know. Women seemed particularly baffled when I asked them about the past. "Old people," they told me, were the ones to ask, but no matter how many old people I queried, nobody seemed to know as much, or be interested in knowing as much, as Abdurrahman.

Abdurrahman considers himself a local intellectual. Like all thinkers, he can do his pondering because other people are providing for him, producing the food, doing the cooking and cleaning. Abdurrahman is the dominant person in a large household, he has more labor available to serve him than most other people and more property for them to work on, and he is well positioned in terms of long-term lineage dynamics. Abdurrahman was also the youngest son of the youngest son of the most powerful person in the historical memory of the village, so there too he has been fortunate. His understanding of himself as linked to Goundafi power (through his father and grandfather) is not a general history, but a very specific one.

For my purposes here, the point is that history is at the service of the powerful, or at least those powerful enough to have the time to ponder the meaning of events in time, and who benefit by such remembering. Abdurrahman has charged himself with his family's history and the history of his village, and he sees this knowledge as important to his other self-appointed position as the interface between the village and the state. As we will see, sometimes the state agrees with him about the usefulness of providing such an interface, even if his fellow villagers are not so happy about it. Sometimes Abdurrahman's fellow villagers want him to engage the state and he refuses. And sometimes he attempts to take on positions of power but is outwitted by his cousins, uncles, nephews, and neighbors. As in the past, with the arrival of Ibn Tumart and the rise of the Goundafi, a line of men related by birth forms the conceptual entry point for understanding political action, but action itself is dependent on acumen, skill, ruthlessness, ambition, and ultimately, always, God's will. Abdurrahman is quite unusual; his views should not be taken as representative, but they are nonetheless illustrative. What follows is the way he explained Moroccan state politics to me, and then three examples of how the activities of the state and NGOs locally unfolded during the time I lived in Tadrar.

NOTES FROM THE FIELD
July 24, 2004

We were walking, one of our longer hikes up a tributary of the Agoundis River, the Assif n Oumslane. I wanted to see the village of "saints," or *igurramen,* in the village of Zaouite up in the high pass to Glaoui territory, and we stopped to rest in the shade of a boulder about halfway there. Tell me again, I asked, about politics [*siyasa*] in Morocco. I had made this request before, but Abdurrahman likes to demonstrate his mastery of certain realms of knowledge, and so is happy to repeat for me, again, how the world is constructed. He takes a small rock.

"This is me," he begins, "I am a little big in Tadrar." Abdurrahman then proceeds to lay out a line of ever larger rocks, each representing a level of the Moroccan government. The first line is *muqqadem, amghar, caid, 'amil,* and *wazir.* These represent enforcement, officials appointed by Rabat to keep order, and from the *caid* level up, people with the power to imprison, fine, even, many suspect, murder. The *caid* is named in Rabat, and is always an outsider from the perspective of villagers, but he appoints the *amghar* from among the local population. The *amghar* chooses men to act as *muqqademun,* local informants. This is by far the most locally relevant chain of power from the village up to the state.

A second line of rocks are the *adil, qadi imzee, qadi imqor,* and *wazir,* and these represent the judicial system, from lawyers up to judges and the minister. They, too, are concerned with crime and punishment, but in general are not of much importance in the Agoundis as few people have money for a lawyer, and there is generally little to gain from a court. Local justice has to come from local people, which means little is accomplished from a line of officials that begin with outsiders and work up from there.

A third line of rocks radiating up from "little big" Abdurrahman are the elected officials, from *mursheh,* to *rais al-jemaa,* and *'oodu n majlis.* The *'oodu n majlis* makes requests of a *wazir,* too, and there are a number of *wazirs* for different things such as religion, roads, and forests. The three lines of officials are thus joined at the level of ministers. This third group is empowered to spend local tax money in the mountains; they relate the priorities of the populace, and collect and distribute the meager fees garnered, for instance, at market when people have to pay to park their mules. At the apex of all three lines, above the level of ministers, is the biggest rock, the singular king.

Abdurrahman himself belongs to none of these lines. He had no formal office at the time and is not a structural part of the system; his rock is small and he may move it to access one line or another. Abdurrahman is a private citizen, a man among men, though "a little big" in the context of Tadrar because he attempts in some circumstances to link the general dust of "the village" with one or another rock-hard channel to power. Like rocks, and life itself, officials are *ishqa*, hard. Power is not accessed without danger or costs, as we will see.

While it sounds like a mixed metaphor, as Abdurrahman explains it, each rock must "eat" the one below, must exact payments from them in order to feed the person above. This is simply how it is. What outsiders call "corruption" is for Abdurrahman the condition of political action in Morocco. The only person who is exempt—the only fully *nishan* or "straight" person conceptually possible in such a system—is the king, since there is nobody above to "eat" him. The king has nobody to feed above him, and thus no compulsion to eat those below, though Abdurrahman ambivalently noted that the king too needed money. These days everyone, "even saints, even the king has to work." I refrained from asking how all the "eating" gets started if the top level is not hungry; this is the sort of question I had learned not to ask because I knew it would make my host uncomfortable. I never in any circumstance in Morocco asked Abdurrahman or anyone about their opinion of the king, the royal family, or the justice of the political system, only how politics was organized.

Abdurrahman's understanding of politics accords very well with Abdelleh Hammoudi's master and disciple model of Moroccan authoritarianism (1997, 1999). Hammoudi writes that there is in Morocco a cultural norm—what he calls an *episteme,* after Foucault, a framework for the boundaries of the knowable—that men exist in relations of domination and submission. Hammoudi argues that this *episteme* emerged from the Sufi master and disciple model, and that it forms the basis of political authority in Morocco and perhaps over a much larger area. In my view, this cultural model undervalues the potency of fear and repression—the material bases of state power—but it tells us something interesting about how power is exercised. From Abdurrahman's perspective, at least, political viability involves becoming part of a chain of patronage dyads, assuming a position of submission to someone "above" so that you can dominate someone else "below." This is how to get things done, and is exactly what we might characterize as "the cultural foundation of Moroccan authoritarianism," the subtitle of Hammoudi's 1997 book.

However, from the perspective of Tadrar these lines of rocks as linked chains of master/disciple dyads also look something like a schematized, branching segmentary lineage, with the king at the top. Lineages contain a strong ethic of egalitarianism between branches, even if they are characterized as authoritarian up the lines of generations. Thus the difference between the lines of state power from Tadrar up to the king and the lines of lineal relatedness back to ancestors in the village is that lineage ancestors are dead while the officers of the Moroccan state are alive and active—all too active in the view of villagers. Nodes (or rocks) in a lineage system serve as the conceptual linkages that bond living people into an egalitarian social imaginary, while in the world of contemporary state politics the nodes are alive, and thus able to exercise their authority on their also-alive "descendants," the men below them on the chain.

In this sense the linked dyads of patronage that stretch up from the village through the state to the king are a sort of animated lineage—one absent its customary expression over long periods of time and actualized bizarrely in the present. Dealing with the state is thus like encountering vivified, dominating ancestors rather than the safely dead patriarchs who normally link a man to his contemporary equals. This may be why most villagers see this "eating" as corrupt and yet feed their extortionists with exaggerated hospitality—what to me seems a strikingly deferential groveling before men they clearly hate. Everybody talks about bribes as gifts. It may also be why even Abdurrahman is ambivalent, at once attempting to explain the system to me dispassionately, but clearly cognizant of the moral danger of trying to explain away the "eating" associated with political power. Domineering authority (the "master" pole of Hammoudi's "master and disciple" model) is fully legitimate in its context, in the relationship between older and younger men, or men and women. When such domination is taken out of the domestic temporal context, out of "transgenerational time" (Weismantel 2004, 498), it becomes monstrous—even if it retains much of its force. How such an aesthetics of power plays out through institutions and particular circumstances, and how it articulates with other modalities of governance, is, as we will see next, more complicated.

◈ ◈ ◈

As we turn to contemporary development, and the opportunities it holds to engage the state, we see that attempting to assume a dominant position in Tadrar does not go unchallenged. As David Hart writes, "a constant preoccupation of all Berbers is never to let one head rise above the rest" (1981, 77), but if this really is a "constant preoccupation" or a kind of "counterpower" (Graeber 2004, 25), it can only be so if some Berbers are determined to raise their heads. Ambition, submission, egalitarianism, and domination are equally culturally logical if they are done in the right way, between correctly classified participants, in the right time frames. In novel situations ambition takes considerable political skill because contests are in part about establishing the terms of the relevant relationships, the nature of social reality. This is what Lawrence Rosen calls "bargaining for reality" (1984, 4). Before one can argue, one needs to establish the relationship with the opposing member of the argument, whether, at least in public, one man may look into another's eyes or should lower them, whether one can speak arrogantly and dismissively or not, whether one can openly challenge a man's assertions or plans or must do it secretly, behind his back.

After all, the male, public arena is not the total political space even if it is the part of political space I knew best; it is not true that action always occurs on the main stage, that everything in a village is known to everybody (Scott 1985). To give one cautionary example, I was once stopped on the road just outside Tadrar by the *amghar,* the most powerful man in the valley. I was properly deferential, lowering my eyes, shuffling my feet; I had absorbed the *habitus* of submission from the social environment—but perhaps I had absorbed it too well. As the *amghar* left, I was flabbergasted to see that behind our backs (literally) a female neighbor of mine had been quietly but successfully training my two-year old son to throw rocks at the *amghar.* Wee Calum Crawford never found his target, thankfully, but the woman convulsed in barely contained laughter as my toddler waddled down the road gurgling and heaving pebbles at the departing, supposedly esteemed *amghar.* As we talk now about how I came to understand the actualizations of power and politics in Tadrar, it is well to remember that I did not always know what was going on behind me.

Development involves change, and in the delicately orchestrated sociopolitical world of Tadrar, change is never harmonious. As I noted at the very outset of this book, "progress" is swamping Tadrar, with a new road in 1995, a new school in 1998 (the first-ever official state school in the village), a potable water system finished that same year, a diesel grain mill installed by 2002, and a World Bank-funded cement canal almost finished in 2004. Each of these projects presented its own challenges for the development agents and the villagers, and each played differently upon the dynamics of inequality that undergird village life. This is not meant as an exhaustive report on development in the region; for interested readers there is a detailed master's thesis by Dennis Ryan Russell (2003) and a terrifically thorough Ph.D. dissertation by Fatima Gebrati (2004).

September 19, 1998

The new schoolteacher arrived, her parents and brother in tow. The family departed after a week or so of rural idyll (though one brother remained longer to look after his sister), but the sister, our new *mualima,* or teacher, could not begin work until the school was done. She and her brother (and her other family members while they were in the village) stayed with Abdurrahman. Abdurrahman knew enough Arabic to converse with them, and while, in my view, they treated him with condescension, they were something closer to appalled by the rest of the village. Allegedly teachers have to bribe their way into training, then into a job, and when that job turns out to be located in a dirty village of illiterates without electricity or indoor plumbing, disappointment easily turns to bitterness.

October 26, 1998

The school is finally done. The *mualima* does not move in to her room there, however, but continues to stay with Abdurrahman's family. [In fact, she will never move in over the course of her entire first year.] The idea that a young woman fresh out of college—especially a young city woman—would live alone in a room is unthinkable. The idea that she would pay rent to stay with Abdurrahman is equally unthinkable, partly at least because during her first year the teacher will never get paid. The government is slow to get new employees on to its rolls. Worse, however, it is late October with a teacher in situ and well fed and the school building done and painted Pepto Bismol pink, but the term cannot start. There are no desks, no books, no paper. The school remains an empty cement room.

October 29, 1998

Abdurrahman roars triumphantly into the village atop a truckload of school supplies—desks with chairs, a blackboard, and backpacks, one for each student stuffed with the requisite materials for an official state education: chalk, pencils, a ruler, books, paper. The children are ecstatic, mobbing the truck and then marching around the village in their new backpacks, assaulting any reasonably flat surface with the new chalk and lording their great luck over the students too young or too old to begin first grade. The village hums with excitement. This is a great relief to me as I had made some aborted attempts to run a kindergarten class with students anxious to begin. My first and only class lasted 45 minutes. We played a game that involved arithmetic and learned the English sentence, "Hello, my name is Daoud." Some of the children to this day think their name is Daoud. I do not envy the new, young teacher her challenge.

November 5, 1998

A chill has descended. Yesterday at souk my neighbor Belaid accused Abdurrahman of stealing; Belaid had taken the case to the *caid*. Because Belaid and Fatima are one of three families I eat with, and Fatima is one of my best friends and my only "employee" in the village besides Abdurrahman, I am more involved than usual. Nobody takes a complaint to the *caid* that is not serious. The *caid* is an Arabic speaker from outside of the region. He holds tremendous power and to bring a case to him is necessarily to risk jail, at least. Belaid is very angry, and now Abdurrahman is angry too, and worried.

The facts of the case emerge slowly. Some are not in dispute. Abdurrahman had collected money for the school supplies, perhaps about 10 dirhams [$1 US] per pupil. Belaid believed that the money was for the backpacks, which are government property and have "forbidden to sell" emblazoned on each one. Abdurrahman says that the money was for the truck to bring the supplies, not the backpacks, and that he paid 500 dirhams for the truck—more money, in fact, than he had even collected. He alludes that he needed money to get the supplies released at the regional depot, too, even though he had "a paper" from the commissioner of schools. Belaid and Abdurrahman have to "make another paper" in the government office in Talat n

Yacoub, which I take to mean they have to produce sworn statements. Things are never good when paper is involved.

The issue reverberates around the village, and with me. Abdurrahman warns me to stay away from Belaid and to stop paying Fatima to do laundry. Fatima is bruised—her left eye is swollen, and despite her claim that she fell, it looks like she's been hit. Abdurrahman's son Mohammed suggests that Belaid can sometimes go crazy. Belaid tells me over lunch that I am his neighbor, that Fatima is therefore supposed to take care of me, and that if she fails to bring me anything I need he will beat her. This is a perverse twist on what I had been warned Belaid might think, and it seems that the argument about school supplies is collapsing into my lap. I laugh uncomfortably, and suggest beating is not necessary, that Fatima is a perfect neighbor. Privately I ask Fatima if it is better that I stop paying her to do work for me, that people may talk, but as usual she laughs. "People talk like chickens," she says, "let them talk." She laughs despite her black eye. Privately Belaid says to me, with disgust, "we have no democracy here. Only you Christians have democracy." I think he means justice rather than democracy, or at least that he conflates the two. I am not the savior he hopes for.

The resolution of the money-for-school-supplies conflict is illuminating: Abdurrahman was legally exonerated even though some of the charges against him were determined to be true. It was determined, for instance, that he had taken the money, and even that he had taken more money than was strictly needed to bring the truckload of material to the village. Thus his initial argument that he had spent more than he received did not seem to hold up under examination. However, from the perspective of the state, Abdurrahman had been hosting the teacher now for more than a month, feeding and housing her for free, and translating so the Arabic-speaking teacher could function in the Berber-speaking village. More significantly for the case at hand, *somebody* needed to pick up the supplies. A village is not an administrative unit, it has no elected or appointed leader, and yet the school was bequeathed to this village alone. A village of equal men can be paralyzed by its lack of hierarchy. If Abdurrahman had not taken the initiative to get the supplies, the school would never have opened. From the perspective of the state, Abdurrahman is a man who gets things done. By Abdurrahman's own admission, the only way to do this is to "eat" those below you so as to feed those above. While distasteful to some, most people see nothing particularly wrong with this so long at it is done among the right people and in the right proportions. After all, *iqaridin ar tsoualin,* Abdurrahman told me one day, "money talks." Eating those below you is a precondition of political action.

This does not mean that Abdurrahman's fellow villagers were happy with the outcome, though the tension did diffuse relatively soon thereafter and I kept eating with and talking to whomever I wished. While Abdurrahman had used the activities of the state for his own benefit, and while the state seemed to believe that this benefited the village as a whole, many people were determined to keep Abdurrahman's from defining himself as "above" them, to keep his head from rising above the rest. This was made clear later, in 2004, when a new cement canal was installed.

After years of wrangling, in the fall of 2003 World Bank money had finally become available to the village of Tadrar to accomplish one of their most desired development projects: cement a canal named Taforikht. Abdurrahman had made himself *rais,* or president of the project, and organized people to work on it. At first, it was a voluntary village-wide project, but as order broke down it was decided that they needed a proper labor rotation. They based this on lineages, something like the irrigation rotation. Here they allocated the work by meter of canal rather than time worked. The rotation allocations in Table 7 are revealing.

The math seems to support the Arbuz assertion that the canal Taforikht was "Ben Ouchen." If we calculate the division by *ighsan* (and thus lump the four Ben Ouchen sublineages with the Arbuz and Lukstaf sublineages, see Table 3), we see that there are ninety meters for the Ait Yousef, ten for

Table 7. Lineage labor obligations to reconstruct Canal Taforikht

Lineage	Sublineage (if any)	No. of meters
Ben Ouchen	Ait Ali	20
Ben Ouchen	Ait Hussein	20
Ben Ouchen	Ait Bil Qas	20
Ben Ouchen	Ait l'Haj	20
Arbuz and Lukstaf		10
Idzdo		10
Id Baj		10

the Idzdo, and ten for the Id Baj—with the Ben Ouchen getting eighty of the ninety Ait Yousef meters. Presumably the number of meters the teams need to work roughly corresponds to the amount of land they have adjoining the canal. Perhaps the latter two *ighsan* managed to talk their way out of doing a fair share of the labor, but it seems more likely that the Ben Ouchen (in particular) talked the development people into starting work on a canal that benefited them disproportionately.

The canal was built in a U shape, with three rods of rebar supporting the cement on the outside wall, three rods on the bottom, and two on the mountain side of the canal. Crossbars were supposed to be placed every twenty centimeters, and Abdurrahman reported that it was his job to ensure that these specifications were followed. Unfortunately, for him at least, Abdurrahman got very sick in the middle of the project and had to be hospitalized in Marrakech. He eventually recovered, only to find that he had been voted out of the *rais* position and his nephew, Hamad, voted in. Hamad is also Ben Ouchen, in fact he is also Ait Ali, so in some sense this was not any sort of dramatic revolution.

What happened next is not so clear. From Abdurrahman's perspective, Hamad and some of his friends began to cheat on the proportions and sell the extra cement and rebar. It was not clear if they kept the money or distributed it more widely. Abdurrahman took me down and showed me the spot on the canal where he stopped being in charge, and it is true that workmanship is notably less exacting after this spot. I cannot confirm or deny whether the correct amount of iron or cement was used before or after, though in an area I checked that was under construction in the summer of 2004, there was clearly economizing going on.

Interestingly, Abdurrahman's main argument was not that he wanted to be *rais* again, but that the state agencies involved wanted him to do it. From the state perspective, claimed Abdurrahman, he was an ideal candidate because he had taught himself some Arabic, and could thus communicate with the translators for the foreign development agencies, and he was a good, moral man who did his prayers. It is also true that by this time (late 2003 to early 2004) Abdurrahman had become much more comfortable than when I first met him. He had secured government help to build his tourist hostel, he had one son working permanently outside the village and two working part-time, and thus he had an income beyond his land. As I have noted several times now, he also had more land than anybody else, and was comfortably situated in the lineage labor scheme, so that he was not very burdened by this either. The state agents involved did not understand all of these dynamics, but they did come to believe that Abdurrahman was *nishan,* straight or honest, and that he always seemed to have time to host representatives from the outside.

One could argue that it was precisely Abdurrahman's good fortune that made it possible (or at least more likely) for him to be "straight." His local power, and in particular the time he had at his disposal to work with outside agencies, made him seem an ideal candidate. Abdurrahman was perceived by the state as useful, and this inclined Abdurrahman to work for long-term benefits rather than try to profit off of a single project in the short term. Abdurrahman's nephew, on the other hand, does not speak Arabic, does not know the people in government, and may never get another chance to make anything personal off of the transformation of his village. He and his younger age mates are more likely to want to gain as much as possible in the short term—and to benefit as many of their intra-village allies in the process—than they are to worry about the way they are perceived by outsiders the village may never see again. Everyone knows development money is fickle. Those who are not presently positioned to benefit from the village transformation are unlikely to be the most willing participants in development.

While I cannot know all the facts of the case, it would not surprise me if Hamad opted for immediate gain rather than trying to build a longer-term relationship with the state. He probably knows that if Abdurrahman really wants to become *rais* again, his uncle can probably do so over his objections and those of other villagers who would like for Hamad to keep the job. In the era of development, relations with the state matter in new ways—and outsiders have new ways to meddle with village attempts to keep everyone's head level. Abdurrahman is hoping to secure long-term alliances with "the outside" that will allow him to benefit, to "raise his head" above those of his fellow villagers, at least in some situations. A final excerpt from my fieldnotes will illustrate the perils of Abdurrahman's position and show some of the ambivalence my friend experienced in his rise to being "a little big."

The next section is comprised of largely unedited fieldnotes from a single day, May 7, 1999. They are incomplete in places, misspelled in others, simply wrong about some details, and are sometimes written in an accusative tone owing to my frustration at the time. I include them here to capture a more vibrant sense of what development feels like in the moment, while it is happening, and the confusion that attends dealing with "the outside" in a multilingual environment. I mean these to complement the passionless, explanatory sections above by trying to capture some of what it feels like to sit in a meeting with development agents as they come to Tadrar, and as my own personality comes through in ways proper "academic writing" has typically excluded. It also shows how I, as an actor in the events as well as a participant, am nothing like neutral. I have removed some names and changed others because of the sensitive nature of the material.

May 7, 1999

The big news is that the [big funding] people were here yesterday trailing every big wig this wretched region could assemble. Calling it a circus grants it too much entertainment value, and a sophistication of production that was totally absent. I will try to record the relevant bits, but it has taken me almost 20 hours to recover from the thing sufficiently that I can write it down without wincing in physical pain. I reconstruct the following imaginatively, as I was not able to take notes.

Present: leading the parade was the guy from the [big funding agency], an overweight Frenchman with wet, rubbery lips and a sulfurous aura of superiority. He had with him a guy named [H.], from a German development agency. [H.] seemed obnoxious also, though he didn't talk as much so it was hard to tell for sure. The third *rumi* [foreigner] was a biologist specializing in wild mammal populations, a guy who has lived and worked in Marrakech for 18 years. I liked him, though he said nothing at all during the main part of the meeting and he smoked continuously, like the other ingrate Christians, indoors in a tightly packed room.

There appeared to be two main factions of Arabs. Heading one was a guy from Rabat, a neat, balding, bespectacled man said to be some sort of liaison for the Toubkal [National] Park. With him, of course, was Larbi, who is locally in charge of things, or at least as locally as Marrakech. Both of them seem to be decent enough. The other faction was comprised of the Eau et Fôrets (or "Eaux" as they write it here). This bunch is headed by the nefarious Si Rahal, the consummate extortionist of the region, and his sidekick who I just call [B.]. Rahal is a vicious, toad-like animal, five feet tall, wearing his little khaki cap like a tank wears its armor. I consider him dangerous. [B.] is nice enough, but his limbs are too long for his body and he's got an irritating "aw shucks" sort attitude. He's stuck with a permanent drooling grin, and so, with his limbs at odd angles, looks like a retarded spider. Two more Arabs were present, one seemingly with Rahal, the other seemingly with Larbi. Khalid [the Peace Corps volunteer, Dennis "Ryan" Russell] was in the room for much of the fun, as was I. Abdurrahman was there some of the time, but spent much effort scurrying about seeing to the needs of his guests. Despite the scholarly shame of going missing in action, I had to leave several times to keep from chomping my tongue off at the nub. In fact, I tried to leave altogether but messengers were dispatched to return me to my part in the production. This seemed to mean sitting in the corner quietly, not a specialty of mine. I spent much time with one hand on my forehead and one clamped over my mouth.

In addition to those listed above, the middle part of the meeting featured a special appearance by "the villagers," who were shuttled in, packed together near the door, and then shuffled out when it had been determined by some secret mechanism that they had "participated." The "villagers" were essentially any man over thirty who happened to be in the village at the time. The beginning and the end of the meeting—the parts when food was served—were reserved for us special folks who were white and those urbane brown folks who spoke Arabized French.

It is hard to say exactly what happened, since in essence nothing really happened. First we ate and all the guys guffawed and kibitzed, pretending not to loathe each other, or at least showing that while they loathed each other, they were stuck in this business together. Then the "villagers" were herded in. Nobody made room for them, so they all sat crammed against one wall, knees in each other's backs like school children. I was already on that side of the room and so was included in the group who spent their time rocking back and forth and flexing our butt muscles to keep the circulation going.

The [big funding, hereafter BF] guy began with a windy speech [in French] about public money and transparent accounting, about sharing the burden of rural development. The liaison from Rabat attempted to translate this into Arabic, which Abdurrahman fumbled to figure out and attempted to at least partially translate into

Tashelhit [Berber]. BF guy would only wait for about two thirds of the Arabic translation before he would start speaking again, and so the Tashelhit portion of the translation was necessarily excised from most of the storm. What words did make the three language voyage tended to transform things like "transparent accounting" into "invisible money," and "the burden of rural development" into the "difficulty of growing up farming." These are examples I made up. In fact, it was not even this comprehensible. I could understand the French most of the time, and I could understand the Tashelhit most of the time. The Arabic made no sense to me. Calling the relationship between the two ends of the language chain "tenuous" is to grant that there was any chain and any relationship at all. This was sometimes the case. Sitting there, I was bored silly even though I understood what was being said. I looked at the faces of my comrades in discomfort. They had mastered a look of mesmerized interest, and even nodded at appropriate times. I believe they were thinking about the prices of seed at souk, whether they will get to eat lunch, and the details of their daughters' weddings. A few clandestine winks, shrugs, and eyebrow raisings support this view.

So then BF guy says that he has questions for the villagers, that he wants to hear from them and not—he points around the room—from the Eaux et Fôrets or the [Toubkal] Park people. He is unctuously condescending to his Arabic-speaking colleagues, snorting at their mild attempts to seem officious. Evidently BF guy thinks they are all crooks, but relatively stupid ones. His manner conveys that he is going to do his best to overcome their malicious incompetence, but is not hopeful. In Rahal's case I find this rather sweet, but I am embarrassed for some of the other Moroccan officials who, for all I know, do their jobs with integrity and what efficiency is possible in this country. On the whole I feel rather uncomfortably aligned with a racist [because I am sympathetic to the French distrust of some of the Moroccan officials].

With a deep breath BF guy launches into another soliloquy, this time so abstract and untranslatable that the liaison/translator starts to sputter and beg for time to begin getting the message across. He is told to shush, that the BF guy is talking with the people, "them," as he says with a poke of his thumb. Nonetheless, BF guy is halted at several points by the attempt to render the French into Arabic, first by the liaison, but when he gets frustrated, by one of the other guys. BF guy is clearly irritated at having the eloquence of his questioning interrupted by the inconvenience of audience comprehension. In fact, however, the "audience" doesn't understand a fucking word of it. While the liaison at least had the sense to aim his Arabic at Abdurrahman, who would at least sometimes fire a sort of summation off to the peanut gallery, the newly self-appointed translator now talks directly to the *Ishalheen* [Berbers from the Moroccan south] clustered at the far corner of the room. He speaks slowly and with exaggerated clarity, evidently figuring that pronouncing the syllables loudly enough will somehow cause the villagers to be miraculously stricken with Arabic comprehension. I am hoping it will work for me, too, since I have no idea what he is saying. This goes on for some time. Finally the BF guy can't stand it and he resolves to simplify the questions he had himself lost track of.

The first question took about five minutes to formulate in French, and included lots of phraseology about the responsibility of public funds. The Arabic version reduced the bullshit to a (relatively concise) two minutes. The Tashelhit was rendered, "do you want money." The crowd nods enthusiastically. An old one-eyed man is suspicious. He asks, "What do we have to do for it? Do we get it for nothing?" Abdurrahman attempts to answer this question himself and both of them are shushed by the BF guy, who had a pencil ready and wants to move on.

The second question involves being willing to work for it, being willing to pay for part of the project. This included lots of hypothetical percentages, like what would happen if in the third of five years' worth of funding the [big funding people] only provided 80% of what a given aspect of the project required. In Tashelhit this comes out as, "Like the last project, they pay, we work, what do you think?" The crowd nods enthusiastically.

The third question concerns the disbursement of funds. The [big funding] arrogance is ratcheted up a notch here, as BF explains how they will provide the funds to the Moroccan government, but he needs to know how to distribute the funds, how they will get from the bank to the project meant to benefit the people. He explains that he doesn't understand Moroccan law, but that he figures that any sort of association would have to be legally sanctioned to receive and spend funds, especially outside funds. Do the villagers want to have the money administered by the [notoriously corrupt] Eaux et Fôrets, or do they want it themselves?

To Abdurrahman this seems like a trick question and he grins broadly, nodding his huge head and says that they are all like one, Rahal [representative of the Eaux et Fôrets] and the villagers. "Everything is great," he continues. I snort loudly. Khalid claps his hand to his forehead. BF guy realizes this is silly, shakes his head. One of the other Eaux et Fôrets guys points out that the villagers cannot receive the funds directly, they have no "association." The normal [local] word for "association" is *jemaa,* which is [also] what they call the collective decision making body of household . . . heads. It is not a formal, chartered, legalized institution, of course, and so we are having a hard time translating the idea that an "association" will be necessary if funds are to be delivered. In fact, Khalid has been trying to get this idea across to the villagers for about a year now. I am not clear exactly what they would have to do. I don't know the law, and neither does Khalid or the people themselves. No problem, says the crowd, who remain totally ignorant of what is going on. They all nod enthusiastically. It seems Abdurrahman has agreed to have the Eaux et Fôrets, with Rahal at the helm, administer the funds.

Another question concerns who will do the work. Abdurrahman basically understands this and so tries to explain that there are five lineages [or lineage-based work groups] in the village and that each provides a certain amount of labor. It is more complicated than this, of course, since money that is paid out is done by household rather than lineage and, as I am trying to show, the lineages are not exactly equal. This is the only time I say anything, urging Abdurrahman to explain that they also do things by "takat," household.

After the "questions" have been "answered," the villagers are sent on their way so that the adults can talk. I am now refusing to be on the official side of things, and go with them to stand in the next room feverishly discussing what just happened and what should or might happen next. Abdurrahman is concerned that if they have an association, he will be in charge and will get in trouble. Cynically, I would think he would himself jump at the chance to skim funds, but he cites the example of another association head who "ate" all the money and got in trouble. Maybe he remembers his own trouble after he collected money for the school supplies. Khalid tried to explain that an association doesn't have to have one guy in charge, that it can be basically the system as it stands. Ben Salah points out that if the money goes through the Eaux et Fôrets they will eat it all. People seem to want the money directly and are arguing with Abdurrahman about it, though it is also the case that nobody will himself agree to be the guy who signs on the paper.

Abdurrahman refused to be the one to sign the paper; the Eaux et Fôrets were charged with distributing the money, to the obvious dismay of the granting agencies who had hoped to funnel more of the money directly to the village and keep the agents they saw as corrupt from playing a role. Clearly, these were early days for Abdurrahman. It was a big project worth a lot of money, and while both the villagers and some officers of the state seemed to want to place him in a pivotal position, he was scared of other officers, other branches of government, other lines of power. Letting those above him skim the funds first and making do with what was left seemed wiser than getting stuck between the unknowable funding agency and the powerful Department of Waters and Forests. Abdurrahman is too little a rock to dwell between two such hard places.

I can apologize now for my uncharitable characterizations of some of the men involved. I had been working in Tadrar for close to a year and I had clearly incorporated some of the local distrust of outsiders. This project did go forward and I think it did benefit all villagers to some degree, even if it helped some more than others. The point is that, from the perspective of Tadrar, contact with "the state" is not a singular thing. Each of the men involved has his own personality, his own power base, his own moral compass, and his own mode of interacting. Something "cultural" was surely going on, but so too was much that remains determinedly personal. To be seen by the state the villagers have to render themselves visible, and this requires somebody to speak, somebody to take a chance, somebody to sign a form. It requires political labor, some danger, and much time to engage the power of state agents who can do good or ill—or both at once. It also requires locals to understand the state, and inevitably they do so in terms that make sense to them, terms they draw from other domains of authority, including the lineage and, ultimately, the patriarchal household.

◈ ◈ ◈

To summarize, Tadrar has long been involved with the outside world. I gave two examples of political involvement—one from the twelfth century and one from the nineteenth—and tried to show how today the main interface between the village and the state involves development. How this happens as it does is not easy to explain, but we can start with three main veins of scholarly writings. First, there are writings on the mountains that focus on lineages and egalitarianism, with Ernest Gellner and David Hart providing the most important examples. Second, there is an interpretivist literature mostly done in urban areas that focuses on culture as a kind of text that begs translation and interpretation. Here Moroccans are argued to use cultural categories as points of departure, and identity is negotiated in an essentially agonistic social environment. Many people could be cited here, but particularly Clifford Geertz and Lawrence Rosen. Finally, a more contemporary set of writings has emerged that emphasizes the power of the state, and a cultural emphasis of authoritarianism, writings that are in some ways the precise opposite of the egalitarian emphasis of the earlier tribal work. I would cite the edited volume by Bourqia and Gilson Miller, some of Elaine Combs-Schilling's research, and the work of Abdelleh Hammoudi here.

While these three foci might seem unrelated, I have tried to offer a synthesis. First, I am very sympathetic to the suggestion that Moroccans negotiate their positions in society. In fact, they negotiate almost everything, and I can see why Geertz chose the bazaar as one of his central metaphors for Moroccan society. However, the terms of the negotiations are not open-ended or fairly adjudicated, and both the egalitarian "tribal" literature and the more contemporary writings on the cultural roots of authoritarianism offer insight into how culturally appropriate terms of negotiation influence the possible social outcomes. We have seen that in Tadrar some relationships are accepted as authoritarian, some are meant to be egalitarian, and some are ambiguous, left open to question. The negotiation in the new, dynamic world of local development is precisely over what cultural model ought to be employed in each context, a negotiation that suggests a notion of "culture" that is less an integrated whole than a reservoir of meaningful frameworks more or less artfully deployed.

In this sense, the hierarchical state system of linked dyads and patronage can be seen as parallel rather than counterpoised to the rural lineage system—or at least it is understood that way by some people in the mountains, particularly those who know something about the larger system and hope to put it to work. I argue that the lines of authority ramifying from king down to the village are like a lineage taken out of time. The "ancestors"—the nodes in a segmentary system—are in the government's case living officials. Because they are located "up" a line of authority, these men have the right to dominate those "below" them. In a lineage system most of the men with authority, those "up" the line, are dead, and certainly the apical ancestors, the ones with the most authority over the most descendants, are dead. Only fathers and sons remain, so the pyramid of authority is very flat. While this does not tell us about the sources of power—land in the case of fathers, violence in the case of the state—it does suggest something about the aesthetics of the expression of power in Morocco, the notable extremes of dominance and submission in some interactions, combined with a prickly pride and deep conviction of egalitarianism in other areas.

Lineages stretch back in time through ancestors who each have authority over their sons, but the living, breathing men using the concept of lineages are all equally related as equidistant from these dead patriarchs, at least above the level of the household. The authoritarian part of the system, the part that holds it together, is safely buried in the past and contained within households in the present, allowing men associated through lineages to function in some sense "equally" in the present. The state system has been argued to be exactly the opposite—authoritarian rather than egalitarian—but my argument is that it is structurally analogous, simply wrenched out of time and actualized in the present. State bureaucrats thus have the power of the dead. Why—and especially how—farmers should defer in such an exaggerated way to such beings is part of what I have tried to understand.

Some of the work on the power of the state emphasizes too-easy acceptance of royal pomp, in my view, too much credit to the theater of legitimacy (Combs Schilling 1989, 1996, 1999). My toddler's being taught to throw rocks at the *amghar* suggests reservoirs of resistance beneath the surface of deference. Surely Moroccan citizens are not cowed simply by the king's white robes and the televised rituals of state. The Moroccan government has real, material mechanisms of power—police, an army, bureaucratic records, paper, prisons, fines. But the way villagers understand the "how" of state power cannot be reduced to fearful reaction; the power to imprison does not in itself explain why dread is expressed as groveling solicitude, or why such solicitude is accepted as a form of payment by the powerful (McMurray 2001). Domination and submission are aesthetically complex, culturally mediated acts that have to be performed; the cement and rebar of development, the walnuts, cash, and goats that form "gifts" to officials all have to be transacted by men who understand one another, or at least misunderstand one another coherently (Bourdieu 1984). These mis/ understandings are critical to making sense what state power is and how it works in Tadrar.

6

⚜

GLOBALIZATION BEGINS
AT HOME

However significant the dynamics of state-guided development discussed in the previous chapter, by far the most important contemporary interchange between Tadrar and the outside world is migration for wage labor. The ability to access wage-paying jobs in the plains and cities is becoming a crucial means by which the community of Tadrar is constituted, both locally in the mountains and in the broader sense; wages are ever more important in village life. In the last chapter Abdurrahman Ait Ben Ouchen was often a singular interface between the local economy of Tadrar and exogenous (ultimately state-controlled) resources; wage labor is far more diffuse, with many different families seeking money in different places, for different reasons, at different points in their domestic cycles, and with different results. The capitalist economy is volatile, fertile, and perilous, and its capacities are becoming vital to contradictory processes: the reconstitution of the traditional patriarchal order of the village, and its transformation, including the extension of the village community into the broader Moroccan sociogeographic context. This chapter thus ties the local sociopolitical dynamics of earlier chapters—beginning with households—into an argument about globalization.

In essence, globalization, as I will use the term, is about interconnectedness, a particularly profound interconnectedness spawned by the global expansion of the economic system we call capitalism. That capitalism is necessarily global has been recognized since at least the middle of the nineteenth century, even if its origins can be traced much further back (Mielants 2007). A famous quote from the *Communist Manifesto* suggests that the business class must "nestle everywhere, settle everywhere, establish connections everywhere," must constantly grow to create a "universal inter-dependence of nations" if the system is to stay alive (Marx and Engels 1967, 83). Some have suggested that this capitalist dependence on growth leads to a condition of continuous "dynamic disequilibrium" (Desai 2002, 254), the productivity of the system grounded in "creative destruction" (Schumpeter 1976). But if it is clear why the capitalists are so energetic (they are seeking profits), what of the places where capitalism is expanding *to,* the viewpoints, motivations, actions, and reactions of people being globalized?

The Liberal view's most rosy assessment—or what in the United States is called the conservative position—is simply that capitalism offers a better deal than traditional social orders, and thus people choose it for rational, material reasons. There would seem a certain amount of evidence for this in Tadrar, as we will see. Slightly more ominously, however, some argue that capitalism is more productive, and thus outcompetes other forms of economic organization. This view emphasizes the destructive part of capitalist growth, but portrays it as necessary to the creativity and fecundity of the system. This too has some support in the village where I worked. And most pessimistically, scholars on the Left suggest that capitalist economic organization is foisted upon regular people by elites (both national and international) without regard to what regular folks *really* desire, or by manipulating desire such that folks are drawn into wage labor because they are mystified, because they do not understand their own best interests. I did not find people to be especially confused, but did find that wage labor was foisted on people rather than simply chosen. This last, most pessimistic view has elicited much scholarly attention from those interested in the marginal, pre- or newly capitalized world.

Perhaps the most celebrated work on the victims of (or new participants in) globalization has been the work on "resistance" begun by James Scott (1985). In *Weapons of the Weak,* Scott argues that capitalism happens *to* regular people (the "weak"), but that they do not merely accept it or misunderstand what is happening. Scott thus criticizes an earlier Marxist position that viewed the peasantry as either mystified (i.e., unaware or uncaring that they were being dominated) or absolutely powerless. He showed that peasants in Malaysia understood very well that the Green Revolution, the arrival of capitalist farming methods and their accompanying forms of social organization, was a terrible deal for the poor. However, the poor did not fail to openly revolt because they were stupid or unaware, but rather because they very rationally calculated the likelihood of success. An open revolt was sure to be violently repressed, so peasants instead "resisted" the landlords through myriad acts of work slowdown, wasting time, and sabotage. Scott's work begat a flurry of studies seeking to find similar dynamics in other places, and launched a frenzy of scholarly debate about just how conscious and intentional actions had to be for scholars to label them legitimate forms of resistance. Many who were sympathetic to the plight of the poor were relieved to find that the poor were not unaware of their disadvantage.[1]

In the Malaysian case, however, Scott was observing the behavior of peasants who had *already suffered* the effects of capitalist transformation, and their historical perspective is crucial. The Malaysians had their previous lives to look back upon, and used their memory of the traditional social order to weigh the changes they had experienced. Unsurprisingly, peasants dispossessed of control over their land did not view the arrival of large-scale, "efficient" capitalist agriculture very positively. The physical experience of wage labor was less than exhilarating, and they were not happy that the values that had sustained the previous economic order were undermined by the new, profit-oriented system. These Malaysian peasants were unfortunate to have been in control of land that turned out to be valuable for the purposes of Capital, and once the potential for profit was realized, the poor were summarily divested of their resources. What, then, of Tadrar, another poor community of farmers being integrated with "the outside"?

At the outset it is important to note that Tadrar is not a blank canvas, a laboratory for the arrival of capitalism on virgin territory. Even if local production remains largely for local consumption, and even if the main way labor is organized is still through households and lineages rather than contracted wage labor, Tadrar has long been in contact with the outside world. In previous chapters I have noted interactions from the twelfth century to the nineteenth, and on this basis we can say that the village as it exists today has come into being along with the larger state and global economy. There may now be relatively little a capitalist would want in these high, rugged mountains, but in the middle of the twentieth century, for instance, the French identified valuable lumber and mineral resources in the mountains— and set about its removal and sale. Today the mines are closed and the hillsides deforested. This unfortunate situation has nevertheless allowed villagers to again be left more or less alone for the latter part of the twentieth century. This brief example is meant to illustrate that Tadrar and the capitalist economy of the plains have been mutually constituted, exist at the same point in history, and have come into their present relationship after

---

1. See Fletcher (2007).

cycles of contact and retrenchment. This long-term engagement does not mean that the two systems have merged into identical economies, cultures, or social orders.

Tadrar remains substantively distinct from the city. Here I agree with Jonathan Friedman's observation that "the fact that people occupying a particular place and living and constructing a particular world are in their entirety integrated into a larger system of relationships does not contradict the fact that they make their world where they are and with the people that are part of their local lives" (2002, 31). Social entities can exist "within" or "in relation to" larger entities or processes without being subsumed by them. The emphasis on globalization can obscure local distinctiveness, and can cause us to overvalue large processes and ignore the particularities of local engagement with them. After all, "most people in the world—if we are speaking in absolute numbers—do still live in what they see as recognizable communities, believe themselves to be individuals, and think of their values and way of life as relatively coherent" (Moore 1999, 16). In Tadrar, local distinction has been quietly resilient over a very long period (which is to say it has been doggedly reproduced over a very long period) despite a diversity of types and intensities of exchanges with the world beyond the valley.

The issue today is that people in Tadrar appear to be *choosing* to participate in the capitalist economy—and in record numbers—suggesting a very different dynamic than simple "resistance." Villagers in Tadrar do not appear like Scott's peasants, with capitalist landlords taking over the land. Instead, villagers leave the village to come to the city, and not at gunpoint.

My argument will be that different villagers in Tadrar are using the potential of the larger economy at cross purposes—some to escape the rural patriarchal order, some to evade particular restrictions of that order, but with an eye to returning to it, and some to solidify their positions in, and the reconstitution of, the traditional village. The effect of using the capitalist system for various and contradictory purposes, some of which seem thoroughly traditional, may yet be the destruction of the village political economy. It may be that by putting the dynamics of the capitalist system to local uses villagers inevitably usher in the atomization and individualization of the larger social order. But that is beyond the scope of this present study, and will only become clear in time. Here I will focus on how the people in Tadrar extract resources from the larger, wage labor economy, and what this may tell us about how capitalism expands. In essence, this is not simply because capitalists are chasing profit everywhere, but because non-capitalists (and household patriarchs, in particular) are seeking to use aspects of the capitalist system for their own culturally sensible purposes. It is not always the person using the system who pays the human costs of such use. Both the benefits and the costs of capitalist integration can only be calculated across time.

Significantly for this argument about globalization, and any theory about villagers' own purposes, life in Tadrar is produced through households. It is not possible to understand the decisions villagers make without reference to the social organization of the households in which they live, without contending with the dynamics of authority within households, and without accounting for villagers' deep faith in the importance of family, the emotionally charged ties through which households are formed and by which they are linked together. It is not possible to greet anyone in Tadrar without asking them about the health and well-being of their family, and they never greeted me after any absence at all without inquiring into the status of a whole string of my relatives that I have to admit I rarely think of at all. People in Tadrar were more concerned about my family than I am, in other words, and this says something about the importance they ascribe to their own family networks. We should not confuse households and families, but household-based production in Tadrar is wed to a deeply resonant ideology of the importance of family. There is a rich anthropological literature on the household, but somehow this social unit has never received due emphasis in Morocco, where it is all-important.[2]

The literature on migration often divides motivation into "push" and "pull" factors. In Tadrar, I found these to be complicatedly intertwined, though there were clear regularities in how people balanced the desirable and undesirable aspects of urban life. Older, propertied men were far less interested in moving to the city than anyone else. Older women did not seem so keen on it either, but understood why people would seek an urban life, and wanted to visit their children who had moved there. Like all women, older women complained bitterly about the difficulty of life in the mountains. Younger men were ambivalent, with some saying they would like to spend half the year in each place (particularly the winter down in the warmer cities and the summer up in the cooler mountains), or that they liked some aspects of

2. There are terrific accounts of household life in the region, such as Singerman (1995), Hoodfar (1997), and Mernissi (1994). However, these focus on urban households, not agricultural ones, and the differences are significant. The main, outstanding exception is Martha Mundy's work linking households, kinship, and politics in Yemen (1995).

the city but found others hard to deal with. Those who had never been to the city were apprehensive, but curious. Those who had lived in both the mountains and the cities insightfully compared the difficulties of both places.

Young women were most insistent on the positive nature of urban life, though casual conversations with village women who had migrated showed they had much less enthusiasm for the city than their rural sisters and cousins who had no direct urban experience. Young women were not interested in moving to the city to work, however, and did not want to go alone. They wanted the advantages of urban life, but they wanted to obtain them by marrying someone "rich," someone who had a job in the city and would set the young woman up with her own urban household

It is not difficult to figure out why these general trends should be. What follows are parts of conversations I had with different villagers about their views of the city, conversations that reveal something of what villagers might want to change about their lives, and why wage labor outside of the mountains might or might not seem desirable to differently positioned people.

Interview with Rqia Ait Ouakarim and her husband, Mohammed Id Baj

October 30, 1998

David: What's your name?

Rqia: Rqia . . . from Agerda.

David: Agerda? [the name of her natal village]

Rqia: Agerda.

David: Your 'asl [origins] are in Agerda?

Rqia: Agerda.

David: Do you want to talk about women's lives?

Rqia: Yeah. Women. You want to speak about women's lives in [Tadrar.] Yes. We go to the mountains to bring wood, and fodder. We come back and light the ovens, we make bread and put it in the ovens, we milk cows. We make lunch. We do everything like that. We go to fetch water. We go to the river and wash clothes. Everything like this we do. And we prepare wool. We wash wool and card it.

We put it on the loom and work on it. Like this women work. They bring fodder for the cows, and give it to them. We milk them and if there is a calf we take him to his mother for some milk. We give them food. We wash dishes, sweep, and shake out the blankets. We fold up the carpets and take them out in the sun to get rid of the bedbugs, if there are any. We feed the chickens and rabbits, if we have any. That's all we do. We go up there, and come back. [We] spend the whole day moving.

David: Moving.

Rqia: Yeah, moving around. To the mountains for wood, and fodder for the animals. They bring *aouri* [a local shrub] and they give it to cows to eat. They prepare something for themselves to eat, they eat it. . . . They go to the fields to bring the cows something to eat, so we can milk her. Because if you don't give them any fodder, they won't give you any milk. They come back and prepare dinner. They churn buttermilk . . .

[Her small son chimes in: they churn buttermilk . . .]

Rqia: They eat a little butter and a little buttermilk. They stir a little *tagoula* [a sort of soupy, curdled-milk concoction]. They prepare *bedaz* [corn flour porridge]. They prepare couscous, bread, press it in the ovens when they're hot. They sweep the kitchen, wash the pots, wash the serving dishes, and they take the trash from the cooking area and throw it out. They carry it in bags and take it far from the house, so that it won't come back in. Everything they do is like this.

David: Is the life of women harder than men's life, or easier?

Rqia: Oh no, women's lives are harder than men's [laughter]. Their activities [*tizla n timgharin*] are harder. They go to the mountains for wood and bring food for the cows. When they come in the late afternoon, they light the ovens and prepare food. Men, when they come back from the fields, they "take off their belts" and go to pray. After prayers, they say to women, "what have you done, have you prepared lunch or something to eat? You haven't prepared anything?" [laughter]. You have not prepared anything!? I am rushing around, but I have not done anything! The oven does not want to light. The wood does not want to light. Like this . . . men, their job is easy and near by. Women, it's hard. They spend the whole day rushing, from morning to night.

David: Until afternoon? Until night?

Rqia: Until night, then they can rest. At first light they get up again, and they start hurrying around. And men, they have a little job. They don't have lots to do. Right?

At this point Rqia's husband, Mohammed, is looking slightly uncomfortable, like he is waiting to speak.

David: Yeah . . . [addressing Mohammed]. Do you know it's like this?

Mohammed: Huh?

Rqia: He said to you, do you know that this is true or not?

Mohammed: Oh yes!

Rqia: [To David.] Have you seen? [Laughter.]

Mohammed: Women of the mountains are always like this, always, always. They bring kindling from the forest. *Aouri* from the forest. They carry it on their backs. Then they take their sickle to the fields, and they gather fodder. They bundle it . . .

Rqia: We put it here. [indicating on her back]

Mohammed: They carry it on their backs . . .

Rqia: *Hba* [a word meaning things carried on the back, whether babies, fodder, or wood] . . . here [indicating her back].

Mohammed: . . . when they arrive, they parcel it out to the cows, and they go to see if there is any *askeef* [barley flour gruel] to drink. If there is none, they light the oven. This is what they do until ten at night. At ten they go to bed. And she gets up at four and goes to the oven. She makes coffee, she makes *askeef*. She prepares food for the children, and they eat it. She takes her rope to the mountains [i.e., the rope used to carry the bundles of wood]. To bring wood to make fire. After, when she brings the wood, she comes down and eats a little. She takes her basket to the river to bring fodder for the cows. She feeds the cows, and she makes lunch. She feeds the children and she takes grain to grind in the river [there was at this time a water-powered mill wheel in the river]. She makes *tagoula* for the children.

David: Yeah . . .

Mohammed: That's all. She does not rest. Never, never.

David: Never.

Mohammed: When she finishes one thing, another thing comes. . . . Men, no. When they irrigate and plough the plots, they go up to the fields. They come back and sit. That's all their job. That's all.

David: That's all?

Mohammed: That's all their job.

Ten days before this, on October 20, I had interviewed Mohammed and Rqia's daughter Fatima Id Baj. Fatima had moved to the city after she divorced her first husband, her patrilateral parallel cousin. She lived with her sister for some time in Rabat before returning to Tadrar to marry her present husband, Mohammed Belaid. Like her mother, Fatima too gave a long, passionate, and gruelingly detailed iteration on the difficulties of women's labor. Then I asked her, "Do you think life in the city is easier?"

Fatima: Life in the city is easy, because I have seen it. Life in the city, you find a job, you will work there and your children will go to school. Women work [for money] and men. Some might work in a *nadi* (a factory). Men, God knows, whatever he finds [to do,] he can work in the city. But in the mountains, there is *no* [paying] work. Only wood, fields, that's all. That's all [there is to do] in the mountains. But the life in the city is nice [*teshwa*].

From these interviews it might seem that any woman would want to move to the city, and any man would be reluctant to do so. This is not entirely accurate, however. Rqia, Mohammed, and Fatima are not emphasizing the benefits of village life (the safety and security of living among people you have known a lifetime, making a living in ways that are difficult but at least reliable) and they are not expounding on the difficulties of urban life. After all, Fatima did come back to the village, and Mohammed has never discussed taking his household to the city no matter how much Rqia complains about women's fate. The interviews above were done at a time when Mohammed had one grown son at home, a son who did most of the family's male-gendered labor and left his father to, as Rqia says, "take his belt off" and just sit. It is not surprising that Mohammed found mountain life pretty good: he was a leisured, propertied patriarch. By 2004, when Mohammed's son had married and the new bride was brought into the household, Rqia's life had eased some. Rqia became more involved with raising her granddaughter while her daughter-in-law took over some of the heavy labor of wood, fodder, and grain transport. Fatima's opinion of city life is based on her sister's situation: married to a man with a job, the kids in school. Fatima did not suggest that she wanted to go look for a job, only that a good life could be had in the city, that city life was "nice."

Some of this is clearer in another interview, this one with Lahcen Lukstaf (who lived in the city but returned his wages to his parents' household) and his mother, Aisha Ben Ouchen, in 1999. Lahcen's wife remained in the mountains with his natal household during 1998–1999, though by 2004 Lahcen's father had died and he had brought his wife to the city with him, starting an independent household. The interview is somewhat choppy, as it was an afternoon in Ramadan and I (at least) was famished and thirsty, but also because one of Aisha's grandchildren has started a small fire down the hill that gradually grew out of control while we spoke.

Interview with Aisha Ait Ben Ouchen and her son Lahcen Lukstaf

January 7, 1999

David: What is the difference between life in the mountains and life in the city?

Lahcen: What's the difference? The city is clean. There is money if you work. You bring a little money home. If you have your own house, you do not rent. It's not like the mountains. In the mountains there is no money, people just sit, that's all. They do not do anything.

This line begs some explanation. Part of Lahcen's assertion that in the mountains "people just sit" has to do with the season; we were doing the interview in winter, and there was very little for men to do. But I believe there is more to it than this. Lahcen has lived for many years in the city and his vision of seasonal fluctuation is telling of a particular understanding of time, an urban understanding that sees time as something empty to fill. His understanding of "unemployment" or "not working" is wage-based, one that sees time as money, and inactivity as potential activity not undertaken. In Tadrar villagers do what work needs doing; they do not tend to work within clock-based time frames or according to predetermined hours. As Pierre Bourdieu argues for rural Algerian Berbers, "Entrance into the money economy is coupled with the discovery of time as something that can be wasted, that is, the distinction between empty, or lost, time and full or well-filled time. These are unknown notions in the logic of a precapitalist economy" (1973, 83). Lahcen's time working for wages has reorganized his conception of time. Continuing the interview, Aisha discusses "work," a concept closely related to time.

Aisha: Me, I only visit [the city]. I only go there and come back. There is no work there [for women] like they work here. It's only here. That's all. When I go I just cook some [indistinguishable]. That's all. Only here . . .

David: [To Aisha.] What's your work here?

Aisha: Carding wool and spinning wool. I bring fodder for the animals. When I was able I carried loads on my back from the mountains. Now, no.

David: Now no?

Aisha: Now I am no longer able. [Aisha is quite old.]

David: Because Khadija [her granddaughter] brings it now?

Aisha: I have Khadija, I have Kiltoum [Lahcen's wife] . . .

[Pause. There is some commotion.]

Aisha: I want to go to the city again. I want to go when Ramadan is over.

David: In Ramadan maybe?

Aisha: When I finish the loom that I am preparing now, then I will go again to the city.

David: How many times in a year do your [urban] children visit [Tadrar]?

Aisha: Me, I did not spend a year there. [Aisha has misunderstood the question.]

David: But how many times?

Aisha: I visited only one time per year, only at the end of the year.

David: Only one time? That's hard. But Lahcen, no.

[Everyone talks at once. The fire is getting larger.]

Lahcen: No, I always come.

Aisha: He always comes. At the *'eid* [*al-Kebir,* also called *tafaska,* the biggest holiday of the year] he always comes, and in Ramadan. Because he doesn't have a lot of work [then]. Work is not stable. There is no work where you can earn money. It's sporadic. So we are just sitting here. [Laughter.] We do not even earn our dinner.

In another part of this interview Lahcen summed up his position succinctly when he said of life in the city, "Yeah, it's good. *When* there is money. It's good when there is money."

Among people who had not lived in the city I rarely heard about winter as "not working." In fact, for women in particular winter is a more difficult season because of the amount of wood required to stay warm, but for men it is indeed a slow time of year for agricultural labor. Men do not discuss it this way, however. They focus on it being cold. When Lahcen says "there is no work," he means paying work. The issue for him is that there is nothing to do for money in the mountains. Lahcen's brother, father, and nephews do all of the rural labor, and indeed when Lahcen visits, he mostly sits. That is why he was available to talk to me; the other men in his family were off working. Lahcen is charged with returning wages to his household, thus he and his mother have come to think of Lahcen's period of relative inactivity as "lost wages," time lost when paying work could have been done.

Lahcen's uncle Hamad, who has also lived most of his life in the city, also focuses on money as the centrally important element of life in the city, though his much longer period outside the village burnishes his glorification of the city with the sheen of rural nostalgia.

INTERVIEW WITH HAMAD LUKSTAF

November 5, 1998

David: Do you think that people in the cities are different from people in the mountains, or not?

Hamad: Oh yeah. They are different. There is a difference. Mountains are apart from the city. They have to plant vegetables. They gather wood. They have to fetch water. They have to buy candles. They stay in their houses without paying rent. They have their own houses, they do not rent them. *They have the good life of the mountains.* They do not know meat. If he has animals, if one of his animals dies, he will eat it. And if he goes to the *souk,* he may bring half a kilo or a quarter of a kilo and eat it with his children.

In the city, no. In the city, no. We buy vegetables. We pay for electricity and water. We pay rent. We buy meat. We buy oil. We buy flour or bread. We buy noodles. We buy rice. We buy fish. If we don't want meat we buy fish, if we don't want fish we buy chicken. That's how it is. The one who lives in the city is always working, he always gets money, in the morning and in the afternoon. In the mountains, no. If he does not sell a cow or a goat, there is nowhere to get money. What he ploughs is only enough for his donkey or mule. And he has lots of children, there are some who have ten, some of have five, some who have seven, some who have eight, and others have one. They are not all the same.

Most striking here is Hamad's assertion that "they have the good life in the mountains," an opinion sandwiched between "they don't pay rent" (Hamad is, among other things, a landlord) and "they don't know meat." Meat is highly desired, and together these three sentences seem to indicate a kind of cognitive dissonance.

Hamad was never able to claim his portion of his inheritance, and it seems clear he feels that he was driven to the city rather than lured. Still, he has done very well for himself, and now owns a small *funduq* (a kind of extremely modest hotel for rural people that has a place for any animals they might bring to the city with them), as well as rental property. In other conversations Hamad showed evident contempt for many aspects of village life, and for most villagers. However, while he extols the many material virtues of city life—most especially in relation to food—he lets slip that the mountains are, at some emotional level, the epitome of "the good life." There is no doubt that the city represents opportunity, though both migrants and non-migrants are realistic about the limitations of urban life. Opinions seem tied to fluctuations in the rhythm of the domestic cycle, with differently positioned men and women differently enthused (or not) about wage labor. Sometimes, however, patriarchs, the propertied men who benefit most from the rural patriarchal order, do move to the city. In the next section I deal with the structural conditions under which this happens.

Between 1999 and 2004, three households—more than 10 percent of the total households in Tadrar—abandoned the village for the city. This does not include the many inchoate households that left—newly independent *tikatin* produced when a patriarch and his wife die and divide the family property. Because each son can, in the best of circumstances, establish his own household at the death of his father, and because fathers can have many sons while sons only have one father, the total number of households in Tadrar can increase upon a patriarch's death even as households or individuals migrate out. This does not mean people depart in order to felicitously manage the village population; people leave for a variety of reasons, but often because they cannot support a household with their limited resources. Marriage and establishing a household is the main life goal of all young villagers, a point so obvious to them that it scarcely needs mentioning. Sometimes urban wage labor is the only way to fulfill this goal.

The three migrations I examine next were not products of death and the subsequent redistribution of household property, but are households that by 1999 had existed for some period of time. The issue, then, is what inspired them to move when they did. Each household was headed by a neighbor of mine—men named Mohammed, Hussein, and Hassan—and each has a somewhat different and illustrative trajectory. Schematically, the three households have one important thing in common: they are all members of the Ait l'Haj sublineage of the Ait Ben Ouchen. In chapters 3 and 4, I showed how a single man (Mohammed Ouchen) bequeathed a considerable inheritance to four sons, each of whom became the apical ancestor of a contemporary Ben Ouchen sublineage: the Ait Ali, Ait Hussein, Ait Bil Qas, and Ait l'Haj. We might suspect that each of these four brothers inherited something like equal quarters of the original stake and passed these on to their respective descendants. I showed some of the ways women's inheritance complicates this idealized branching lineage system; in the examples that follow we will see further complications.

Whatever might have happened in property devolution since the time the original *"Ouchen"* died, the sublineage groups of his descendants had very different dimensions in 1999. The Ait Ali had three households, the Ait Hussein had three, the Ait Bil Qas was comprised of only one official household, while the Ait l'Haj had grown to seven independent households. This suggests that the Ait l'Haj might have a lot less property per household, a lot less room for families to grow. While I need repeat that it is not the case that property exactly devolves along the lines of simple, branching lineages, father to son transfers do form the core of property exchange, and we should not be surprised that Mohammed, Hussein, and Hassan, the three who took their households to the city, were all from the Ait l'Haj. While the original Ait l'Haj ancestor was the oldest of the four Ouchen brothers, while he had houses in Marrakech and managed to accompany the Goundafi *caid* on the pilgrimage to Mecca (one of the five central pillars of Islam, which qualifies the pilgrim to use the honorific "Haj"), and while he supposedly returned from his voyage to the other end of the Mediterranean with a car (one of the first in the country!) and a Turkish wife, his descendants have been left not only the most miserable among the children of the Ouchen, but among the most impoverished in the generally poor village of Tadrar.

The story of Haj Ouahman has many lessons, among them: global integration in one generation can be followed by a retreat into a local context; power is not necessarily or unproblematically reproduced through time; and the traditional order is hardly static. Upon returning from the Haj, the eldest son of Mohammed the Ouchen was never able to reclaim his father's title of *amghar*, which passed out of Tadrar at that time and has never returned. Still, as we will see, the stories of the three recently migrating "People of the Haj" *tikatin* are interestingly distinct despite this shared history, and such differences vastly complicate the faith we can have in a schematic understanding of the history of Tadrar, or any general story about how globalization happens.

The migration of each of these three households is unique. They each left a different kind of "hole," created a different kind of absence in the village. As they were entire household units that left rather than individuals, the organizational level on which the absence is most apparent is lineages, which are the conceptual way that households are strung together. Even so, the departure of these three households did not equally handicap the rest of the Ait l'Haj lineage when it comes to communal labor obligations, for reasons other than pure demography. We will examine this below, especially in the context of the third household that left, that of Hassan.

Emigrating households do not just leave behind an absence, of course, but also establish new connections and facilitate new sorts of relationships. The fact that these households will be living in the city means that friends and relatives in the village now have someplace to go, stay, and eat while they learn the skills necessary for life in the city. It also means that whatever resources these families left in the village can be bequeathed in one form or another to other village households. Sometimes this encourages the development of *amshrek* relationships, sharecropping, where patriarchs from other households (typically from elsewhere in the Ait l'Haj) take over the farming of land and split the crop proportionally with their urban brethren.

Departure may mean changing the nature of farming. One important thrust of development in this part of the mountains is encouraging farmers to plant fruit trees. Supported by NGOs such as the High Atlas Foundation and by the Moroccan government, the idea is to establish new means of generating cash in the mountains so as to improve rural life and lessen the need for migration. However, this also results in villagers being more securely tied to global markets in fruit. Villagers are nervous about this—cash crops are desirable, but as they cut into the production of the life-sustaining barley, villagers are cautious. Therefore, only relatively wealthy villagers are generally willing to risk much of their land on speculative, cash-generating fruit production as opposed to growing the barley that keeps families alive.

Emigrant households are under less direct pressure. City dwellers are already at the mercy of the global wage labor economy, they are already dependent upon finding and keeping a job, pleasing a boss, living from paycheck to paycheck, and attempting to save money (rather than barley) to weather economic uncertainties. It is possible such people might be more willing to turn their mountain properties over to fruit cultivation since what income they derive from the mountains is an addition to, rather than the substance of, the family budget. There is much less labor involved in fruit trees than barley farming, and much more profit, at least in a good year, when prices are up. The economic calculations important for urban life (thinking in terms of profits and losses) are appropriate to fruit production, but do not make sense for barley (which is never sold, only eaten or given away to families too poor to eat anything else).[3]

Most importantly, fruit cultivation is something that can be done with a minimal personal presence in the village. This is true of almond and walnut trees, too, which might make us suspect that the future of farming in this region involves arboculture and absentee landlords rather than patriarchal household production of barley. If one significant aspect of migration involves the withdrawal of labor from the village, another is the migrant household's contribution to the transformation—arguably the capitalization—of the traditional farming regime. Trees take a long time to mature, only need care at certain times of the year, and cannot be easily removed to return back to farming barley. The introduction of fruit trees is likely to have a long-term, dramatic impact on the populations of the mountains and the things they do to stay there.

Despite the complicated significance of the departures of the households of Mohammed, Hussein, and Hassan, the impact on the village does not tell us much about why the families departed. Surely there is on one hand fate, *rezq,* which might be thought of in this context as simple economic desperation. But economics are never simple in a subsistence economy. In Tadrar property is bafflingly, sensually particular both in its materiality (different sizes and shapes of fields, each differently positioned vis-à-vis the sun and canals) and its ownership (men and women linked through households and lineages). The labor necessary to render the property productive is no less complicated to organize, a point I think I have made apparent by the sheer multitude of words I have exhausted trying to explain it. A thousand acres of identical wheat precessed by a single, huge combine tractor is stupefyingly simple by comparison to agriculture in Tadrar.

EN MASSE DEPARTURE NO. 1:
THE HOUSEHOLD OF MOHAMMED "AZOOMZOOM"

Mohammed is a kind man, smart, engaging, and, as near as I can tell, well trusted. He is also unlucky. From my calculations he is among the poorest landowners in the village. His wife is from a village up the valley, and brought no land with her. Mohammed ranks eighteenth (out of twenty-six)

3. See Michel (1997, 4) on the importance of grain in rural Moroccan society.

in the village in terms of the number of fields he owns, but is dead last in the all-important category of total irrigation time. (Appropriately enough, he is household 13 in Table 1.) His father, Omar, is still alive, but many years ago Omar had an accident that left him unable to speak (*azoomzoom* means "mute," so "Mohammed Azoomzoom" is "Mohammed son of the mute"). Omar has for a long time been both mentally and physically disabled, and his son, Mohammed, and his wife thus take care of Omar and their own seven children. If they had more land, these seven children would be a useful labor force. Without land, it is difficult to find ways to put them to work in the mountains.

One solution has been to send the older boys to the city. One left for Essaouira around the time I arrived in the village in 1998. He tried to make a living working in cafes, while another tried to find agricultural work in the Sous Valley. One of them was eventually imprisoned for allegedly stealing clothes from another worker, but was let out and came home after his sentence was served. Mohammed himself also took jobs such as *amshardo,* guardian of the walnut and almond harvest in the village, less to protect his own crop than to earn the small wage that came with it. In 1999 Mohammed and his wife, Fatima, had two babies below school age, one child beginning to go to the mosque to learn his prayers, and two more who were still not full-fledged workers. As these five dependants grew into workers, there was no work for them to do; the children thus grew burdensome rather than useful for a family with few fields; they needed work. Inevitably, perhaps, by 2004 Mohammed and his family left their house (the one just next to Abdurrahman's) and settled in a village on the plain outside of Taroudant, a half day's travel from Tadrar. From there they can more easily access the shifting opportunities available on the big, wage-paying farms of the valley.

This is a classic case that reveals the "push" out of the mountains and the "pull" of wage labor. Young men lead, searching out wage labor opportunities and making contacts, and eventually the rest of family follows. In terms of the impact on Tadrar, Mohammed did not sell his meager lands. Instead, he kept the trees for himself and sharecropped the land. He can do this because his trees are planted among the fields, and whoever irrigates the fields will necessarily water the trees. All Mohammed needs to do is return at harvest time to collect his walnuts and almonds, and to get his portion of the barley from his fields. Mohammed is thus simultaneously an absentee owner of trees in Tadrar, a partner in sharecropped land, and an employee on the big capitalist farms on the plains.[4]

EN MASSE DEPARTURE NO. 2: HUSSEIN'S HOUSEHOLD

Hussein's case is somewhat different. Although Hussein is about my age, in his late thirties at the time I lived in the village, his father is still alive, and so the only way Hussein could start his own household was by moving to the city to work. He chose an unusual destination: Sidi Kacem, in the north of the country near Fes. Evidently he chose this because his brother, who had abandoned his father's household much earlier, had contacts there. Hussein's brother was considered by some to be a bit disreputable, and was rumored to have been in prison for some time for allegedly selling drugs. This brother seems to have broken with his father's household long ago. While I only met him once, I found him engaging enough; his only local indiscretion was smoking cigarettes in the village. The old men, especially the pious ones, do not like this.

Hussein married a woman from Tadrar, Yemna Lukstaf, who remained in the village as the couple produced three children in a row, all of whom were still small in 1999. Despite the new, well-appointed house that Hussein built for his family, Yemna spent most of her time in her natal family's house—with her mother, Aisha, and her brothers' wives, Fatime and Kiltoum. I spent much of my time with the Lukstaf family also, and so I saw Yemna quite often. I saw Hussein only occasionally, in late summer when he returned to the village to help his father with harvesting, and during brief periods at other times of the year when he came to spend precious moments with his wife and babies.

Hussein is smart, ambitious, and much worldlier than most villagers. He asked pointed questions about methods of illegal migration to Spain and moving legally to the United States, about the economic conditions in Belgium and France, and the linguistic skills needed to labor in these places. Hussein was one of the people to ask directly what I planned to do with the profits of my "book" (my Ph.D. dissertation), and how my writing was likely to benefit him or Tadrar. Hussein had a grasp of a wider range of re-

4. See Robertson (1987) for a detailed analytical discussion of how farmers integrate different economic arrangements like sharecropping and wage labor.

ligious concepts than most villagers, too, pointing out to me that the traditional village dances were, according to "correct" Islam, shameful. Presumably for him "correct" Islam is the strident, international sort available in sermons for sale on cassettes in the city—yet another interpretation of what tradition is or should be.

By 2002, Hussein found work in Marrakech and moved his family there, abandoning his village house to swarms of mice and slow disintegration. The move to Marrakech isolated Yemna from her natal household, and all manner of reciprocity and mutual aid from her mother, sisters-in-law, and nieces. However, in Marrakech Yemna joined a growing Lukstaf community. Two Lukstaf sisters had already married there, and from 2002 to 2004 Yemna's unmarried younger brothers Mohammed and Omar both came to live with these sisters for periods of time.

I do not know if Hussein will bring his family back to Tadrar upon the death of his father, or return one or more of his boys to take care of his land. His social world seems to have far more to do with his wife's Lukstaf relatives than his own Ait l'Haj lineage. If Hussein does return upon the death of his father, it will be with much tough-won knowledge about how the world works. Hussein's departure removes a capable political actor from village affairs, as well as labor from his father's household and the Ait l'Haj lineage; Hussein's possible return as a household head would inject a new sort of perspective into the village council, new religious ideas, fresh understandings of proper relations with the state, as well as new sorts of linguistic capacities.

En Masse Departure No. 3: Hassan's Household

The situations of Mohammed and Hussein represent two of the standard forms of migration: poor families with too little land to sustain their growing members, and sons who strike out alone and labor in the city to support a rural household, eventually bringing their household to the city. Both of these dynamics extend the range of the village community, in the first case by maintaining property in Tadrar along with an urban wage-labor household, in the second through expanding the network of kin that village households use to access the city.

Hassan's story complicates this picture of poor men being driven from the village to take their households to the city. To start, he is not especially poor, by Tadrar's standards. Hassan is ranked tenth in terms of total fields, fifteenth in terms of irrigation time. While this hardly puts him in position to be a political powerhouse, neither is he among those who receive *l'ashour* charity at the end of the year, people beholden to the communal generosity prescribed by the Qur'an. Hassan is the paternal uncle of the Hussein discussed above, the only brother of Hussein's father (see households 8 and 10 in Figure 2). Thus, two of the Ait l'Haj households to emigrate would seem to be splitting the same fifth of the Ait l'Haj patrimony, and yet empirically, by my calculations, Hassan is approximately "middle class" for Tadrar. It is the unusual way Hassan got to be middle class that makes his departure revealing.

Hassan was a grown man by 1999, married to his second wife. His first wife was Khadija Ait Bil Qas, one of the daughters of the original four Ouchen boys, and one of the only sisters in her generation to receive her Islamically just portion of her inheritance. Hassan was Khadija's second husband; she originally married a patrilateral parallel cousin—one of her father's brothers' sons. In this case it was her uncle Haj Ouahman Ben Ouchen's son Hejmi. The marriage of Khadija (Ait Bil Qas) and Hejmi (Ait l'Haj) thus linked two of the four Ben Ouchen sublineages. They had a daughter named Fatima, who married to the new center of power in the Agoundis, the village of Tijrisht, where the *amghar* lives.

When Hejmi died, Khadija married Hassan, bringing to her new household the portion of the Ait Bil Qas land she got from her father, as well as the Ait l'Haj lands of her late husband, Hejmi Ait l'Haj. Hassan, her new husband, is himself Ait l'Haj, but at this point he had inherited no land, as his father was still alive. In fact, Hassan's father is Khadija's late husband Hejmi's brother. Young Hassan married his aunt. While not seen as specifically forbidden (or *haram*) in local understandings of Islamic propriety, this evidently did not please Hassan's father, and the boy was disinherited from what would have been his Ait l'Haj patrimony. If this hurt his relations with his lineal kin, it seems to have benefited Hassan economically, especially as Khadija died and left her second husband the lands of Hassan's late patrilateral uncle in addition to her own (more significant) Bil Qas land. Thus Hassan got his share of Ait l'Haj land—but through his uncle rather than his father—and he picked up a significant portion of Ait Bil Qas land. In interviews, some villagers considered him to be "really" Ait Bil Qas because that's where the bulk of his land came from. Most of his irrigation cooperation was undertaken with the one remaining Ait Bil Qas household (as the inherited lands are often contiguous), thus it is the Ait Bil Qas and not his native Ait l'Haj lineage with which Hassan mostly cooperated.

It does not seem like this cooperation went very well, though I could get little direct information because I did not tend to press questions that seemed to make people uncomfortable. What I know is that by 1999 Hassan—Ait l'Haj or Ait Bil Qas, depending on who you ask—had remarried again to Zaina, a woman from a neighboring valley; they had two small sons together. Zaina brought with her a daughter from a previous marriage, and by 2002 they added yet another daughter to the family. With one younger girl and three very young children, by 2004 Zaina and Hassan chose to move to the city, presumably sharecropping their mountain land with the one remaining Ait Bil Qas household, headed by Mohammed Ben Salah. I do not know where they went or with whom they might have stayed.

Hassan's story illustrates several things, not least the mutability of households in time, and the limits of accepting the "ideal type" of lineage relatedness as political or economic reality on the ground. Hassan seems to have built himself a better position than some of his other Ait l'Haj lineage mates through a fortuitous marriage he arranged himself, apparently in defiance of his father. However, if the difficulty of getting people to discuss the matter counts as evidence, Hassan seems to have isolated himself, first from his father and then from his extended lineage. In Tadrar, the means of exercising one's ambition are limited; these limits can be material (lack of productive property) but also social (lack of cooperation). While Hassan acquired property, the process of acquiring it cost him respect, or what theorists refer to as social capital. It takes both luck and political skill to prosper in Tadrar in ways that are acceptable to village mores. The absence left by the departure of Hassan's household, and the possibilities it might engender for other villagers, are as enigmatic as the means by which Hassan first made himself a life in Tadrar.

There is far more to the story of migration in Tadrar than households lacking the land or social resources to make their lives farming. Far more common, and far more influential to the long-term dynamics of village life, is migration from *within* households, that is, the way households send members out to work in the city without losing the rights to the migrants' wages. This is the main way the village social order is becoming articulated with the wage labor economy (Mayer 2002).

ARTICULATED HOUSEHOLD NO. 1:
THE DAUGHTERS OF MOHAMMED OMAR HUSSEIN

In chapter 1, I discussed the case of Mohammed Omar Hussein, who has established an independent household in Tadrar despite the fact that his father is still alive. He does this by sending his daughters to work in the city (he has only one young son) and by working periodically in the city himself. Mohammed's oldest daughter, Fatime, works in Casablanca as a domestic servant, and previously worked in Agadir. The next oldest, Naima, remains in the village to assist her mother with the younger children and other labor in the household. The third oldest daughter, Mina, worked in Marrakech as a maid as of 1999, and her younger sister Fatima began working in Marrakech in 2002.

It was very difficult for me as a male and an outsider to interview these or any other daughters. The fact that I was single during the bulk of my research, and understood to be wealthy, made me a frequent object of marriage proposals, and made interviews with unmarried women awkward. Compounding the difficulty further is the sensitive nature of sending young girls to the city. It is widely known that conditions for young rural girls working in the cities can be quite awful.[5] In the best of circumstances they work girls very hard, very long hours; in the worst situations girls suffer physical and sexual abuse, isolation, and are in some cases no better off than slaves. The problem is recognized in Morocco, but there is little agreement over what to do about it. Village life is very difficult, too, and many village girls actually want to move to the city despite the hardships and danger. Most I spoke to want to move through marriage rather than for wage labor, and they want to move where they have relatives; but young women realistically appraise rural and urban life, and neither option is very easy.

Whatever they want, girls migrating for work in the homes of urban families are not making their own independent contracts. It is not the case

---

5. According to a July 1, 2000, BBC report: "'Parents are raising their children for sale,' says Bashir Nzaggi, news editor with the respected Moroccan newspaper, *Liberation*. 'They send them to work in the towns, and never see them except to collect their pay-packets.' . . . According to a recent government survey, 2.5 million children aged under 15 drop out of school, and more than half a million work. Many pursue the tradition of toil in the fields. But in exchange for $30 a month, tens of thousands of parents are now contracting their children to urban families to work as domestic servants in conditions of near slavery. Dealers earn up to $200 per child. It's so institutionalized that kitchens are designed with low counters for child-maids to wash and cut vegetables" (http://www.bbc.co.uk/worldservice/people/highlights/streetlife.shtml, by Nick Pelham [accessed October 18, 2005]).

of "choosing" the capitalist economy, of entering into an exchange that (like any exchange in classical economics) benefits both parties. Girls are *sent* to work; whether they desire that work is immaterial, and even the question of desire is complicated by the valuation of household needs over one's individual wants. Girls have no control over the wages produced by their labor; wages are repatriated to the rural patriarchal household.

This does *not* mean that these girls hate their fathers for sending them away or that they resent having to support their natal households. They may, of course, and some surely do. It would be unlikely they would tell me (as an older, exotic male), but in casual conversations while they were visiting the village it seemed perfectly reasonable to most migrant girls that they should be supporting their households. Most wished to be married and work for their own households, of course, and most definitely wished to have their own children, but serving their fathers and by extension their households seemed to make much cultural sense while waiting for a husband. I do not know of any cases of sexual abuse, but the normally grueling conditions of urban labor did not shock the girls, for the simple reason that rural conditions are no easier. There are horror stories of life for girls in the city, but to put them into context we need to understand the rural world the girls themselves use as a basis of comparison.[6]

ARTICULATED HOUSEHOLD NO. 2:
THE DAUGHTERS OF MOHAMMED BEN SALAH

The culturally valued fidelity to a household does not prevent girls from breaking away. Young women do not pursue independence like young men, however, by heading off to work to make money to establish a household. Instead, girls seek to arrange marriages, to link themselves to a male wage laborer and thereby establish a household where they can raise children of their own; young women seek to accomplish this with the help of other (usually female) relatives in the city.

The case of Mohammed Ben Salah's household is illustrative. Mohammed has one of the largest families in the village—nine girls and five boys in my 1999 census—in part because he has more land than almost anyone. As the sole heir of the Bil Qas quarter of the Ait Ben Ouchen lands, Mohammed

6. There is a growing literature on the global phenomenon of migration and domestic servants. See Chang 2000, Ehrenreich and Hochschild 2003, Hondagneu-Sotelo 1994, and Parreñas 2001.

Ben Salah is, on paper at least, one of the wealthiest men in the village. He is ranked second in the village in irrigation time, behind only Abdurrahman Ait Ben Ouchen

Ben Salah has not been blessed with Abdurrahman's demographics, however. Ben Salah's five oldest children are all girls, and cannot be used for male agricultural work. While it is a good household in which to be a woman (i.e., there are many women to share the labor), it is hard for Mohammed to find a way to put his girls to work in the village context, even with a surfeit of agricultural land. By 1999, Mohammed had sent three of the girls to work as maids in the city, Fatima to Casablanca, Kebira and Zahra to Marrakech. All of their wages were returned to their rural household. I only spoke to one of these young women, when she visited the village, but she seemed happy enough. She was an eager participant in water fights with the village boys (fights facilitated by the newly installed water taps), and evinced little passion over her urban work, positive or negative. She struck me as more urbane than her rural sisters and cousins—more forthright, certainly more opinionated, and less respectful of the older men.

However, by 2004 this young woman and her two sisters were all married in the city, depriving their natal household of income even as they extended its social resources out in space. Ben Salah thus sent another daughter to the city to work, Zaina, and sent his oldest son to study in the city, living with his oldest sister and her new husband (now moved to Marrakech, too). Mohammed Ben Salah is thus depriving himself of male agricultural labor in order to better prepare one son for the future. Five of Ben Salah's children now live in Marrakech, forming a kind of urban network of rural offspring, and providing some support for one another.

ARTICULATED HOUSEHOLD NO. 3:
THE SONS OF ABDURRAHMAN AIT ALI

Throughout this book I have been referring to Abdurrahman's position in the village, and his rise to being "a little big." Abdurrahman's political trajectory is related to having land, manipulating his fortunate position in the lineage-based labor allocation system, and using development contacts and other state-based resources for his own benefit. Here I want to suggest that another vital resource has been the wages remitted by Abdurrahman's sons. Not everyone has the excess labor to send migrants out, and it is the synthesis of his different forms of luck, acuity, and action that have allowed

Abdurrahman to prosper by using urban wages for rural political and economic gains.

Mohammed was sent first, many years ago. He did not do well in the city, having had a hard time learning Arabic, but eventually he found some work moving around the countryside helping to build rural schools. His brother Lahcen migrated next, working on a dairy farm near the Middle Atlas town of Demnat. By 2002 Mohammed had returned to the village, but Lahcen had found work in (relatively) nearby Marrakech. In 2006 Lahcen worked in a commercial bakery. Hussein, Lahcen's next younger brother, also worked in Marrakech by 2006. Hussein was rarely able to return to the village, though Lahcen's boss has been more flexible and allowed him to spend some time in his natal household with his new wife, Zahra. All of the money ever made by these boys has been handled by Abdurrahman, who has collected their paychecks, paid their rent in the city, and left them an allowance for food.

While Abdurrahman had two daughters also, they both married long ago. To replace the feminine labor lost to marriages, Abdurrahman found wives for his sons Mohammed and Lahcen. Mohammed had never seen his wife, Fatime, before they were married; Lachen did know Zahra, as she is from Tadrar also. Because their husbands had no independent household, both Fatime and Zahra came to work for Khadija, Abdurrahman's wife. Both were ultimately dependent on Abdurrahman for all their needs, from food to clothing to the question of if and when they could visit their relatives. We might not be surprised if either Fatime or Zahra were to press her husband to abandon the natal *takat* and try their luck in the city. Both women have relatives working in Marrakech. Of course, neither of them would admit such a thing to me, a friend of the father of their husbands, even if they might wonder if I could be a resource in setting up an independent urban household.

Still, by 2004, I suspected that change was on the horizon. By 2007, we will see in the concluding chapter, Abdurrahman's household was reconfigured again, and not in a way chosen by the patriarch.

So, why and how does "globalization" happen? It is commendable that anthropologists and others who have written about the Moroccan mountains have not focused on what is lacking—electricity, toilets, motorized vehicles—but instead have looked to culture, to the way local people themselves see their world and their place in it. However, it is apparent that villagers today understand their world explicitly in relation to what it lacks, specifically in terms of what we call "poverty." In other words, the cultural self-understanding I found in Tadrar includes a notion of poverty generated through the comparison of the village to a larger global community. This is not to argue that villages have a "culture of poverty," or that their cultural values *cause* poverty, either in their own view or mine. Rather, people in Tadrar understand themselves as being poor in addition to being Tashelhit (Berber) speakers, Moroccans, farmers, men and women, Muslims. Poverty is thus part of their cultural understanding of the world. The means villagers employ to address their poverty are also, of course, culturally informed.

A central aspect of rural Moroccan self-consciousness today is an understanding that villagers are *miskin,* poor. Rural people understand that they lack many things at least some urban people have, but perhaps more importantly they lack things people *should* have, like medical care. Villagers carefully observed, for instance, that when my wife became sick in the summer of 2004, I took her hurriedly, by four-wheel-drive ambulance, out of the mountains to a well-equipped hospital that no villager could ever afford. It was about $150 for two nights—very inexpensive by U.S. medical standards—while maids working in the city earn the equivalent of $30 a month. Villagers visited my wife in the hospital in Marrakech, which unlike its mountain counterpart has medicine, efficient staff, beds, even televisions, and does not have pools of blood coagulating on the floor and tightly packed swarms of very ill people waiting endlessly for professional care. The doctor we first visited in the mountains in Talat n Yacoub (the regional capital) was very good, and tremendously kind to my wife, but he was obviously overwhelmed by the proliferation and severity of the medical problems he faced.

Villagers understand, in other words, their poor position vis-à-vis relatively rich people within Morocco and beyond, people who have access to things like medical care. This is only one kind of comparison, but it serves as an example. While villagers report many desirable aspects of life in Tadrar, they view other parts as wretched, and the wretched parts of village life are invariably reported to come from being *miskin.*

In contemporary Tadrar, the main way of dealing with being poor is working very, very hard, and more commonly now, working for wage labor. While I was concerned with toilets, bathing facilities, quality of life, and the romantic *communitas* of living among people who had known one another since birth, the men and women of Tadrar were emphatic that they needed money. With money they could solve their other problems, keep their families together, begin new families, eat better, buy medicine, afford clothes, have easier, healthier, happier lives. Money—*floos, iqaridin*—comes from employers, and employers dwell down the hill, in the plains and cities. The only way to maintain a household and tap the resources of the larger economy is to send migrants down to work.

In the previous section I referred to "articulated households," those that used urban wage labor to support their rural existence. This kind of migration is not economically rational in any neo-Liberal sense because the individuals who do the migrating are not autonomous actors. The value of the time and labor given for the wage is not determined by the worker and the employer, but by the employer and a distant patriarch. Fathers travel to the city to collect the paychecks of their sons and daughters, give the children an allowance to live on, and return to the village. Children work for their households, not for themselves, and the decision to send children to work is necessarily a household decision, preeminently a decision for the patriarch. This is not to say that the young do not have ways of resisting by siphoning off a portion of their earnings for themselves or by avoiding labor that their fathers expect of them. Ultimately, the young resist by abandoning the village altogether, along with their responsibilities to their natal households.

Migration involves a cultural ideal, a shared sense that fathers have a legitimate right to children's labor, and that everyone owes fealty their household. The ideal does not always hold. Some sons abandon their natal households, and many girls sent to the city manage to get themselves married, thus moving from serving their rural natal household to serving a new, urban one. This does not mean these young people are adopting a new, individualistic set of values, however, or at least not wholly. Young men and women may abandon their particular households, but they rarely abandon the ideal of household life. Migrants almost always intend their efforts at wage labor to support a household, either their natal household or a new household with themselves at the center, either in the mountains or in the city.

Foreign understanding of this process portrays it in starkly horrific terms. The BBC, for example, reports that "in exchange for $30 a month, tens of thousands of parents are now contracting their children to urban families to work as domestic servants in conditions of near slavery" (Pelham 2000). The U.S. Department of Labor, in preparing a report related to Morocco's free trade agreement with the United States, paints a similarly depressing picture, writing, "Children, predominantly girls from rural areas, are contracted by their parents or sold by orphanages as maids to wealthy urban families and work for little or no payment" (2004, 5). The Human Rights Internet is still more forthright, summarizing their report as follows:

> General points made under the heading "economic exploitation" included the following: the widespread abuse of young girls working as household maids, or *petites bonnes,* is among the most serious problems confronting children; in most cases, these girls—50 percent of whom are below the age of 10—are sent by their families from rural areas to work as maids in houses in the cities; often the parents genuinely believe that they are doing the best for their child; other parents see their daughters as a lucrative source of revenue; often an agreement will have been reached with the future employer that the child will receive a certain number of hours of education each week. The results of various studies of the situation of these girls, however, showed that, for example: in most cases, the work involved cleaning and general housework, looking after the children and doing the cooking for the whole family; the working day often began before 7:00 a.m. and did not end until after 11:00 p.m.; the child's salary was usually US $30/month and was sent directly to the parents; in some cases, parents were not allowed to visit their daughters; others were allowed only one visit per month with parents; some parents only visited their daughter to collect her salary; up to 70 percent of the girls did not receive any education, regardless of the agreements made before the child left her parents; up to 50 percent had no access to medical care.[7]

Here I have tried to portray the rural side of this dynamic. While I have no desire to exculpate child labor, and certainly not sexual and other forms of abuse that working children suffer in Morocco, to understand why children work we need delve into the economics of rural household production, and the ideology of patriarchal domination. We need to understand the world girls and boys are leaving behind, one of staggering physical difficulty. As Fatima Id Baj summarized village life in a 1998 interview:

7. Human Rights Internet/The United Nations Human Rights System, "Thematic Reports: Morocco." http://www.hri.ca/fortherecord2001/engtext/vol2eng/moroccotr.htm (published 2000, accessed November 24, 2005).

Fatima: When a child is born, he lives for two months. He dies. Another one is born. He lives for one month, he dies. Sometimes four or five die and then she has one that lives. The other ones are dead. And then time passes, she has another one that dies. Then another time there is again one that lives. . . . May God protect us, they call this *tezdait* [bad luck]. And so if God finishes [fulfills] what she wants, she will have children. If not, they will continue dying. Until every child in her stomach is finished [and she reaches menopause]. Until she finishes all the children that are in her life. All she has given birth to dies. They die when they are still very little, still very new. Still very little, they die. There are those who have nine who die.

David: Nine children?

Fatima: Nine children, I swear to God. There are those have five who die. *Everyone* has children who die, everyone has a different number. These die when they are still babies.

In Tadrar most young migrants are *sent* to the city, at least initially. Later some young people do migrate of their own volition, hoping to escape the drudgery of rural agricultural life and begin anew in the city. Sometimes they may be successful; other times they end up in Morocco's growing population of homeless and displaced persons. Some who succeed in finding work return to the village to establish rural households, some do not. The main way that individuals come to labor in the cities, however, is through articulated households. Understanding rural household processes is crucial to understanding the increasing participation of villagers in the wage labor economy. Whether through domestic or other labor, rural migrants like those from Tadrar are the human capital through which the global economy expands.

In Tadrar the word for "city" (*medina, l'medint*) is also used for "cemetery," and there is a genre of morbid humor that plays on this word association. Jokes involve a punch line that equates going "down to the city"— with all its allure and potential—to going to one's death. In both the cities and the mountains of Morocco, death stalks the poor. In ways that are both horrifying and mundane, globalization begins at home.

CONCLUSION
The Market Has No Memory

At the beginning of 2007, I returned to Tadrar to gauge what changes had taken place since 2004, when this book was begun. I knew Mohammed Lukstaf was dead (his wife, Aisha, had cried with me over it in 2004), but now Aisha was dead, too. Fatima Id Baj was again left with only boys in her household; her baby girl, Sumaiya, had died. Venerable Mohammed Ali was dead, and two of his sons returned from the city to claim their inheritance. One of them married a village girl and the three of them set up a new joint household. One of my favorite older ladies (also named Fatima, another Id Baj) had died, as well as other older people I knew less well; numerous children had moved away to the city looking for work, moved to other villages to marry, or moved in to Tadrar from other villages to take up life in a new *takat*. By January of 2007, at least twenty members of village households were living and working in the city (out of a total village population of less than two hundred people). Thirteen households had solar power—nearly half of all households in Tadrar—and twelve had televisions along with either satellite dishes or video disk players. Nearly all households had piped water by 2007. The village seemed to me in the throes of rapid change. Some of this seemed epochal (a shift in the basic arrangements of production) and some (the movement of bodies into this life and out of it) depressingly typical.

Abdurrahman's household had changed more than most. He had already secured funding from the government to open his tourist hostel in 2004, and the new construction was mostly of cement, with a real functioning bathroom and even a shower, albeit with no hot water. Abdurrahman had solar power with a few electric lights, a television, a satellite dish, and a video disk player. But the most important changes to Abdurrahman's household in 2007 did not involve buildings and televisions.

On December 31, 2006, we were celebrating *tafaska,* the feast of the sacrifice, where the head of each *takat* slaughters a ram to commemorate Abraham's willingness to sacrifice a son for God. In Tadrar wealthier households keep the sacrificial ram inside the house for months or even a whole year, feeding it well and treating it more like a member of the family than a farm animal. This is what Abdurrahman had been doing.

When the day arrived, having finished the outdoor communal prayers, we stopped to make a donation at the mosque. Abdurrahman and I then filed back to his home to meet the women and children. I was surprised to see my friend bring out two animals for slaughter, not one. Abdurrahman's oldest son, Mohammed, readied the animals for the ritual, but I now discovered that the next two oldest sons were not absent simply because they were working in the city. They had moved permanently—and independently—to Marrakech just after my previous visit in 2004. The two boys had severed their ties to their father and formed their own household.

It seems that my intuition in 2004 was correct: Abdurrahman's second son, Lahcen, and his wife, Zahra, planned and implemented secession. The couple managed this by convincing Lahcen's next youngest brother, Hussein (Abdurrahman's third son), to marry one of Zahra's sisters, Saida, and the two couples joined together to liberate themselves from their village households and strike out on their own. By spring of 2007, Zahra had given birth to a son, and the new urban household was solidified. Lahcen and Zahra, and Hussein and Saida, had achieved the dream of all young villagers: an independent household, with their own children. They managed this long before their parents passed on and left them productive fields and the rights to water. They achieved the archetypal rural dream not through patient endurance of long-term village dynamics, but in the tumult of the city through the wage labor economy.

Abdurrahman related all this with a heavy heart. I suspect part of the sadness originated in his seriously diminished income—the wages of two sons were now permanently subtracted from the household budget—but there was more to it than material interest. Abdurrahman somberly told me how he had carefully raised the rams for sacrifice, then gone down to *souk* to telephone his sons with the surprise, to tell them they could pick up one of the animals to take back to the city. The sons, he said, decided it would be too much trouble. "We'll buy a sheep here in Marrakech," they told him over the phone, "it's easier." Telling the story, Abdurrahman said "easier" almost as a whisper, his eyes damp and trained on the distance.

A sheep purchased in the market has not been raised in the house, has not been vested with the familial aura that renders its slaughter so poignant a comment on one's obligations to God. But the sons were severing their household ties and they wanted to do it emphatically, with the blood of their own ram sealing their own covenant with God. The boys were making it clear that they were now heads of a household, and they would provide their own sheep, their own way. This does not mean they abandoned their family, only their household. The boys evince no less emotional attachment to their parents or siblings than they ever did, and Abdurrahman and his wife do visit their sons in the city. But economically two of Abdurrahman's sons now manage an independent *takat;* their wives have a hearth of their own.

Abdurrahman had long benefited from the wage labor economy, probably more than any other patriarch in the village. He had been sending sons out for wages since the oldest, Mohammed, had been capable of work, and when he brought Mohammed back he continued to send out the younger boys. The remunerated wages from the capitalist economy had facilitated Abdurrahman's rise in village politics; it had freed his time, eased his ability to provide hospitality, and helped him rise to be "a little big." By 2007 he had also tasted the bitterness of opportunity, the cruel atomization that nourishes the global economy.

Clearly life in Tadrar is based on the household—an institution that is much more than a cluster of rational actors. The bad news about this is that eminent scholars agree that economic understandings of the household are limited at best. Amartya Sen, winner of a Nobel Prize in economics, writes that "inequality inside the household is one of resource-use and of the transformation of the used resources into capability to function, and neither class of information is well captured by *any devised notion* of 'income distribution' within the family" (1992, 122–23, emphasis added). While the focus on "resource use" may be more apposite for non-agricultural, non-subsistence-oriented households, the basic idea that within households people have motivations that cannot be reduced to self-interest confounds Liberal economic theory at its core. Deirdre McCloskey (also an economist, and a neo-Liberal one) puts the issue in broader perspective, writing, "Suppose a big part of the economy—say the household—is, as the economists put it, 'distorted' (e.g., suppose people in households do things for love: you can see that the economists have a somewhat peculiar idea of 'distortion'). Then it follows rigorously (that is to say, mathematically) that free trade in *other* sectors (e.g., manufacturing) will *not* be the best thing. In fact it can make the average person worse off than restricted, protected, tariffed trade would" (2002, 17, emphasis in the original).

In Tadrar households are not "a big part" of the economy, *they are the primary unit of production.* Households are not just where people eat and the thing people spend their wages on; households are the way rural people organize productive labor in the first place. Thus, without taking up the "free trade" part of McCloskey's argument, we can still say that because the economy of Tadrar is based in and on households, economic theories devised to understand globalization writ large are of little use in understanding village-level dynamics. And since villages are where globalization is happening (i.e., villagers are on the productive frontier of capitalist expansion), it would seem we have few theoretical tools in conventional economics to understand why or how the capitalist system expands into places like the High Atlas. The awkward truth is that since economics takes itself as the discipline best positioned to explain to the rest of us how the capitalist economy works, and since expansion is key to how capitalism works, and since capitalism expands precisely in places like Tadrar that are organized through households, and since economists admittedly have little idea how household economies work, we are handicapped in understanding what is arguably the single most significant dynamic in our contemporary social world.

The issue is not, I should add, whether villagers exhibit "rational" economic behavior or perform "utility maximization." All people "maximize" in the sense that they choose between options. Time flows one way and we each must decide which path to walk down, or someone must choose for us. Anthropological attempts to deny this aspect of Liberal economics have failed miserably because it is an argument against tautology. Much of what has been called the substantivist/formalist debate has foundered exactly here.

Substantivists believe that different economic systems are substantively different from one another, with different goals and values and modes of organizing. Not everyone in all societies is looking to profit at the expense of others, they argue, people have different values. Formalists counter that everyone everywhere is choosing *something,* is looking to maximize something even if it is honor, the size of their yams, or their chances of pleasing God. Since people choose, say Formalists, their choices can be formally modeled using conventional economic tools, such as utility maximization curves. The two sides speak past one another, as others have pointed out (Donham 1985).

The central problem is that if people act to get what they want, and we define what they want as what they have self-evidently acted to get, it is hard to say much about "maximizing" other than it is thoroughly inevitable and any behavior—from onanism to suicide—at any time for any person is necessarily "rational." Surely there are cultural differences in what are deemed desirable actions, different kinds of rationality (and we have examined these in Tadrar), but just as surely "in the same environment in which a capitalist firm rationally decreases production, a peasant household rationally increases its output. The difference in response stems not from any supposed contrast in emphasis on material versus nonmaterial *values*, but from the fundamentally different ways in which capitalist and peasant household economies are institutionalized" (Donham 1999, 25–26, emphasis added). The issue is the mode of production, not the associated values. There are indeed different values in different societies, but the salient factor is the way labor is institutionally organized.

In Tadrar, household institutionalization means that a boy serves his father until death. A boy is born in the house he will likely inherit, the house that his father, too, was born in. Girls also serve their households, beginning to work when they are barely old enough to walk. Their mothers, in every case, came from a different house, however, and eventually every girl will, like a young walnut tree, be uprooted from her natal household and sent to grow in another place. In such an institutional framework, what is "rational" for a person to do is what is rational for the household as a unit, and the decision over what is rational for the unit as a whole sits ultimately with each patriarch. Now, fathers are constrained by cultural norms and public opinion (I never found a father who could keep his daughters from marrying, even if he wanted to retain their labor), as well as by the evasions of household members. I watched little boys run screaming when their grandfathers tried to give them work assignments, found teenagers swimming in the river when they were supposed to be irrigating fields, saw a woman teach my own toddler to throw rocks at a minor political official. The patriarchal order is not any more tightly laced than any other; it functions through idealized norms and practical deviations from them. The norm, however, is for households in Tadrar to be organized hierarchically along lines of age and sex.

The microsociological household is not unrelated to the larger dynamics of capitalist expansion more usually discussed, and the key to linking them is to specify how the temporalities of their inequalities relate. All economic regimes, all societies, must organize inequality—at the very least by age and sex. There is no society that attempts to enforce equality between mother and child, for instance, and neither the village economy nor capitalist organization is an exception to the general rule that societies produce and reproduce themselves via their distinctive productive inequalities. "Equality" in any society is complicated by the diversity of human capacities (between individuals and over time) and the multiplicity of variables by which it can be judged (Sen 1992, 1). There is no such thing as equality among all people in a society, across all domains of potential equality, across time. All societies face tough questions about how to allocate social labor over time, and how to distribute the rewards of our inescapably interdependent production and reproduction of society.

Thus, key structures of inequality are integral to capitalist economic organization. As Desai puts it, "No doubt there are many inequalities within capitalism. Alternatives can be devised which, in theory, avoid its disadvantages. But the advantages of capitalism—its wealth-producing ability, its dynamism and innovativeness—are dialectically connected to its disadvantages" (Desai 2002, 295). I would say that the advantages of capitalism are related to *some* of the disadvantages. Racism, sexism, and other forms of discrimination and inequality are not necessarily advantageous to capitalist organization, even if they have persistently accompanied it, and such perduring inequalities may in fact be antithetical to capitalism's most efficient operation. However, *some* inequalities—in capital, talent, and compensation—are functionally necessary to the productive power of the capitalist system as we know it. There are intense scholarly debates over whether globalization is good (usually economists and political scientists) or bad (often sociologists or anthropologists), but I believe it is difficult to argue against the assertion that any social good that might come from capitalism necessarily drags along some bad. Eliminating the productive inequalities of capitalism would eliminate capitalism itself.

Exhausting dynamism, the dislocations of economic growth, and some ineradicable forms of inequality are not necessarily the only disadvantages integral to capitalism, however. Since the nineteenth century a major concern of social theorists has been the fear that the instrumental, self-serving, short-term nature of relations in a capitalist society are too shallow to satisfy our natural human sociality. The move from face to face "community" to anonymous "society" outlined by Ferdinand Tönnies in 1887 was believed to produce "anomie" (in Durkheim's phrasing), a deleterious disconnectedness that Karl Marx termed "alienation." In Marx's thinking, this takes several forms, but ultimately results in alienation from our "species being," or what we would now call our human nature. This scholarly concern has penetrated popular consciousness, or perhaps popular understanding has penetrated social theory: most students I speak to believe that village life must be more peaceful, harmonious, and in some sense more satisfying than the contemporary urban world. This is not to say my students want to live in villages, only that they believe village communities are "simpler," that villages lack an understanding of their material poverty, and that they enjoy a sense of belonging to one another that is absent in the modern world.

Globalization is in this sense thought to destroy communities, flattening them into a worldwide "mass society." In fact, "globalization" is often understood as a synonym for "homogenization," both in the popular mind and in scholarship on both the Left (where such homogenization is bad) and the Right (where it is good). While some sorts of homogeneity under globalization seems inarguable, anthropologists have made a case against a *general* assumption of increasing homogeneity, seeking to leaven the obviously convergent aspects of some global dynamics with attention to countervailing tendencies, especially manifestations of new forms of community via processes of "heterogenization" (Appadurai 1996). From this perspective, some forms of difference and distinctiveness (languages, cultures, social orders) are evidently being absorbed, commoditized, and consolidated, but others are sprouting afresh. Sometimes the "fresh" is not seen as new, but as surface manifestations of deeper, cultural continuities. Marshall Sahlins, for instance, seems to say that no real change is occurring at all, that any evidently "new" communities are in fact constituted of longstanding, culturally distinct forms even if they are built in new circumstances and of new materials. Sahlins would deny my simplification, but he does seem to propose a kind of cultural determination, stating that culture is "atemporal" (1999, 409), that it is the enduring structures of culture that makes both history and historical understandings possible (1985).

Therefore, while globalization surely involves "creative destruction" (Schumpeter 1976), whether "culture" is one of things being destroyed remains an unsettled issue. We cannot say conclusively if the "new" forms of communities spawned in our era are really "new" or merely apparently "new," in the same way that we cannot confidently say whether a house

rebuilt of new materials is a "new" house or simply the old one reconstituted. The issue for most scholars is whether the plan of the house, the
"structure," has changed, but this is the issue of debate rather than the answer to the question. These are old philosophical concerns, dating at least
several thousand years back to curious Greeks asking whether stepping into
the same river at two different moments is really stepping into the same
river. The potentially or putatively "new" forms of community spawned
within the global system are sometimes celebrated or even romanticized,
and other times disparaged as the ersatz leavings of the capitalist order
(Joseph 2002).

The central coordinates that bind any community—traditional and
emergent forms—are shared understandings of space and time. This, too, is
an old idea (it goes back at least to Durkheim), but there remains an argument here about homogenization within globalization. Most scholars agree
that space and time are increasingly de-localized, reordered, and standardized, but disagree about how this process operates and whether it occurs at
the same scale or with the same regularity. Sometimes, in other words, this
new capitalist spatial and temporal order is a unified global phenomenon
(Giddens 2000), or sometimes a sub-global, "national" form of time and
space is emphasized (Anderson 1991). Others find different ethnic experiences of time embedded in larger, dominant but not entirely hegemonic
structures of a major "chronopolis" like New York City (Laguerre 2003).
Still other scholars emphasize how some aspects of global modernity facilitate transnational communities of shared temporality and alternative forms
of coherent, if de-localized, spatiality (Appadurai 1996; Silverstein 2004).
Despite these different emphases there seems some agreement that we are
experiencing a global "speeding up" of time and "compression" of space via
new transportation and communications technologies, technologies that are
ultimately produced through, and reproductive of, a global capitalist order
(Harvey 1989). The situation in Tadrar offers some evidence for this conclusion, but also presents more interesting dynamics, not just acceleration
and compression, but a re-weaving and integration of different modalities
of space and time.

Obviously, scholars and pundits evaluate the desirability of all this very
differently. Liberals and self-described pragmatists—*New York Times* col-
umnists like Thomas Friedman and David Brooks, for instance, or politi-
cians like Bill Clinton and Tony Blair—acknowledge that globalization offers challenges, but suggest in a vaguely utilitarian sense that it offers the

greatest good for the greatest number. Such Liberals are opposed on the Right by jingoists like Pat Buchanan, proponents of protecting what "we" have from the "unfair" competition of (generally melanin-rich but capital-poor) people elsewhere. Unions often end up aligned with this side against "free" trade with the global south, sometimes in a transparent attempt to protect their own (national, safety regulated, unionized) jobs, and sometimes with a broader appeal to institute fair standards and working conditions across national borders before free trade can happen.

Liberals and pragmatists are opposed from the Left, too, but less because of what globalization does to "us" in the affluent parts of the world than what it does to "them," the people of the developing countries. Here the emphasis is often on "resistance," the way poor people oppose the ingestion of their local social orders in the maw of global capitalism (Fletcher 2007; Scott 1985). David Graeber, for instance, writes that global capitalism is "the single greatest and most monolithic system of measurement ever created, a totalizing system that would subordinate everything—every object, every piece of land, every human capacity or relationship—on the planet to a single standard of value" (2001, xi). The danger here is the erasure of difference, and thus the eradication of other potential futures we might discover in our global diversity. Graeber says "would" rather than "will," or "can," but the "would" here means "would" if not resisted at various levels and by various means of "counter-power" (2004). Terry Eagleton (2001, 84) summarizes the Left's position on globalization with his typical verve:

> It is a sign of just how bad things are that even the modest proposal that everyone on the planet gets fresh water and enough to eat is fighting talk. One can imagine launching revolutions in the name of some exorbitant ideal, but to disrupt people's lives in such a spectacular way simply so that everyone may be guaranteed a supply of fresh vegetables seems oddly bathetic. Only extremists could argue against it, just as only extremists could endorse a global capitalist system which in 1992 is said to have paid Michael Jordan more for advertising Nike shoes than it paid to the entire south-east Asian industry which produced them. Revolutionaries are those realist, moderate types who recognize that to put such things to rights would require a thoroughgoing transformation. Anyone who imagines otherwise is an idle utopianist, though they are more commonly known as liberals and pragmatists.

Whether globalization is good, bad, indifferent, inevitable, or but one among many alternative futures is closely tied to understandings of why it happens, how capital comes to reorganize (rationalize, some would say) the spatial, temporal, and interpersonal moorings of human beings. While is it clear enough why the business class would want to expand trade and increase their capital, it has never been very obvious why villagers would want to become workers. The Liberal answer has been that it is simply a rational choice, people choose wage labor as a reasonable means to self-betterment, but we can also ask whether capitalism expands because it:

1. fools people into thinking it is a rational means to self-betterment
2. destroys other social orders, leaving people no choice but to accept it
3. is implemented by national and international elites beyond the control of regular people
4. is more efficient and productive and thus outcompetes other social orders regardless of whether people welcome or oppose it

I believe the evidence from Tadrar supports all four dynamics, and that the multicausal nature of capitalist expansion may be the key to its success *and* the reason scholars can so vehemently disagree about it. In Tadrar, some sons do chafe under their father's authority and abandon the village for the freedom of the atomized economy. Such sons do not figure prominently in my account because I worked in the village, in the world left behind. Clearly, from the occasional meetings I had when they happened to visit, the intimacy of village life is both a blessing and a curse. For a few sons alienation is preferable to the grinding domination of the local patriarchal order, anonymity and isolation are better than a world cloyingly suffused with memory, where every rock has a name, and everyone knows it. For some the city is attractive precisely *because* the market has no memory.

For others, however, the city is an empty promise. I spoke with more than a few men who had been to the city and returned, shaking their heads, muttering about the heartlessness of the people, the noise, the filth, the interminable grasping and jostling of a social world where everyone is on the make and anonymity ensures nobody can be trusted. Even migrants who had become successful businessmen, men who had achieved the dream of creating a successful urban household, came up to the village on vacation and sat silently on boulders beside me, watching the sun set and soaking in the tender ambiance of a village settling down to its evening meal.

While I have done little work with migrants themselves, David McMurray has written eloquently of the emotional costs of foreign migration in a northern Moroccan town. Following the story of Haddou, McMurray shows how a lifetime of migrating for labor in Europe has bought this migrant many of the material benefits he had been hoping for back in Nador, on the southern Mediterranean coast, but through his absence Haddou has gradually become estranged from his children. Haddou's dream of a big house where his sons would live with him has arrived, but arrived empty—with the house built but the sons interested in their own individual dreams. Haddou migrated but retained a set of communal, patriarchal family values; his children, raised in a bustling world of migrants and commodities, international media and global inflections of what is hip and desirable, grew up to value new sorts of relationships, to dream new dreams. Haddou migrated to fulfill his traditional values, but his success ultimately destroyed the transmission of those values to his children. His story is a tragedy, but after my own work in rural Morocco it was hard for me to blame the migrants. Traditional Morocco is no paradise, however recently minted urbanites remember it. Who but propertied fathers would want to stay in the village?

This suggests that beyond calculating the benefits and costs of migration, it is crucial to note the distinction between people doing the labor and people benefiting from it. In Haddou's case, he has spent a lifetime in Europe doing menial labor for the benefit of a family in Morocco that does not much appreciate him (or at least does not appreciate him as he thinks he should be appreciated). In Tadrar the men who make the decision to tap the wage labor economy in the city are *not* those who have to actually do the labor. Patriarchs stay behind. Because Tadrar is based on a household economy, and because those households are strongly patriarchal and rooted in the mountains, "elites" within the household are foisting wage labor on at least some of their offspring for the benefit other offspring, other household members, and the elites themselves. The issue is that "elite" in a rural patriarchal household means "father." Globalization happens *to* most young people from Tadrar who directly encounter it; the young people themselves are not usually choosing it in any simple way. When they do choose it, the motivation is not to own commodities but to establish a household. Village values bring villagers to urban contexts, not any transformation of rural values themselves.

Ultimately, the men who maintain their households and tap the productive world beyond the valley are the biggest beneficiaries. We are not necessarily talking here of the sort of "rural notables" discussed so eloquently by Dale Eickelman (1985), but rather rural nobodies—men who have power over nothing but their household labor. Such men can still make use of the wage labor economy if they have successfully manipulated their local social position, their family and lineage labor organization, to free up sons and daughters who access wages. Such men become hard to contain within the egalitarian village council. It has long been the case that the Moroccan mountains have experienced alternating periods of rapacious and domineering warlords with diffuse (though exclusively masculine) democracy. Perhaps one reason villagers are so concerned with equality between men is that they have historical experience with the results of some men becoming too powerful. In the present situation the main way to become powerful is to *live off the grid*—to maintain a political and social presence in the village, but support it through urban resources. Neighbors without urban resources cannot compete. They are politically outmaneuvered and will find it ever harder to maintain any sort of political equality, or to negotiate the terms of fairness by which villagers maintain a community. Some will eventually give up and head off to the city.

However beneficial for powerful patriarchs, we have also seen that for them the wage labor economy is playing with fire. We saw how Abdurrahman's sons and his daughters-in-law gained experience in the city through their service to their natal households, and how they used this new competence to establish their own independent joint household, something close to their ideal. In this way capitalism drains the life out of villages by facilitating the evacuation of the young. The wage labor economy provides a means to achieve the village dream of household independence even as it removes the labor that sustains the village in the first place. Men like Abdurrahman choose to send their children to work in the city rather than loaning them to relatives at vulnerable points in the domestic cycle. The young are thus absent—whether they are supporting their natal household or beginning a new one—and are not available for the long-term transactions of labor between households that are vital to village survival. If households capitalize independently on their excess labor at moments of strength rather than invest this labor in their less fortunate neighbors, the village—as a village— cannot survive. Villages do not operate in the short-term time frames of the larger economy. If the members of a village lose control over the long-term labor of their young, the village as it has been ordered is doomed.

I will not suggest that the example of Tadrar will settle such vastly complicated questions as how globalization happens, but I do think we can add some evidence to the arguments, evidence from people who are arguably in the midst of being globalized and have some interesting things to say about it. My conclusion from what I know of Tadrar is that different people join the wage labor world for different reasons, and it is precisely the ability of money to be many different things to different people, to be used at the same time to solidify patriarchal control in the village *and* to escape it in the city, that gives the capitalist economy its power. Once you establish a dependence on money, it is hard to stop. The young are particularly susceptible, as the wage labor economy offers the traditional reward of independence *now*, not eventually, after they have worked a lifetime for elders who take a distressingly long time to die.

I suggested at the outset of this book that I think we (literate, comparatively wealthy people) can learn something from a social order like that of Tadrar, and from its transformation. This is not so obvious, perhaps. Anthropologists are famously Romantic, and I am probably no exception. I agree with David Graeber, to cite one fellow traveler, that as a discipline we have been far too fearful of being labeled Romantics, and have thus failed to press upon our audience the lessons we might learn from other worlds. Anthropology is not butterfly collecting, and the achievements of people organizing themselves to survive in tough environments may inspire us to find new, more equitable ways to share the world's resources. I have tried to show that Tadrar is not a simple place, that material survival and the sense of belonging it produces is difficult to maintain and reproduce.

Village life, as villagers emphasized consistently, is very, very hard. While I found the people hauntingly beautiful (inside and out) and while the rhythm of village life beat a kind of peace in my soul, I was never able to stoically watch dead babies be buried in shallow ditches or my neighbors die of snakebite or curable diseases. I was not able to be so culturally relative or awestruck by rural idyll that suffering, especially physical suffering, ever became simply a part of life. Often I could not stand to remain in the village for more than a few days at a time, and I moved back and forth between Taroudant and other cities and the mountains. In the mountains the flies interrupted the beauty, disease consumed my peace, and my inability to help all the people I wanted to help sapped my professional determination to participate, observe, and write things down. Increasingly, I would argue, the people of Tadrar are not so tolerant of rural disadvantage either. The production of new wants (including the desire to be healthy, get dental care, have one's children educated) proceeds as part of the expansion of the global economic order. If I have been at pains to show that migration is fully explicable in terms of the older values villagers maintain, it is also true that new values are emerging.

What can we learn from the people of Tadrar? First, capitalism, too, has costs. It is not the best of all possible worlds, but merely one possible world. Many of the advantages of the global economy (productivity and personal freedom to contract wage labor with whomever you like, at least for some people) are related to its disadvantages (constant change, uncertainty about future employment). Villagers in Tadrar *take care of each other.* The village order may be stifling, but it is organized to provide for its members from birth to death. Children and young people suffer particularly cruelly, especially young women, but unlike the wage labor economy, any young man who survives long enough will eventually be "a boss," will eventually be served by the generations that come after. Even girls will eventually be grandmothers, and will have younger girls to help and care for them. Nobody will ever be alone. This is an economy serving its constituents in a human time frame, not one that beats to an inhumanly standardized rhythm.

Households are organized into lineages precisely because no person or household is an island, neither bodies nor households can contribute to the community in the same way from infancy through adulthood to old age and infirmity. Smaller, weaker households are assisted by larger, stronger ones; interdependence is the core of what makes a village, and what defines us as a species. To accommodate fluctuating dependency, household members employ their genealogical imagination. The bones, or lineages, are arranged, and while this is politically fraught and often untidy, the negotiations are undertaken with fairness in mind—not fairness now, necessarily, but fairness over time. Such calculations are made possible by the genealogical imagination itself, the belief that at some level, if you go back far enough into the deep time of the village body, the bones are all connected. Everybody is, if not a brother or sister, a cousin. It is a small "republic of cousins" (Tillion 1966), and just as nobody would fail to help a baby sister up the hillside or their grandfather get up from a fall, the strong are morally obligated to help the weak. This strikes me as profound because we are all,

as a species, "cousins." We simply ignore this fact most of the time, and focus on our differences rather than our deep and necessary interdependence.

The global economy does not serve human beings. It allows human beings to serve themselves, sometimes, but this is not the same thing. Capitalism may be more efficient, may produce spectacular quantities of stuff to
buy, but it does not produce people to take care of you. We forget, in other
words, that all societies are forged in households, not just the world of village farmers. All societies must make babies, and neither the capitalist order
nor the theoretical tools we have built to understand that order seem capable
of their respective tasks—of making a society that cares for its members, and
of coming to understand how economies can be made to serve people. When
we grow old—and we will all most certainly grow old—we are likely to be
cared for by low-wage workers from elsewhere, by migrants. Village economies like Tadrar build those migrants, provide the people who will work
for little money doing difficult jobs, caring for other bodies that are sag-
ging and failing, bodies that are no longer profitable or productive. If they
cannot spend and cannot work, old people in the so-called first world are
little more than the waste products of a fantastically productive but heart-
less machine.

Paying someone you do not know to serve you is not the same as being cared for by relatives, people devoted to you who are certain that some
day, in their turn, they will be cared for, too. In Tadrar, caring for others is
part of caring for land, part of normal existence, part of *life;* "home" and
"work" are not separate places and are not conceptually separable. As in
other economics, individuals in Tadrar can "opt out" if they like, can move
away or decide not to care for the declining generation, but in a village those
who choose not to care lose resources maintained by the elderly. By contrast, where I live, it is those who choose to care who suffer. In the United
States the people who devote themselves to the infirm and the immature,
who nurture elderly parents and young children, these are the people who
lose wages, who have to explain the gaps in their resumes to "re-enter"
the workforce, who find themselves dependent on wage earners. Their rewards are a flatter career trajectory, smaller social security checks at the end
of their own lives, and no certainty anyone in the generation below them
is likely to return the favor. Thus it seems to me there is much to learn in
Tadrar about love, especially about transacting love and care across time,
between families, through generations. Tadrar has something to teach us
about living in an alternative temporal order, a social order built of its own

inequalities, surely, but one constructed through time frames well aligned with the trajectory of our mortal lives, and less oriented toward our inexhaustible, ephemeral desires.

To end, I want to return to my original impressions, the terrible hardship evident in the village, but also its great warmth, humanity, and elegance. Much of this book has concerned politics, economics, the chilly Apollonian fixations of men and money, property and labor. This is one kind of social operation, one kind of meaning. I will end here with something less exact, less amenable to scholarly arguments and more appropriate for literature. I am no novelist, but I think that sometimes the words that came to me while I lived in Tadrar—almost ten years ago, now—captured some things about village life that I cannot quite resurrect here at my desk. Sometimes the words that flowed from my time in Tadrar have an intimacy and immediacy I can still feel but no longer articulate.

SELECTED FIELDNOTES
October 31, 1998

I continue to be struck by the contradictory nature of the Agoundis, or the contradictory feelings it arouses in me. The weather is changing, fall is easing slowly into winter, and it is quite beautiful. Some days mist hangs in the valley below, and the low orange sun does not so much shine as illuminate the cliffs from within. The tightest bends in the river get no direct light at all and the air there is cold, dead still and moist, like a cave. But up on the slopes the sun is still summer-hot, and you will break a sweat even walking. Evening comes early, the sun ducking south now behind the peaks of Ounein rather than the more westward valleys. There is more night than day and the stars seem to have multiplied. I am using up lots of candles reading *Tashelhit* interviews, social theory, and Faulkner's *The Hamlet*. The rains are late this year and getting later, though people don't yet seem too concerned. The almonds are dropping their leaves, the walnuts turning yellow. Some [trees] are already naked and ready for winter. The carob has been harvested from the lower elevations, packed into bags and hauled off to *souk*. The prickly pear is long since done giving us fruit. Figs are over with. The blackberries that remain on the bushes are desiccated, hard little blackberry candies for those of us who search them out. A few pomegranates still hang on the trees, most of them sprung open to show their sexy, ruby-red innards to the world. Once a week or so, after an early dinner, I build a fire in the *hammam,* heat water, and go steam myself. It's perfectly silent in the small tiled room, just me and the single candle. I shift back and forth from the hot spot just next to the cistern to the cooler end of the room until I have sweated everything in me that I think there is to sweat. I dry off, wrap up, and crawl back between my blankets and my carpet, trolling the shortwave dial for English, reading, or watching the stars through the pane-less window.

There is much here that is beautiful, and some that is terrible. I watched yesterday as Abdurrahman stuffed and sewed me two new pillows. His thick, blunt fingers deftly stitching, rhythmically, evenly, not missing a beat. I sat fascinated for twenty minutes at the sheer confidence his hands evinced stuffing and sewing, stuffing and sewing. Such a powerful form on such a delicate task. It was something like watching Mike Tyson expertly cut origami, or a middle linebacker play Bach on the harpsichord. Then I went to dinner at the Lukstafs', and again was consumed by the sight of hands, this time the variety of hands dipping into the *tajine.* Grandpa Mohammad's thin, gnarled fingers taking small bites. He doesn't eat much anymore. Grandson Hussein's chubby, full-fisted grip of each bite, packing his mouth palmload by palmload, sitting on his grandpa's lap, stretching to reach the *tajine.* Grandma [Aisha's] hennaed palms, old knowing fingers, Fatima [Idzdo's] cracked nails, the baby at her breast sucking the nutrients out of her even while she eats. Little Mohammad's dirty nails and scabbed hands, Khadija's incredibly powerful, beautifully tapered fingers . . . a young lady's hands forged hickory tough by the constant, backbreaking labor that is life for young women here. Little Fatima and little Hassan both have tiny, grubby hands and paper-thin nails, not much bigger than little Hussein's, though quite a bit more coordinated. They tend to bypass the *tanoort* [flat bread used for dipping] and dive straight in for slices of potato, then retreat from the crowd at the low table, away from the penumbra of bodies, where they can kick each other and squeal with delight. The rest of us sit knee to knee, cross-legged, packed together around the *tajine.* Grandpa reaches for the big bowl-shaped bread, tears it into pieces, and distributes them around the table. Each of us mutters, "in the name of God," before the first bite hits our mouths. We squint in the glare of the propane lantern to see what we are dipping our bread in.

There is the smell of meat tonight. And the wax from my extinguished lantern. The littlest ones smell strongly of urine; there are no diapers here, and clothes and carpets are washed less frequently now that the river is icy cold. Mohammed has cleaned up from a day of carrying heavy wool bags of manure on his back, but carries the scent of the stable with him. Khadija's hair is matted to her forehead with the dried sweat from the long hike to the forest, and the longer hike back with a load of wood at least half her own weight. She straps the sticks and branches to her back with a rope slung over her shoulders, held by both hands except where the path is too steep to descend safely. There she holds the rope in her mouth, hangs on to the rock with her hands and feet. She has big, solid, yellow teeth, lucky for her. Not small rotted nubs like her brother.

November 13, 1998

Went to my first *ahowash* [dance]. If this was it, if this was all you got after four years of graduate school and four months in the mountains without plumbing, it would be worth it. A wonderful scene. Really moving. I couldn't understand a word of the singing and I kept getting teary eyed all the same.

Once again I almost missed it. I had passed out by about a quarter after nine and was snoring through the preliminaries when Omar Lukstaf came down and banged on my door until I got up. We staggered up the path to the upper part of the village by the light of my single candle lantern. No moon. Countless stars. Dark in the village and the houses all quiet.

Above Haj Lahcen's house we began to run into other people and all of us snaked our way up the path with candles and the occasional flashlight. We passed the mosque and moved into the covered part of the trail, where the houses merge into a single huge hive of a building, which seems to swallow you up. It is completely dark in here but for the madly swinging shadows of the candles, and we all move carefully, single file up the rock worn smooth by centuries of feet, all the time *salaam aleikum*-ing people moving the other way, dodging kids bombing down the path, moving slowly up in a lengthening train. Granny [Aisha] . . . had made me her project by this time and was huffing and puffing behind me, giving me instructions on what to do between huffs. She looked something like an oversized softball wrapped in lumpy un-spun wool, wrapped again in the bright scarves and rags of a Guatemalan village wedding or a London techno rave . . . about three feet tall, three feet wide, ancient hands and a cherub's face . . . toothless, grinning, laughing, cajoling.

Where the path forks into a Y there is a space open to the sky. A small flat area forms, maybe fifteen feet by twenty, before the two tunnels continue on, leading up and out of the square, one toward the almond fields, one toward the *sherij* [water cistern]. Here the men of Azzaden have gathered to sing and dance for the bride they will take with them, and the people of Tadrar had packed around to see. All of the people I know—Jamoo and Khadija, Belaid and Fatima, Yemna, Ben Edar, and all the Lukstaf boys, Haj Lahcen and Abdurrahman—everyone is piled onto the rocks above the dancers, packed in doorways, squeezed together, lounging on one another. The dull mud of the walls rising above us, shuttered wooden windows, the small mud and stick eaves of the buildings, the bright dress clothes of the women, and especially the girls, the somber earth tone *jellabas* [cloaks] of the men, all are lit by a pair of propane lanterns wedged into ledges above us. Brahim Arbuz tends the fire, and the Azzaden men hand him their drums to heat. The smoke curls up past the propane glare and it all seems quite unearthly.

I take the first bare spot of ground I see as my seat, directly behind the dancers. One patriarch of the Azzaden folks occupies the stable doorway above me, Haj Lahcen is next to him, Abdurrahman packs in underneath me. I am wedged between warm bodies on a cold starry night. It smells strongly of fresh hay and the wax of the extinguished lanterns.

The men begin their calls. Their *rais* [leader, president] will sing out a verse, and the men repeat it, or repeat the appropriate call back to it, and join in with the drums. The verse is repeated again and again as the drums get faster, and someone even brings a big plastic water drum that they beat with a stick for a baseline. On some unrecognizable signal they all rap their drums in unison and finish. The villagers yell out, *bsaht kum,* to your health, with a kind of tone like the Spanish yell out "olé." Then the *rais* calls out a new verse and they begin again. While they sing the men huddle shoulder to shoulder, bobbing, shuffling back and forth, moving forward, packing tighter into a single, multi-footed wool-clad body, dropping their heads further and further, then popping up with the final chorus. Some hand their drums to Brahim for warming and the *rais* calls out again. *Bsaht kum,* people call out. *Bsaht kum*!

They consume this small space, pressing back the walls of what seems a very small amphitheater melting, collapsing in on itself, slowly. Then at some invisible signal a line of women pour down the aisle between the dancers' backs and my feet, press their way past the Azzaden men, and form a line against the wall facing me, facing the men. Too beautiful for words, their bright and distinct faces . . . the Ben Rais girls, young Aisha in particular with her serious pre-adolescent haughtiness, Yemna Lukstaf wry and confident, Fatima Id Baj concentrating, looking self-conscious as the center and sort of leader, Rqia looking like a sultry raccoon in her heavily kohled eyes . . . they line up, their tough, hennaed hands clapping in unison, their eyes flashing then modestly turning down at the ground. They are wearing tartan skirts and satin dresses, bangled country scarves and sheer city headshawls, Chinese print dresses, tie-dyed wraps, polyester exploding with color . . . they look like Scottish Chinese African Muslim princesses, beautiful faces not like anything or anywhere else . . . they continue to press into the line, lime scarves and more tartan skirts over Chinese prints, white satin and sequins and deep royal red overcoats, powder blue and sun yellow silky dresses over rough wool sweaters, phosphorescent orange scarves and dangling bits of silver and tin and copper, coins welded into jangling bracelets, bead collars and bright plastic shoes stirring the dust with small, stuttering unified steps. . . . Clapclap. Clap. Clapclap. Clap. Like ponies prancing, proud and shy and skittish.

From the corridors outside the light, other women ululate and call out an opening verse. The women respond, clapping in rhythm, their voices surging and falling. The men huddle on the ground now, hunched around their drums, twisting their ears to the sky to better catch the rhythm of the women. They find the beat with their drums and drive it faster and faster. Aisha o Rais and her older sister leave the line, dancing in front of it, facing one another. Their hands are at their sides, their shoulders rise and fall, their feet make small, precise steps that carry them to the end of the line. Here, where there are a few feet of space to turn around, they make eye contact with some invisible person off beyond the light, dip their heads, swirl, shimmy their shoulders, swirl the other way, and dance their way back down the line. Sometimes the men will suggest a beat with their drums, sometimes Fatima or Yemna or a woman I don't know . . . will call out, sometimes the women off stage yell out. Then it is taken up, people join in, and they build another slow rise to crescendo.

This goes on for two hours or so, when the women begin to try to leave the line. All the while one granny (a Ben Ouchen? a Baj?) has been dragging girls to the line, the shy ones like Khadija too overcome with the public-ness of their position to do any more than stare at the ground and clap along. The men say, *hashuma,* "shame," to any woman who tries to leave. But it is late now and babies are starting to be lugged off to bed.

The women perform one more song, then scatter to the periphery, and it is the turn of the men from outside [the village]. They are good, practiced. They begin to move in a circle to their beat, voices soaring and dropping. A step toward the center, a step out, a step around the circle . . . they are picking up speed, crammed together, one or two soloing on their drums while they keep the step of the group, around and around until a final bumbum, bam bum. *Bsaht kum,* we yell! *Aoud,* again. But it is late. They go two or three times, then Abdurrahman says, "More tomorrow," and everyone breaks into the opening verses of the Qur'an.

This is deep, sonorous, every man, woman, and child know it . . . palms to the sky, beseeching the one and only God, they chant a long chain of looping, loping syllables, while the *rais* hollers out a contrapuntal string of praise for the prophet, praise for Allah, praise to the bride and the people of Tadrar in a sort of [fiery preacher] invective . . . and finally: *Allahu akbar:* God is great. It is over. Lanterns are lit, random groups of women are repeating the verse, people seep back into the quaking shadows of the corridors, and spill down the hill. I wind down with them, saying goodbye again and again until the lower path—there are only the few of us who live down here left. Final goodbyes and goodnights and promises that, if God wills, we will be back to *ahowash* tomorrow. My door is dark and quiet. High on the

hillside a thin string of lanterns files north, toward the Arbuz com-
pound, toward Hussein Ben Ouchen's house beneath the old fort, and
further, to Ait Moussa and Agerda. The traveling girls sing in small
groups, their voices holding the night back from the narrow trail, until there are only the stars, only the dim echoes of high pretty voices.
Then the village is quiet. There are only stars, cold and far away
in the November sky, and the monstrous dark of the canyon below.

References

Addi, L., ed. 2003. *L'anthropologie du Maghreb son Berque, Bourdieu, Geertz et Gellner*. Paris: Awal/Ibis.

Amahan, Ali. 1998. *Mutations sociales dans le Haut Atlas: Les Ghourjdama*. Paris: Editions de la Maison des Sciences de l'Homme.

Anderson, Benedict. 1991. *Imagined Communities: Reflections on the Origin and Spread of Nationalism*. New York: Verso.

Anzaldúa, Gloria. 1999. *Borderlands = La Frontera*. San Francisco: Aunt Lute Books.

Appadurai, Arjun. 1996. *Modernity at Large: Cultural Dimensions of Globalization*. Minneapolis: Univ. of Minnesota Press.

Arrif, Ahmed. 1985. Compétition caïdale et procès d'intégration d'un canton montagnard: l'Unayn. *Annuaire de l'Afrique du Nord* 22:347–60.

Beck, Ulrich. 2000. "Living Your Life in a Runaway World: Individualisation, Globalisation, and Politics." In *Global Capitalism*, ed. A. Giddens and W. Hutton, 164–74. New York: New Press.

Bédoucha, Geneviève. 1987. *L'eau, l'amie du puissant: une communauté oasienne du sud-tunisien* Paris: Editions des Archives Contemporaines.

Bencherifa, Abdellatif. 1983. "Land Use and Equilibrium of Mountain Ecosystems in the High Atlas of Western Morocco." *Mountain Research and Development* 3 (3): 273–79.

Berque, Jacques. 1938. *Etudes d'histoire rurale maghrébine*. Tanger, Fès: Les Editions Internationales.

———. 1953. "Qu'est-ce qu'une 'tribu' nord-africaine?" In *Éventail de l'histoire vivante: hommage à Lucien Febvre*, ed. Mel Febvre, 261–71. Paris: EHESS.

———. 1967. *French North Africa: The Maghrib Between Two World Wars*. Trans. J. Stewart. New York: Praeger.

———. 1978 [1955]. *Structures sociales du Haut-Atlas*. Paris: Presses Universitaires de France.

Bhabha, Homi. 1994. *The Location of Culture*. London: Routledge.

Bidwell, Robin. 1973. *Morocco under Colonial Rule*. London: Frank Cass.

Boudraa, Nabil, and Joseph Krause, eds. 2007. *North African Mosaic: A Cultural Reappraisal of Ethnic and Religious Minorities.* Cambridge: Cambridge Scholars Press.

Boukous, Ahmed. 1995. "La langue berbere: maintien et changement." *International Journal of the Sociology of Language* (112): 9–28.

Bourdieu, Pierre. 1973. "The Algerian Subproletariat." In *Man, State and Society in the Contemporary Maghrib,* ed. I. W. Zartman, 83–92. London: Praeger.

———. 1984. *Distinction: A Social Critique of the Judgement of Taste.* London: Routledge.

Bourouiba, Rachid. 1974. *Ibn Tumart.* Alger: SNED.

Bourqia, Rahma, and Susan Gilson Miller, eds. 1999. *In the Shadow of the Sultan: Culture, Power and Politics in Morocco.* Cambridge, Mass.: Harvard Univ. Press.

Braudel, Fernand, Roselyne de Ayala, Paule Braudel, and Jean Guilaine. 2001. *The Mediterranean in the Ancient World.* New York: Allen Lane.

Bray, Francesca. 1997. *Technology and Gender: Fabrics of Power in Late Imperial China.* Berkeley: Univ. of California Press.

———. 1998. "Machines for Living: Domestic Architecture and the Engineering of the Social Order in Late Imperial China." *Cambridge Anthropology* 20 (1–2): 92–110.

Brett, Michael, and Elizabeth Fentress. 1996. *The Berbers.* Oxford: Blackwell Publishers.

Brown, Kenneth L. 1976. *People of Sale: Tradition and Change in a Moroccan City.* Manchester: Manchester Univ. Press.

Chaker, Salem. 1989. *Berbéres aujourd'hui.* Paris: Editions l'Harmattan.

Chang, Grace. 2000. *Disposable Domestics: Immigrant Women Workers in the Global Economy.* Cambridge, Mass.: South End Press.

Combs-Schilling, Elaine M. 1985. "Family and Friend in a Moroccan Boom Town: The Segmentary Debate Reconsidered." *American Ethnologist* 12 (4): 659–75.

———. 1989. *Sacred Performances: Islam, Sexuality, and Sacrifice.* New York: Columbia Univ. Press.

———. 1996. "La legitimation rituelle du pouvoir au Moroc." In *Femmes, Culture et Societe au Maghreb,* ed. R. Bourqia, M. Charrad, and N. Gallagher, 71–88. Casablanca: Afrique-Orient.

———. 1999. "Performing Monarchy, Staging Nation." In *In the Shadow of the Sultan: Culture, Power and Politics in Morocco,* ed. R. Bourqia and S. G. Miller, 176–214. Cambridge, Mass.: Harvard Univ. Press.

Conley, Dalton. 2004. *The Pecking Order: Which Siblings Succeed and Why.* New York: Pantheon Books.

Cornell, Vincent I. 1987. "Understanding Is the Mother of Ability: Responsibility and Action in the Doctrine of Ibn Tumart." *Studia Islamica* 66:71–103.

Crapanzano, Vincent. 1973. *The Hamadsha.* Berkeley: Univ. of California Press.

———. 1980. *Tuhami: Portrait of a Moroccan.* Chicago: Univ. of Chicago Press.

Crawford, David. 2001. "Work and Identity in the Moroccan High Atlas." Ph.D. diss., Anthropology, University of California, Santa Barbara.

——. 2002. "Morocco's Invisible Imazighen." *Journal of North African Studies* 7 (1): 53–70.

——. 2003. "Arranging the Bones: Culture, Time and In/Equality in Berber Labor Organization." *Ethnos* 68 (4): 463–86.

——. 2005. "Royal Interest in Local Culture: The Politics and Potential of Morocco's Imazighen." In *Nationalism and Minority Identities in Islamic Societies,* ed. M. Shatzmiller, 164–94. Montreal: McGill-Queens Press.

——. 2007a. "On the Sluggishness of Cities." *Anthropology News* (April): 30.

——. 2007b. "Making Imazighen: Rural Berber Women, Household Organization, and the Production of Free Men." In *North African Mosaic: A Cultural Reappraisal of Ethnic and Religious Minorities,* ed. Nabil Boudraa and Joseph Krause, 329–46. Cambridge: Cambridge Scholars Press.

Crawford, David, and Katherine Hoffman. 2000. "Essentially Amazigh: Urban Berbers and the Global Village." In *The Arab-African and Islamic Worlds: Interdisciplinary Studies,* ed. R. K. Lacey and R. M. Coury, 117–34. New York: Peter Lang.

Cunninghame Graham, R. B. 1997 [1898]. *Mogreb-El-Acksa: A Journey in Morocco.* Evanston, Ill.: Marlboro Press.

Dahrendorf, R. 1969. "On the Origin of Inequality Among Men." In *Social Inequality,* ed. A. Béteille, 16–44. Baltimore: Penguin.

Desai, Meghnad. 2002. *Marx's Revenge: The Resurgence of Capitalism and the Death of Statist Socialism.* New York: Verso.

Donham, Donald L. 1985 [1979]. *Work and Power in Maale, Ethiopia.* Ann Arbor, Mich.: UMI Research Press.

——. 1999 [1990]. *History, Power, Ideology.* Berkeley: Univ. of California Press.

Doutté, Edmond. 1914. *Missions au Maroc: en tribu.* Paris: Librairie Paul Geuthner.

Dresch, Paul. 1986. "The Significance of the Course Events Take in Segmentary Systems." *American Ethnologist* 13 (2): 309–24.

Dunn, Ross. 1977. *Resistance in the Desert: Moroccan Responses to French Imperialism.* London: Croom Helm.

Durkheim, Émile. 1964 [1893]. *The Division of Labor in Society.* Trans. G. Simpson. New York: Free Press.

Dwyer, Daisy Hilse. 1978. "Ideologies of Sexual Inequality and Strategies for Change in Male-Female Relations." *American Ethnologist* 5 (2): 227–40.

Dwyer, Kevin. 1982. *Moroccan Dialogues.* Baltimore: John Hopkins Univ. Press.

Eagleton, Terry. 2001. *The Gatekeeper.* New York: St. Martin's Press.

Edwards, Brian. 2005. *Morocco Bound.* Durham: Duke Univ. Press.

Ehrenreich, Barbara, and Arlie Russell Hochschild. 2003. *Global Woman: Nannies, Maids, and Sex Workers in the New Economy.* New York: Metropolitan Books.

Eickelman, Dale F. 1985. *Knowledge and Power in Morocco.* Princeton: Princeton Univ. Press.

——. 2002. *The Middle East and Central Asia: An Anthropological Approach,* 4th ed. Upper Saddle River, N.J.: Prentice Hall.

El Guindi, Fadwa. 1999. *Veil: Modesty, Privacy, and Resistance (Dress, Body, Culture)*. New York: Berg.

Elias, Norbert. 1994 [1939]. *The Civilizing Process*. Cambridge, Mass.: Blackwell.

Ensel, Remco. 1999. *Saints and Servants in Southern Morocco*. Leiden: Brill.

Evans-Pritchard, E. E. 1940. *The Nuer: A Description of the Modes of Livelihood and Political Institutions of a Nilotic People*. Oxford: Oxford Univ. Press.

Fabian, Johannes. 1983. *Time and the Other: How Anthropology Makes Its Object*. New York: Columbia Univ. Press.

Fletcher, Robert. 2007. *Beyond Resistance: The Future of Freedom*. New York: Nova Science Publishers.

Fleuret, Patrick. 1985. "The Social Organization of Water Control in the Taita Hills, Kenya." *American Ethnologist* 12:103–18.

Foucault, Michel. 1975. *Surveiller, et Punir*. Paris: Gallimard.

———. 1983. "The Subject and Power." In *Michel Foucault: Beyond Structuralism and Hermeneutics*, ed. H. L. Dreyfus and P. Rabinow, 208–26. New York: Harvester.

———. 1994. "Two Lectures." In *Culture/Power/History*, ed. N. Dirks, G. Eley, and S. B. Ortner, 200–221. Princeton: Princeton Univ. Press.

Freud, Sigmund, and Joan Riviere. 1930. *Civilization and Its Discontents*. London: Hogarth Press.

Friedman, Jonathan. 1985. "Our Time, Their Time, World Time: The Transformation of Temporal Modes." *Ethnos* 50 (3/4): 168–83.

———. 2002. "From Roots to Routes: Tropes for Trippers." *Anthropological Theory* 2 (1): 21–36.

Friedman, Thomas L. 2005. *The World Is Flat: A Brief History of the Twenty-First Century*. New York: Farrar, Straus, and Giroux.

Gebrati, Fatima. 2004. *La mobilisation territoriale des acteurs du développement local dans le Haut-Atlas de Marrakech*. Ph.D. diss., Géographie, Université Joseph Fourier, Grenoble, France.

Geertz, Clifford. 1973. *The Interpretation of Cultures*. New York: Basic Books.

Geertz, Hildred. 1979. "The Meanings of Family Ties." In *Meaning and Order in Moroccan Society: Three Essays in Cultural Analysis*, ed. C. Geertz, H. Geertz, and P. Rosen, 315–79. New York: Cambridge Univ. Press.

Gell, Alfred. 1992. *The Anthropology of Time: Cultural Constructions of Temporal Maps and Images*. Oxford: Berg.

Gellner, Ernest. 1969. *Saints of the Atlas*. London: Weidenfeld and Nicholson.

———. 1987. *Culture, Identity, and Politics*. Cambridge: Cambridge Univ. Press.

———. 1996. "Reply to Critics." In *The Social Philosophy of Ernest Gellner*, ed. J. A. Hall and I. C. Jarvie, 623–86. Atlanta, Ga.: Rodopi.

Giddens, Anthony. 2000. *Runaway World: How Globalization Is Reshaping Our Lives*. New York: Routledge.

Gluckman, Max. 1968. "The Utility of the Equilibrium Model in the Study of Social Change." *American Anthropologist* 70 (2): 219–37.

Goodman, Jane E. 2005. *Berber Culture on the World Stage: From Village to Video.* Bloomington: Indiana Univ. Press.

Goody, Jack. 1983. *The Development of the Family and Marriage in Europe.* Cambridge: Cambridge Univ. Press.

Graeber, David. 2001. *Toward an Anthropological Theory of Value: The False Coin of Our Own Dreams.* New York: Palgrave.

———. 2004. *Fragments of an Anarchist Anthropology.* Chicago: Prickly Paradigm Press.

———. 2006. "Turning Modes of Production Inside Out, or Why Capitalism Is a Transformation of Slavery." *Critique of Anthropology* 26 (1): 61–85.

Hammoudi, Abdellah. 1980. "Segmentarity, Social Stratification, Political Power, and Sainthood: Reflections on Gellner's Thesis." *Economy and Society* 9 (3): 279–303.

———. 1997. *Master and Disciple: The Cultural Foundations of Moroccan Authoritarianism.* Chicago: Univ. of Chicago Press.

———. 1999. "The Reinvention of the *Dar al-mulk:* The Moroccan Political System and Its Legitimation." In *In the Shadow of the Sultan: Culture, Power and Politics in Morocco,* ed. R. Bourqia and S. G. Miller, 129–75. Cambridge, Mass.: Harvard Univ. Press.

Hannerz, Ulf. 1996. *Transnational Connections: Culture, People, Places.* London: Routledge.

Hart, David M. 1981. *Dadda 'Atta and his Forty Grandsons: The Socio-Political Organization of the Ait Atta of Southern Morocco.* Boulder: Middle East and North African Studies Press.

———. 1989. "Rejoinder to Henry Munson Jr." *American Anthropologist* 91:765–69.

———. 1996. "Berber Tribal Alliance Networks in Pre-Colonial North Africa: The Algerian *Saff,* the Moroccan *Liff* and the Chessboard Model of Robert Montagne." *Journal of North African Studies* 1 (2): 192–205.

Harvey, David. 1989. *The Condition of Postmodernity: An Enquiry into the Origins of Cultural Change.* Oxford: Blackwell

Hayden, Corinne P. 2003. *When Nature Goes Public: The Making and Unmaking of Bioprospecting in Mexico.* Princeton: Princeton Univ. Press.

Hoffman, Katherine E. 2000a. "Administering Identities." *Journal of North African Studies* 5 (3): 85–100.

———. 2000b. *The Place of Language: Song, Talk and Land in Southwestern Morocco,* Ph.D. diss., Anthropology, Columbia University, New York City.

———. 2002. "Moving and Dwelling: Building the Moroccan Ashelhi Homeland." *American Ethnologist* 29 (4): 928–62.

———. 2008. *We Share Walls: Language, Land, and Gender in Berber Morocco.* New York: Blackwell.

Hoodfar, Homa. 1997. *Between Marriage and the Market: Intimate Politics and Survival in Cairo.* Berkeley: Univ. of California Press.

Hondagneu-Sotelo, Pierrette. 1994. *Gendered Transitions: Mexican Experiences of Immigration.* Berkeley, Calif.: Univ. of California Press.

Hopper, Kim. 2002. *Reckoning with Homelessness.* Ithaca: Cornell Univ. Press.

Howe, Marvine. 2005. *Morocco: The Islamist Awakening and Other Challenges.* Oxford: Oxford Univ. Press.

Ilahiane, Hsain. 1996. "Small-Scale Irrigation in a Multiethnic Oasis Environment: The Case of Zaouit Amelkis Village, Southeast Morocco." *Journal of Political Ecology* 3:89–106.

———. 1998. "The Power of the Dagger, the Seeds of the Koran, and the Sweat of the Ploughman: Ethnic Stratification and Agricultural Intensification in the Ziz Valley, Southeast Morocco." Ph.D. diss., Anthropology, University of Arizona.

———. 2005. "Water Conflict and Berber (Amazigh) Perception of Time in the Upper Ziz Valley, Morocco." *Prologues: revue maghrébine du livre* 32:66–74.

International Union of Prehistoric and Protohistoric Sciences et al. 1984, 1958–1960. *Encyclopédie berbère.* Aix-en-Provence, France: Edisud.

Jamous, Raymond. 1982. *Honneur et baraka: les structures sociales traditionnelles dans le Rif.* Cambridge: Cambridge Univ. Press.

Joseph, Miranda. 2002. *Against the Romance of Community.* Minneapolis: Univ. of Minnesota Press.

Justinard. 1951. *Le caïd Goundafi; un grand chef berbère.* Casablanca: Éditions Atlantides.

Kraus, Wolfgang. 1998. "Contestable Identities: Tribal Structures in the Moroccan High Atlas." *Journal of the Royal Anthropological Institute* 4 (1): 1–22.

Lagnaoui, Ahmed. 1999. *Aux Frontières de la Tradition Marocaine.* Casablanca: Les Editions Toubkal.

Laguerre, Michel S. 2003. *Urban Multiculturalism and Globalization in New York City: An Analysis of Diasporic Temporalities.* New York: Palgrave Macmillan.

Landau, Rom. 1969. *The Kasbas of Southern Morocco.* London: Faber and Faber.

Laroui (al 'Arawi) Abdallah. 1977. *The History of the Maghreb.* Princeton: Princeton Univ. Press.

Leveau, Remy. 1985. *Le Fellah marocain: défenseur du trône,* 2nd ed. Paris: Presses de la Fondation Nationale des Sciences Politiques.

MacDougall, James. 2006. *History and the Culture of Nationalism in Algeria.* Cambridge: Cambridge Univ. Press.

Maghraoui, Abdeslam. 2001. "Political Authority in Crisis." *Middle East Report* 218:12–17.

Mahdi, Mohamed. 1999. *Pasteur de l'Atlas: Production Pastoral, Droit et Rituel.* El Jadida and Casablanca: Imprimerie Najah.

Maher, Vanessa. 1974. *Women and Property in Morocco: Their Changing Relation to the Process of Social Stratification in the Middle Atlas.* Cambridge: Cambridge Univ. Press.

Malinowski, Bronislaw. 1984 [1922]. *Argonauts of the Western Pacific.* Prospect Heights, Ill.: Waveland Press.

Marcus, George. 1995. "Ethnography in/of the World System: The Emergence of Multi-Sited Ethnography." *Annual Review of Anthropology* 24:95–117.

Marx, Karl, and Frederich Engels. 1967. *The Communist Manifesto.* Trans. S. Moore. Baltimore: Penguin.

Masqueray, Émile. 1983 [1886]. *Formation des cité chez les populations sedentaires de l'Algerie. Kabyles du Djurjura, Chaouia de l'Aouras, Beni Mezab.* Reimpression de l'ouvrage publie en 1886 chez l'editeur Ernest Leroux a Paris ed. Aix-en-Provence: Centre de Recherches et d'Etudes sur les Societes Mediterraneens, and Edisud.

Mayer, Enrique. 2002. *The Articulated Peasant: Household Economies in the Andes.* Boulder: Westview Press.

McCloskey, Deirdre. 2002. *The Secret Sins of Economics.* Chicago: Prickly Paradigm Press.

McMurray, David A. 2001. *In and Out of Morocco.* Minneapolis: Univ. of Minnesota Press.

Mernissi, Fatima. 1994. *Dreams of Trespass: Tales of a Harem Girlhood.* Reading, Mass.: Addison-Wesley.

Michel, Nicolas. 1997. *Une économie de subsistances: le Maroc précolonial.* Le Caire: Institut français d'archéologie orientale.

Mielants, Eric. 2007. *The Origins of Capitalism and the "Rise of the West."* Philadelphia: Temple Univ. Press.

Mikesell, Marvin W. 1973. "The Role of Tribal Markets in Morocco." In *Man, State, and Society in the Contemporary Maghrib,* ed. I. W. Zartman, 415–23. London: Pall Mall Press.

Mojuetan, B. A. 1995. *History and Underdevelopment in Morocco: The Structural Roots of Conjuncture.* Münster [London]: International African Institute.

Montagne, Robert. 1930a. *Les Berbères et le Makhzen dans le sud du Maroc: essai sur la transformation politique des Berbères sédentaires (groupe Chleuh).* Paris: F. Alcan.

———. 1930b. *Villages et Kasbas Berbéres: tableau de la vie sociale des berbéres sédentaires dans le sud du Maroc.* Paris: Felix Alcan.

———. 1973 [1930]. *The Berbers.* Trans. D. Seddon. London: Frank Cass.

Moore, Henrietta L. 1994. *A Passion for Difference.* Cambridge: Polity Press.

———. 1999. "Anthropological Theory at the Turn of the Century." In *Anthropological Theory Today,* ed. H. L. Moore, 1–23. Cambridge: Polity Press.

Mundy, Martha. 1995. *Domestic Government: Kinship, Community and Polity in North Yemen.* London: I. B. Tauris.

Munn, Nancy D. 1992. "The Cultural Anthropology of Time: A Critical Essay." *Annual Review of Anthropology* 21:93–123.

Munson, Henry, Jr. 1991. "The Segmentary Lineage Model in the Jebalan Highlands of Morocco." In *Tribe and State: Essays in Honour of David Montgomery Hart,* ed. E. G. H. Joffe and C. R. Pennell, 48–68. Cambridgeshire: Middle East and North African Studies Press.

———. 1993. *Religion and Power in Morocco.* New Haven: Yale Univ. Press.

——. 1996. "Rethinking Gellner's Segmentary Analysis of Morocco's Ait 'Atta." In *The Social Philosophy of Ernest Gellner,* ed. J. A. Hall and I. C. Jarvie, 291–308. Atlanta, Ga.: Rodopi.

——. 1997. Review of "Anthropology and Politics" by Ernest Gellner. *Journal of the Royal Anthropological Institute* 3 (2): 385.

Parreñas, Rhacel Salazar. 2001. *Servants of Globalization: Women, Migration and Domestic Work.* Stanford, Calif.: Stanford Univ. Press.

Parry, Jonathan, and Maurice Bloch. 1989. "Money and the Morality of Exchange." In *Money and the Morality of Exchange,* ed. J. Parry and M. Bloch, 1–32. Cambridge: Cambridge Univ. Press.

Pascon, Paul. 1979. "Segmentation et stratification dans la société rurale Marocaine." *Bulletin economique et social du Maroc* 138–39:105–19.

Pelham, Nick. "Street Life," July 1, 2000. www.bbc.co.uk/worldservice/people/highlights/streetlife.shtml (accessed October 18, 2005).

Persichetti, A. 2004. "La parenté rahim." *L'Homme* 169:89–126.

Petrzelka, Peggy, and Michael M. Bell. 2000. "Rationality and Solidarities: The Social Organization of Common Property Resources in the Imdrhas Valley of Morocco." *Human Organization* 59 (3): 343–52.

Phillips, Anne. 1999. *Which Equalities Matter?* Malden, Mass.: Polity Press.

Pouillon, François. 2005. "La société segmentaire et ses enemies: notes sur un moment des sciences sociales au Maghreb." *Prologues: revue maghrébine du livre* 32:14–23.

Rabinow, Paul. 1975. *Symbolic Domination.* Chicago: Univ. of Chicago Press.

Rachik, Hassan. 1990. *Sacré et sacrifice dans le Haut Atlas marocain.* Casablanca: Afrique Orient.

——. 1992. *Le sultan des autres: rituel et politique dans le Haut Atlas.* Casablanca: Afrique Orient.

——. 1993. "Espace pastoral et conflit de gestion collective dans une vallée du Haut Atlas occidental." In *Utilisation et Conservation des Ressources: Montagnes et Hauts Pays de l'Afrique,* ed. A. Bencherifa, 181–200. Rabat: Faculte des Lettres et des Sciences Humaines, Universite Mohammed V.

——. 2004. "Le fantôme de la tribu: politique et tradition." *Prologues: revue maghrébine du livre* (29/30): 59–63.

Radcliffe-Brown, A. R. 1940. "Preface." In *African Political Systems,* ed. M. Fortes and E. E. Evans-Pritchard, xi–xxiii. London: Oxford Univ. Press.

Roberts, Hugh. 2002. "Perspectives on Berber Politics: On Gellner and Masqueray, or Durkheim's Mistake." *Journal of the Royal Anthropological Institute* 8 (1): 107–26.

Robertson, A. F. 1987. *The Dynamics of Productive Relationships: African Share Contracts in Comparative Perspective.* Cambridge: Cambridge Univ. Press.

——. 1991. *Beyond the Family: The Social Organization of Human Reproduction.* Berkeley: Univ. of California Press.

——. 2001. *Greed: Gut Feelings, Growth, and History.* Cambridge: Polity Press.

Roseberry, William. 1989. *Anthropologies and Histories: Essays in Culture, History, and Political Economy.* London: Rutgers Univ. Press.

Rosen, Lawrence. 1984. *Bargaining for Reality: The Construction of Social Relations in a Muslim Community*. Chicago: Univ. of Chicago Press.

Rosenberger, Bernard. 2001. *Société, pouvoir et alimentation: nourriture et précarité au Maroc précolonial*. Rabat: Alizés.

Russell, Dennis Ryan. 2003. *Conservation, Culture, and Development in the High Atlas of Morocco: Making the Case for Collaborative Management of Natural Resources for Biodiversity Protection and Local Livelihoods at Toubkal National Park*. Master's thesis, International Development Program, Clark University, Worcester, Mass.

Sabry, Tarik. 2004. "Young Amazighs, the Land of Eromen and Pamela Anderson as the Embodiment of Modernity." *Westminster Papers in Communication and Culture* 1 (1): 38–52.

Sadiqi, Fatima. 1997. "The Place of Berber in Morocco." *International Journal of the Sociology of Language* 123:7–21.

Sahlins, Marshall. 1983. "Other Times, Other Customs: The Anthropology of History." *American Anthropologist* 85 (3): 517–44.

———. 1999. "Two or Three Things That I Know about Culture." *Journal of Royal Anthropological Institute* 5 (3): 399–421.

Schumpeter, Joseph Alois. 1976. *Capitalism, Socialism and Democracy*. New York: Harper and Row.

Scott, James C. 1985. *Weapons of the Weak*. New Haven: Yale Univ. Press.

———. 1998. *Seeing Like a State: How Certain Schemes to Improve the Human Condition Have Failed*, Yale Agrarian Studies. New Haven: Yale Univ. Press.

Segonzac, Édouard Marie René, marquis de. 1903. *Voyages au Maroc (1899–1901)*. Paris: A. Colin.

Sen, Amartya. 1992. *Inequality Reexamined*, 6th ed. Cambridge: Harvard Univ. Press.

Silverstein, Paul. 2004. *Algeria in France: Race, Nation, Trans-Politics*. Bloomington: Indiana Univ. Press.

Silverstein, Paul, and David Crawford. 2004. "Amazigh Activism and the Moroccan State." *Middle East Report* 233:44–48.

Singerman, Diane. 1995. *Avenues of Participation: Family, Politics, and Networks in Urban Quarters of Cairo*. Princeton: Princeton Univ. Press.

Slyomovics, Susan. 2001. "A Truth Commission for Morocco." *Middle East Report* 218:18–21.

———. 2003. "No Buying Off the Past: Moroccan Indemnities and the Opposition." *Middle East Report* 33 (4): 34–37.

———. 2005a. *The Performance of Human Rights in Morocco*. Philadelphia: Univ. of Pennsylvania Press.

———. 2005b. "Self-Determination as Self-Definition: The Case of Morocco." In *Negotiating Self-Determination*, ed. H. Hannum and E. F. Babbitt, 135–57. New York: Lexington Books.

Smith, Joan, and Immanuel Wallerstein. 1992. *Creating and Transforming Households: The Constraints of the World Economy*. Cambridge: Cambridge Univ. Press.

Tillion, Germaine. 1966. *Le harem et les cousins*. Paris: Editions du Seuil.

U.S. Department of Labor, Bureau of International Labor Affairs. 2004. "Morocco Labor Rights Report." Washington, D.C.: GPO.

Valensi, Lucette. 1977. *Fellahs tunisiens: l'économie rurale et la vie des campagnes aux 18e et 19e siècles.* Paris: Mouton.

———. 1985. *Tunisian Peasants in the Eighteenth and Nineteenth Centuries.* Cambridge: Cambridge Univ. Press.

Verdery, Katherine. 1996. *What Was Socialism, and What Comes Next?* Princeton: Princeton Univ. Press.

———. 2001. "Inequality as Temporal Process: Property and Time in Transylvania's Land Restitution." *Anthropological Theory* 1 (3): 373–92.

Wallerstein, Immanuel Maurice. 2004. *The Modern World-System in the Longue Durée.* Boulder: Paradigm Publishers.

Waterbury, John. 1970. *Commander of the Faithful.* New York: Columbia Univ. Press.

———. 1991. "Bargaining for Segmentarity." In *Tribe and State: Essays in Honour of David Montgomery Hart,* ed. E. G. H. Joffé and C. R. Pennell, 4–13. Cambridgeshire: Middle East and North Africa Studies Press.

Weismantel, Mary. 2004. "Moche Sex Pots: Reproduction and Temporality in Ancient South America." *American Anthropologist* 106 (3): 495–505.

Wolf, Eric. 1982. *Europe and the People without History.* Berkeley: Univ. of California Press.

Zwingle, Erla. 1996. "Morocco: North Africa's Timeless Mosaic." *National Geographic* 190 (4): 98–125.

Index